SACRED HEALING

"*Sacred Healing* is the onramp to a spiritual highway whether you are a beginner, a spiritual practitioner, teacher, or healer. Dr. Mann integrates years of professional practice in the field of psychology with lifetimes of spiritual development."

—Larry Payne, Ph.D., Chairman, International Association of Yoga Therapists Founder, User Friendly Yoga™

"*Sacred Healing* is an invaluable resource not only for therapists and their clients, but for any human being. It extends the confines of Western psychology to include the sacred and spiritual in a wise and practical way. One outstanding aspect of Dr. Mann's work is his emphasis on the value of alignment with the Higher Self to infuse spiritual energies in ourselves and others. In my experience, the positive effects of this practice can be remarkable and lasting."

—Robert Gerard, Ph.D., President, International Foundation for Integral Psychology

SACRED HEALING

Integrating Spirituality
with Psychotherapy

RONALD L. MANN, PH.D.

BLUE DOLPHIN PUBLISHING

Published by
Blue Dolphin Publishing, Inc.
P.O. Box 8, Nevada City, CA 95959
Orders: 1-800-643-0765

ISBN: 1-57733-016-1, $14.95 paper
ISBN: 1-57733-028-5, $19.95 CD edition,
includes CD, *Inspiration for Meditation,* guided chakra meditations
spoken by the author with music by Aryeh David

Library of Congress Cataloging-in-Publication Data

Mann, Ronald L.
    Sacred healing : integrating spirituality with psychotherapy /
Ronald L. Mann.
        p.   cm.
    Includes bibliographical references and index.
    ISBN 1-57733-028-5 (with CD). — ISBN 1-57733-016-1
    1. Spiritual healing.   2. Yoga, Kriya—Therapeutic use.
3. Psychotherapy—Religious aspects.   I. Title.
BL65.M5M36   1998
291.3'1—dc21   97-48821
                                                        CIP

Cover art: Judith Cornell
Cover design: Lito Castro
Chapter opening graphic: BBL Typographic

Excerpts from *God Talks with Arjuna, The Bhagavad Gita: Royal Science of
God-Realization* by Paramahansa Yogananda (Los Angeles: Self-Realization
Fellowship, 1995), reprinted with permission.

Printed in the United States of America

10   9   8   7   6   5   4   3   2   1

Dedication

To those souls who are sincere in their search for God

Table of Contents

Acknowledgments

This book has been in process over the last fifteen years. I want to express my sincere appreciation to the following:

All those individuals, patients, students, and friends with whom I have had the privilege of participating in their healing.

Elisabeth Kübler-Ross, M.D., whose love and awareness ignited the spark of my consciousness.

Paramahansa Yogananda and Mahavatar Babaji, whose eternal Love has fed my soul and taught me the difference between Divine wisdom and human understanding.

To my mother and father, Mae Mann and Albert W. Mann, M.D., whose undying love, understanding, and support, spiritually, emotionally, and financially, have allowed this work to be published. I also want to thank my parents for their open-mindedness, integrity, and capacity to support my service to others, even when it pushed them into new territory.

Paul and Nancy Clemens, of Blue Dolphin Publishing, whose friendship and support has lasted for years. Their belief in me and the value of spiritual teachings has led to the publishing of this work.

Corinn Codye, my editor with Blue Dolphin, whose editorial gifts, clarity of mind, and personal development allowed her to clarify my thinking and fine-tune the concepts presented in this manuscript. The final book is much better because of her involvement.

Foreword

by Elisabeth Kübler-Ross, M.D.

I FIRST MET RON MANN twenty years ago when he attended one of my workshops in Hawaii and he was still a regular, straight, square psychologist. Since the emphasis on my workshop was to help others finish unfinished business in order to open up their own spiritual quadrant, to realize that we are all spiritual beings in a physical body, I was impressed by his ability to perceive and follow through with my intended teachings.

I have not seen Ron since the end of the 1970s, for approximately eighteen years, and it is with great delight that I was able to read his book and meet him on a personal level. What he is sharing in his book, *Sacred Healing,* exceeded all my expectations and dreams of functioning as a catalyst for spiritual growth.

As you probably know, I have had several strokes which resulted in total left-side paralysis and agonizing pain for two-and-one-half years until Joseph Bortniak, a spiritual healer, entered my life. In a few months after working with him, on a once-a-week basis, I am no longer paralyzed and totally pain free. Joseph has an extraordinary gift to work on the subtle realms and touch the healing power of the soul. He exemplifies what Ron has described in *Sacred Healing.* He was able to help me in ways that conventional, Western medicine could not. To bring Ron and Joseph together gives me the first joy since I have lived in Arizona. Our physically oriented medicine has a chance to change with people like these two men who will be able to teach people to become whole human beings with equal value of the physical, emotional, mental, and spiritual quadrants co-existing in harmony. Living this way ultimately leads to total health and well-being, which is the medicine of the twenty-first century and the beginning of the new millennium, which I have already experienced in my own being. My three years of anguish and agony have been worthwhile to live long enough to see the possibility of totally changed human beings where love and light is the essence of the future of medicine, and where wholeness and well-being is the natural status of humanity without violence and abuse.

I was delighted to see Ron's change and Joseph and Ron's dedication to making their learning and insights available to others. Joseph is also in the process of completing a book on this important topic. This information regarding spiritual wholeness needs to be shared with others who have the courage to discard all outmoded twentieth-century behavior and who have the willingness to become whole, a prerequisite to survive future earth changes and be ready for the next millennium of love and peace.

Elisabeth Kübler-Ross, M.D.
September 14, 1997

Introduction

THIS BOOK IS ABOUT THE PROFOUND HEALING that occurs when Spirit and the ancient wisdom of spiritual traditions are consciously brought into our lives. The current crisis in our American health care system makes this information even more timely for health care practitioners, patients, and non-patients alike. The focus of this book transcends any specific form of medical or psychological treatment. The theory and techniques presented here are designed to transform consciousness, which leads to spiritual realization and healing at the most profound level of our Being. Furthermore, the overriding theme throughout is that our consciousness is the most potent ingredient in any healing and our interconnectedness in Spirit can result in a direct transmission of subtle energy that is potentially life changing. Whether or not this is accepted professionally, the truth remains: the power in our consciousness, when united with the Divine, is unlimited.

During the past twenty-five years that I have been practicing psychotherapy, I have learned to trust the healing capacity in one's deepest Self or soul. Although I was trained very traditionally to diagnose and look for pathological states, I have found that my intent to perceive the soul or the "perfection" in another, facilitates a shift in my consciousness to an unconditionally loving state which nurtures and promotes a healing environment. My state of consciousness, if you will, creates a container and presence that invites the other to open to deeper aspects of their Being. This work seems to honor the original meaning of the word "psyche," the soul. Furthermore, my clinical experience has taught me that many physical and emotional problems are the result of alienation and separation from the True Self or soul. In fact, some suggest that childhood autism, a very serious developmental disorder, may be a disease of the soul, and in Chapter Twelve I present a brief story of a healing with an autistic child. Society's larger escalation of violence and abuse may well be another symptom of our collective spiritual alienation.

The current crisis in our American health care system appears to be the result of rising costs and overwhelming patient medical needs. Many Americans may not realize that the current health care crisis in America is forcing professionals to provide short-term, symptom-oriented, crisis management. Medical professionals are under tremendous pressure to treat psychological problems with drugs, and many primary-care physicians are advised to prescribe antidepressant medication without any consultation with a psychologist or psychiatrist. While biology certainly plays an important part in determining our behavior, this biochemical, "cost effective" approach to mental health does not serve society.

Furthermore, psychotherapy, which aims to explore deeper issues within the psyche, at both psychological and spiritual levels, has become a luxury for many Americans. The current direction in our health care system, where a physician is given approximately five minutes to properly diagnose and treat each patient, or where a psychologist is asked to address long-standing psychological problems in one to eight sessions, makes a mockery of the entire mental health profession and is imminently dangerous to quality health care. Adding to the problem, the managed care companies clearly focus their treatment on short-term, crisis management, in which the goal is merely to restore the prior level of functioning, rather than address true healing. On the other hand, most individuals in the healing profession would agree that a crisis represents a valuable opportunity to change, grow, and evolve to a higher level. This type of change or transformation typically requires a little time for realization and integration at the higher level. Thus, the goal of our current health system, although most Americans may not realize it, is to keep things as they are, to return to the status quo, and preferably to accomplish that with drugs. This symptom-oriented focus perpetuates the illusion that most problems can be solved by attending only to the patient's thinking and behavior patterns, without equal consideration of relevant spiritual issues and concerns.

Our society can benefit from preventive approaches that honor the integration and balance of mind, body, and soul. Health care cost can be reduced with more enlightened medical approaches that draw upon spiritual realities as well as biochemical, cognitive interventions. I have witnessed in my own therapy practice, life-threatening disease states quickly healed through interventions that honor subtle, spiritual forces, along with conventional medical and psychological methods. Thousands of dollars in potential medical expenses have been saved through simple, loving approaches that address body, mind, and soul. Chapter Twelve discusses several of these "spontaneous healings."

My hope is that this book will help to create a social understanding and dialogue that openly addresses and honors those qualities within the human soul that unite us, nourish us, inspire us, and promote health and well-being. In this regard, educational approaches that provide preventive measures will prove to be the best way to contain health care costs, and understanding the underlying source for many societal and individual problems and developing interventions that speak to those core issues will prove to be a better method for long-term health care than what currently exists.

Our current focus on disease and symptoms can shift to health, balance, wellness, and the deeper underlying spiritual needs of our Being. This change could dramatically alter the nature of American society as individuals are encouraged to become more conscious about creating love, harmony, peace, and cooperation in all aspects of their lives: in business, in family life, and in communities. The methods and techniques for obtaining higher states of love, joy, and health can be integrated into all aspects of our society if we have the collective will to do so. Our society has demonstrated that we can achieve our goal once we have clearly set our will and intention. We have done it in times of war, and we can do it in times of peace, to shift the nature of health care through individual transformation.

There is a calling here for us all. The power of the Divine resides within us all and can be more deeply experienced with spiritual practice and discipline. This book aims to inspire more professionals to expand their experience of spiritual awareness and to integrate a more spiritually-conscious perspective into their professional work.

Towards a New Paradigm

In my experience, healing and transformation occur when one is made whole again by the infusion of Love and Spirit. To assist this process, the healer learns to shift his or her consciousness to a state in which the union between Self and Spirit can be clearly recognized and experienced. In this union between Self and Spirit, a *transmission of energy* occurs, in which Divine intelligence guides and directs the flow and quality of energy. The healer thus becomes both a participant and an observer to the experience. This union with the Divine dissolves all boundaries of separation: the therapist and the patient both become infused with the Love and Peace that is inherent to the presence of the Holy Spirit, and all illusions of separation dissolve in this sacred process. Clearly, a prescription of prozac will not accomplish this goal, although it may help to stabilize an individual so that he or she can become capable of exploring this deeper, more valuable work.

This book is for those who are interested in deepening the quality of their lives and work. It is not designed for those who simply want more techniques, with the hope of quickly solving some presented symptoms. However, it will be very helpful to those who want to integrate spiritual principles into the practice of psychotherapy. A guiding principal in this approach sounds like a paradox: *We can do more to help resolve problems when we learn to "do" less, wherein nothing becomes everything and something profound emerges when we work from the universally-connected place of our Being.* This cosmic shift provides an array of new ways to be involved in the healing process. It may require a new vocabulary and an appreciation for nonlinear approaches to problem solving. Personally, this work has been so very rewarding and extremely nurturing to my soul that I hope I can adequately share its wonder and magnitude with you.

The ancient philosophy of yoga and its techniques are included in this book because of the "mystical" rewards associated with yogic meditation and practice. After all, why not look directly into those systems, such as yoga or the ancient Indian spiritual traditions, which have been proven to foster love, peace, and joy in the individual, and integrate those systems within our traditional approaches?

Yogic philosophy and techniques are presented here not as "the only approach to enlightenment," but because they are the method with which I have the most personal experience. The yoga system is a scientific method for developing a personal relationship with God. One of the by-products of yogic meditation is an awareness of the transcendent, energetic reality of consciousness. Consciousness, in this context, refers to an awareness and concept that is greater than the "mind" alone. Unfortunately, the narrow and limited focus on the "mind," without giving enough credence to the vast, universal reaches of consciousness, is yet another limitation of the current Western model of psychotherapy. In this state of transcendent awareness, the conscious experience of subtle energies, in various forms, opens new and profound opportunities for healing that are much more effective than traditional methods of psychotherapy alone, and can result in a deeper, fuller, more authentic integration of the self.

Yoga literally means union: the union of the soul with God, or the union of the individualized aspect of creation with the creator itself. Thus, psychotherapy also offers the potential to address the process of union: the union of the Self as an integration of all aspects of the self—mind, body, and soul. This type of psychotherapy is, therefore, *conscious and sacred,* as it seeks to explore and incorporate rather than exclude the deepest expanses of spiritual reality and integrate this knowledge into both the process of healing and the lives of both therapist and patient.

The ancient wisdom of the *Bhagavad Gita* is also included because this eternal text provides profound guidance that has endured for centuries. The ancient principles of the *Gita* will be applied within our Western perspectives, to point the way to an expansion of consciousness in the psychotherapeutic realm.

Consciousness wants to evolve through us. We are all on a journey of returning to the source of Love. On our way, we can either coast along with the current or use a paddle to speed our journey. We are all going home. It is up to us how long that journey takes. This book provides a paddle for those who have coasted long enough.

Definition of Terms

Sacred Healing

The blending of traditional methods of psychotherapy with the conscious experience of subtle energies and spiritual awareness can be called *sacred healing,* because one has to be awakened to a higher state of consciousness to engage in it. The terms *conscious psychotherapy, sacred psychotherapy,* and *sacred healing* all refer herein to this ideal of an integrated approach. This work deserves to be called sacred because the soul is touched in this process. Sacred healing occurs when the power of the soul is accessed, which awakens tremendous latent healing forces. Moreover, in this heightened conscious state, psychotherapy becomes an aspect of spiritual practice because it is a sacred experience in which Spirit heals others through us. The discipline, discernment, and devotion that we must have as professionals to help heal the wounded, brings us closer to the Divine. This sacred work continues to purify us as we offer ourselves as instruments of the Divine in the healing process.

Consciousness

The term *consciousness* is used extensively throughout this book. It refers to the state of awareness in which an individual is cognizant of his or her state of being. The state of being "conscious" implies an awareness of one's immediate existence and one's relationship to the universe. There are different states of consciousness, from sleeping, dreaming, waking, to the superconscious. Consciousness might best be understood as awareness, and there are different levels on which awareness can exist.

Ego

The word *ego* is subject to great confusion and is used widely and loosely in both psychological and spiritual circles. For clarity's sake, two symbols will represent two different meanings of this word herein. The Greek letter *psy* (ψ) follows the term *ego* when its meaning is within the psychological realm. The Greek letter *iota* (ι) follows the term *ego* when it is used in its spiritual sense.

In the psychological context, the ego (ψ) performs a very positive function for the self. The ego (ψ) is a hypothetical construct for those functions of thinking, perceiving, organizing, and integrating. It is psychologically important to have a strong ego (ψ) in order to function well in daily life. Those with a weak ego (ψ) structure have difficulty with their own emotional life. They feel overwhelmed by their feelings; they are confused about their inner experience; and they have difficulty accurately perceiving outer reality without projecting their own unconscious material.

A strong ego (ψ) allows one to confront the difficulties of life with confidence and have the strength and flexibility to be open to other people's thoughts and feelings without feeling threatened or overwhelmed. A strong ego (ψ), in this context, allows one to be intimate and to merge psychologically with another person without the need to create conflict and anger as a way of defining one's sense of self. Knowing what one feels and thinks is a great asset. Knowing how to communicate that information to another person is a great gift in any relationship. A strong ego (ψ) results from integrating all parts of the psyche, the light and the dark, the masculine and the feminine, and the various aspects of the personality, such as the child, adult, and parent. A strong ego (ψ) allows one to let go and explore new territory when one's consciousness begins to expand. If one has a very solid and well-integrated sense of self at a psychological level, then one can more easily allow for an inner shift of self-perception that includes a greater sense of one's own being.

This leads to the other meaning of ego (ι). From a spiritual perspective, ego (ι) is the aspect of self that experiences a separation from God. Ego-consciousness (ι) is believing that "I" am in total control of "my" life, that "I" am the total creator of "my" existence. The inherent limitation of this notion is that it does not allow for the full, expansive understanding and experience of God-consciousness. This limited ego-identity (ι) creates a contracted and reduced field of awareness. For example, when a disciple asks his/her *guru*[1] for cosmic consciousness, the *guru* may reply, "If I were to give it to you now, it would kill you. It would be like placing a million watts of electricity through a one-hundred-watt light bulb." This ego-obstacle (ι) occurs as long as consciousness is identified with the limited aspects of the self, which does not allow for the flow of higher vibrational energy.

Ego (ι) consciousness restricts the amount of higher energy that is able to flow through us. Every level of consciousness is like a sheath of energy that vibrates at different levels. If we identify only with a particular level of Being, we limit how much energy can flow through us. The physical experience of receiving an influx of Divine energy that is larger than we are able to handle can be painful or emotionally damaging. The process of transformation, however, through spiritual practices and disciplines, allows for a gradual changing of consciousness as well as a strengthening and conditioning of the physical body, so that the entire Self or Being can conduct and resonate at higher energetic frequencies. Physical cells actually need to be purified in order to receive these higher vibrations.

Many years ago, I participated in a retreat for children with Joan Halifax, Edith Sullwold, and Sun Bear, in Ojai, California. Half of the children present had terminal illnesses. On the first evening, I awoke around two o'clock in the morning, feeling a great pulsing of energy around me. My tent was located in the center of all these young participants. I opened to their energetic presence and realized that I was actually feeling the process of life and the development of the personal self that was emerging within these children. I realized then that one cannot transcend the ego (ι) until one has enough ego (ψ) to transcend it. I realized that spiritual life develops and evolves in its own organic way, with its own developmental timing so to speak, and this process was literally breathing all around me.

This little story illustrates the relationship between the two forms of ego, for many individuals are not ready and able to carry out the profound and difficult work of spiritual development. They do not yet have the inner strength and personal integration that is required of one who is devoted to spiritual unfolding and of anyone who seeks to assist in the healing process on these levels. In fact, such an aspirant finds eventually that his/her ego (ι) must be burned, sacrificed, in the fire of purification. The little ego (ι) gradually dissolves as the greater Higher Self or soul awareness becomes revealed. Therefore, spiritual life is truly for the strong at heart and the dedicated, for only the courageous survive the supreme tests that are given to purify the heart, foster growth, and awaken the consciousness to the reality of cosmic forces.

In the process of spiritual growth or sacred healing, one does not actually "get rid of the ego." Rather, through spiritual practice we shift the identification of the self beyond the ego (ι) to the Soul. This is a process of transformation in which we transcend our attachment to and identity with the little ego (ι). Deep states of meditation provide the experiences in which one actually perceives, through subtle and intuitive levels of perception, the distinction between ego-consciousness and soul-consciousness. The ego (ι) tends to claim personal responsibility for an experience, since it is totally identified with thought, physicality, and emotion. On the other hand, the soul perceives itself as being a channel or instrument of the Divine, through which experience flows. To the soul, knowledge, information, wisdom, healing, and action are experienced as coming from something greater: the Infinite.

Ultimately, all these aspects of the Self are merely energies or levels of consciousness. The shift from ego-consciousness to soul-consciousness actually produces a change in vibration. Yogic meditation practices facilitate this change in consciousness because they provide a relatively precise means of quieting the mind, withdrawing the life-force energy, and shifting the identification of consciousness away from the outer senses of perception to the deep, inner reality of soul awareness.

Many years ago I had a very interesting experience in meditation, in which I was given the perception of my ego (ι) as an energy sheath. I thought that perhaps I could pry that energy body away from me and then be free of my ego (ι). I imagined that I had a crowbar and began to pry at this energy body. Immediately I felt a great pain in my physical body and realized that the ego (ι) could not just be scrapped. Thereafter, I developed a much greater appreciation and acceptance for the process of transformation of energy as a major aspect of spiritual transformation.

Self/self

Throughout this book the word "self" will be used in two different contexts. When Self is used with a capital "S," it refers to the Higher Self or Soul. When self is used with a lower case "s," the term refers to personal identity in a cognitive psychological context.

Spirit

Throughout this book, the term "Spirit" refers to the omnipresent aspect of God which exists both in creation and beyond creation. The inherent qualities of Spirit are love, joy, peace, wisdom, and bliss. Throughout this entire discussion, reference is made to the direct experience wherein the individual feels the presence of Spirit and receives guidance and inspiration in many aspects of life. The soul *is*

Spirit; hence there is no separation between our essential Self and God.

Spirituality

Throughout this entire book, the terms *spiritual* and *spirituality* are used without reference to any particular religion. Often people become offended or put off at the mention of spirituality, because of prior negative experiences with traditional religious practices. Indeed, many have experienced religion as a restrictive force in their life, because the particular practices and beliefs involved may have instilled fear, guilt, and shame. In this book, *spirituality* refers to one's direct, personal relationship with God, without prescribing any particular path or way for sustaining that relationship, or any one specific conception of God. The discussion of yogic philosophy and practices is based both upon my personal experience and the fact that yoga is a scientific method designed to assist individuals in having a direct, personal relationship with the Divine.

The many existing beliefs and concepts about the nature of Omnipresent Spirit give evidence that God can be experienced in many different ways. The form, or no-form, is not the issue here. Whether a person knows God as Christ, Buddha, Krishna, Allah, Mohammad, or whomever or whatever formless state of Being, does not matter. Spirituality is that state of Being in which the unity and sacredness of all life is revered. Spirituality is the conscious knowingness that we are Divine Beings and a reflection and expression of the Divine, that the Holy Spirit moves through us all. How we define, conceive, and worship that sacred presence is an individual matter. At their basis, all the great spiritual traditions share the same goal: the direct personal experience of God.

Subtle Energy

The entire universe is composed of vibratory elements or energy. All physical matter, thought, and consciousness are essentially energy resonating at various frequencies. This subtle energy can be perceived with the intuitive senses when one is able to refine his or her consciousness to higher vibratory rates.

Yoga

As stated previously, *yoga* literally means union: the union of the soul with God, or the union of the individualized aspect of creation with the creator itself. The yoga system is a scientific method for developing a personal relationship with God. The complete system of yoga includes instruction for moral development, correct posture, life force energy control, internalization of the mind, concentration, meditation, and superconscious experience. The Western conception of yoga is often limited to the system of *hatha yoga,* an elaborate system of physical postures to help prepare the student for deep meditation. The final goal of yoga is more than mere physical exercise; it is union with the Divine. One of the by-products of yogic meditation is the awareness of a transcendent energetic reality of consciousness.

Sacred Healing is about a process of personal transformation and the awakening of consciousness to the Divine reality. The following chapters offer practical theoretical information, concrete clinical material, and direct stories regarding the process of spiritual development and "spontaneous healing." Designed for both the general public and professionals in the mental health field, the overriding theme throughout is that consciousness can be experienced as tangible energy that has profound healing properties and is an expression of our Divine nature.

The essence of our Being radiates with Divine light and exists across time and space. Our Divine consciousness is encoded in the depths of our soul and contains profound wisdom. Every individual can learn to access the inner reality of spiritual consciousness, and awakened psychotherapists can help to facilitate this process.

The following chapters provide detailed information about our Divine nature and the multiple possibilities that exist for healing of body, mind, and soul, and for living a well balanced life when we attune our consciousness to Spirit.

God-Realization is a legitimate and obtainable goal. As more and more individuals turn inward to obtain Self-realization, health care professionals will need to be educated and personally available to relate to the soul as an integral part of the entire person. Complementary health care and holistic perspectives will need to consider the soul along with the rest of the human experience to be relevant in the next millennium. This book is offered as a resource for this spiritual journey.

Psychotherapy for the Next Millennium

Blending Traditional & Spiritual Approaches

RECENTLY I SPOKE WITH A YOUNG MAN who was working on his Marriage and Family Child Counselor's license. He had been practicing meditation for over twenty years and believed that the Board of Behavioral Science Examiners actually had a rule that he could not mention spirituality in his work. I was astounded at his belief and willingness to comply passively with this ridiculous notion. There is no reason why psychotherapists should not function to reawaken the lost connection to the soul, once they have done that work within themselves, or why the spiritual unfoldment of an individual should not be a legitimate goal within the mental health system. Especially ironic in this regard is the fact that our country was founded on the premise, "In God We Trust," yet the current if not predominant environment among traditional psychology profession-als seems to be one of atheism and intellectualism. Furthermore, the focus of Western psychological thought rests largely upon "doing" and not one's "Being." Freud regarded one's ability to love and work as the measure of health. Both of these concepts, as he held them, require a lot of "doing" in the outer world, as accomplishment, rather than "Being," which is an aspect of spiritual growth and realization. George Bernard Shaw said, "To me the sole hope of human salvation lies in teaching Man to regard himself as an experiment in the realization of God, to regard his hands as God's hand, his brain as God's brain, his purpose as God's purpose."[2]

Viewed from within the context of spirituality, life becomes a moment in eternity, in which the soul incarnates in a physical body to learn additional lessons and complete the cycle of birth and rebirth. The spiritually-conscious individual sees each life within a larger context and views individual problems as part of the soul's evolution back into God-consciousness. Psychotherapy, when placed in this spiritual context, becomes a vehicle to help an individual understand, accept, and work with life's challenges. In my experience, when yogic practices are also combined with this process, great healing can occur, in which Divine forces are activated that may ease karmic patterns[3] and speed up the healing process tenfold. The illusion of time and space dissolves in deeper states of consciousness, and healing occurs when the truth of our Divine nature is activated and our natural state of wholeness reemerges from the hidden realm in which it patiently waits.

This process of rediscovering our wholeness of Being can be illustrated by a story. There was once a great king who had the most prized music-stand maker in all the kingdoms. A group of people asked the music-stand maker how he could create such wonderful pieces of art, for his music stands were truly the best to be found anywhere. The music-stand maker said, "It is actually quite simple. First I fast for five days and then go into the forest. I walk around in circles for another five days, until I am totally disoriented. Then I continue fasting for another five days, until I am delirious. Then, I just look around until I see the most exquisite music stand inside a tree. At that point, I simply cut away everything that is around the music stand."

Likewise, our true nature is within. A psychotherapist who is spiritually awake may very well have the clear vision (clairvoyance) to perceive the true Self, the soul consciousness, in another. The "work" of psychotherapy, in this sacred context, becomes the loving, compassionate, and patient process of clearing away all the aspects of delusion that separate one from one's true Self. The essential tools in this work include, but are not limited to, discernment, intuition, love, and wisdom. Furthermore, sincerity of the heart in this process is necessary in order to call forth God's grace. By clearly stepping out of the way, the healer makes room for God to help. This collaborative process is utterly sacred. It brings wholeness and wisdom to both the patient and the healer, who become mirrors for each other. As another aspect to the process, as therapists, we teach what we need to learn, and we have the opportunity for furthered personal spiritual growth through seeing ourselves reflected in our patients' problems.

Overcoming Our Lack of Connectedness

The contrast between Eastern and Western notions of human consciousness and human potential are striking. Conventional Western psychological wisdom leaves us with the hope of living a good life that is filled with love, friendship, great sex, children, and material gain. This life is all you get, so you better make it good. If you happen to have a very poor worldly circumstance, i.e. poverty, disease, dysfunctional family environment, bad genes, etc., you really have bad luck. The best thing to do is to learn how to survive and be thankful that death comes to end your suffering. This life is your one shot at happiness.

America is a brilliant country with unparalleled material and mental resources. We are suffering, however, because of our lost connection to spirit, our lost experience of unity, and our lost connection to the Earth. Western scientific rationalism creates a mind, body, spirit separation, resulting in a dualism and delusion regarding a truer, deeper reality. The most respected in our culture seem to be great athletes and wealthy businessmen. Those with worldly power are honored and respected. However, these values will not serve the development of a generation of young people who must learn to care about each other, care about the Earth, and care about their own personal psychological-spiritual development.

This book suggests a higher vision of psychotherapy that offers an understanding of the purpose of life, an understanding of our place in the universe, keys to finding joy and bliss, and the deepening of one's relationship with the Divine. These lofty goals cannot be met through conventional psychological approaches alone. Given that traditional psychological methods do not allow for the inclusion and understanding of spiritual realities, can traditional Western psychological methods actually address the healing of the whole person when parts of the person are ignored? While many parts of the self may be addressed in more conventional therapies, individuals may have to look elsewhere to find healing systems that speak to all levels of their Being.

Is it possible to find wholeness without realizing the spiritual unity that is inherent in one's own being? I think not. The limitation and inherent lack of wisdom within traditional Western psychological thought is that it ignores the spiritual consciousness of the individual and the spiritual foundation of the universe. No small matters to ignore! Rather, it would be more helpful for psychotherapy as a whole to adopt a broader definition of the human psyche and to incorporate beliefs and techniques to address our true and fullest nature.

Our society is ripe for a more integrated approach to mental health and health care in general. America being what it is, a capitalistic society, market-driven forces determine what Americans will receive for their health-care dollars. Insurance companies are beginning to fund complementary health care services because they realize there is money to be made. American citizens spend billions of dollars each year on alternative and complementary health care approaches, and the "mainstream" medical community and insurance companies are waking up to this fact and do not want to be left out. Holistic healing centers are popping up around the country, and individuals are looking for health professionals who honor the Spirit along with traditional views of human development and functioning. Over the last twenty years, acceptance has grown for alternative approaches that embrace Spirit and energy.

Expanded Value of the Psychotherapeutic Relationship

Integrating spiritual knowledge and skills into the psychotherapeutic realm will also serve to broaden the therapists' role in society. For psychotherapy, in the hands of a spiritually-conscious individual, is useful not only for those with psychological and mental problems, but also for those in our society who are interested in spiritual development. Psychotherapy's success with phobias, anxiety, panic, depression, early childhood wounds, abuse issues, and so on, is well documented. However, there is an important role for psychotherapy in the spiritual process as well. Growth, both psychological and spiritual, has been proven to be maximally facilitated within a relationship. We all need mirrors in order to evolve. Jack Kornfield, a noted meditation teacher in the Buddhist tradition, has said, "Mindfulness works only when we are willing to direct attention to every area of our suffering. This doesn't mean getting caught in our personal histories, as many people fear, but learning how to address them so that we can actually free ourselves from the big and painful 'blocks' of our past. Such healing work is often best done in a therapeutic relationship with another person."[4] And, as Jesus said, "Wherever two or more are gathered, I will be there also."

Relationship, or people interacting with people, seems to be an essential form for our collective progress. It takes two individuals, a therapist and a client, to create the process in which psychotherapy flourishes. The unique value of psychotherapy, as opposed to other relationships, is that it provides a stable, safe, secure environment in which to recreate and explore one's deepest issues. The relationship becomes a training ground in which the client can learn to lovingly tolerate his or her deepest secrets and fears, the shadow parts of the self. The therapist therefore becomes a mirror to reflect aspects of the self, a guide to help explore new and frightening territory, and a wise counselor to explain the meaning and value of deep processes within the psyche.

This kind of therapy presupposes that the therapist has traveled the terrain and knows the landscape. The therapist must be a guide who knows the map and has the ability to intuitively perceive what the client needs along this road. Without such a relationship, it is often too easy for an individual to avoid pertinent deeper issues, because sometimes we need to be confronted. Sometimes we are unable to interpret our own dreams and comprehend the messages that the unconscious is attempting to provide. And sometimes we need the boost of another person's energy or consciousness to open and awaken our consciousness to higher possibilities and more expanded realms. In my professional work with others, some report that they enter the therapeutic relationship not because they need it for some form of symptom resolution, but because they seek to experience new aspects of themselves and feel a quickening in their spiritual awareness: the energy of the relationship and the wisdom and insights provided are more than they can obtain in their own personal spiritual practice. It almost goes without saying that this level of work will probably occur only in an environment in which the individual feels very secure, very safe, and is treated with respect and unconditional love for all parts of their Being.

Many individuals naively believe that the spiritual path is one of light, bliss, love, and joy. While that may be the goal, many obstacles occur along the way. The clearing away of the tree to find the music stand inside is a powerful process. We are so identified with the bark, the sap, the limbs, and the leaves, that we typically do not want to let go of those aspects of ourselves. We tend to be very attached to who we think we are, i.e., mother, father, son, doctor, mechanic, lover, student. A popular prayer within the Self-Realization Fellowship states, "O Divine Sculptor, chisel out my life according to Thy desire." This can be a very powerful prayer. Some suggest that it takes a very courageous person to offer it. One monk, Brother Ananda-moy, a direct disciple of Paramahansa Yogananda, uses the following example to drive this point home. He suggests that we are all like raw marble in the hands of God. The Divine Sculptor is chipping away in order to create a perfect Self, and each time a little chip flies off, we want to grab it and put it back, saying, "Hey, stop it, that hurts!" We pray for purity of the heart, for awakening of the Self, but it is not an easy process and does require great fortitude and perseverance.

The hard fact of life is that some individuals are not ready for the transformation of consciousness. The spiritual path is a serious and difficult one. It takes a strong and well-integrated ego (ψ) to survive and succeed on it, and many on the path of spiritual awakening are resistant to doing the hard psychological work that is required. Some think, "Just give it to God, and all will be fine." Paramahansa Yogananda said, "God does fifty percent to help you, the *guru* does twenty-five percent, and you do twenty-five percent. Your twenty-five percent is a one-hundred-percent effort."

The aspects of the ego (ι) that must be purified are painful to confront. Our shadow parts offend our sensibilities. We do not like to see ourselves as angry, prideful, vengeful, perverted, selfish, insensitive, hateful, lustful, manipulative, dishonest, greedy, etc. These shadow aspects of the self are strong and can only be transformed when brought into full, conscious awareness. In this context, the psychotherapeutic relationship can be extremely valuable. Besides, being able to admit to one's problems and difficulties fosters honesty and humility. It also allows for real intimacy, without avoiding the pain and discomfort that is essential to true growth of consciousness.

Even the Great Ones suffer. Cancer hurts! Pain and suffering is a part of this reality. A spiritual Master who lives in *samadhi*[5] does not avoid suffering; however, his or her relationship to suffering is different than that of the unenlightened person. A Master lives simultaneously on many planes of consciousness and does not identify with the changes to which the physical body, mind, and emotions are subject. Pain can exist at the level of the body, mind, or the emotions, but bliss is constantly present in the deep, true experience of the Self. This permanent state of bliss is very different from someone who is simply attempting to cover up inner suffering by adopting an outer presentation of "joyousness."

Sacred psychotherapy provides a context to honor one's spiritual nature and openly work to transform those aspects of the self that keep us removed from our Divine nature. A spiritually loving relationship offers a way to move through one's fears of being emotionally vulnerable, one's shadow material, and one's unresolved issues concerning trust and dependency. A loving relationship helps one to avoid denial and overcome the shame that promotes avoidance of the open and direct exploration of one's inner life,

The greatest obstacle to growth is fear. Once we contract and move away from the situation that is challenging us, we have lost the battle. "The only way is through" becomes the battle cry of the spiritual warrior, and the determination to carry on the work despite the difficulties encountered is a key part of the process. While love and devotion are important, courage, fortitude, and inner strength are essential qualities for those on the path.

In this regard, competent traditional psychotherapy has a very good success rate in strengthening the ego (ψ). An individual who has not been fortunate enough to have had good parenting or to have learned the basic skills for intimate communication, to tolerate frustration, and to establish appropriate reality tests and boundaries, needs more help than a spiritual practice alone can provide. The hard and cold reality is that without a solid foundation of a strong ego (ψ) structure, an individual will become overwhelmed and totally confused when confronted with the powerful spiritual energies and experiences that are designed to dissolve the ego (ι). Thus, a spiritual practice with the support of good, spiritually-conscious psychotherapy offers the best of both worlds.

In fact, sacred psychotherapy with spiritually oriented individuals reveals a different process for change than with other clients. It seems rather simple, yet amazing, that the two individuals, the "therapist" and the "client," can merge into a unified state of energy or consciousness that is one with spirit and not identified with any of the contents of the personality. Conscious awareness, on the part of both client and therapist, assists the therapist in helping the client to release the energy that is being organized into a coherent structure and existing as the specific conflict, issue, or thought.

For example, a common problem results when we identify with our parents' negative feelings and beliefs. When our parents are filled with fear and self-doubt, we often unconsciously identify with these qualities and also become fearful and insecure. These psychic identifications can be experienced by both the patient and the therapist as tangible sensations of subtle energy, since all consciousness manifests as energy. When we focus on the energetic level and consciously release the energy, sending it back into light, the psychological conflict is often immediately released and resolved. If one has little or no attachment and identification with the issue, this allows for an internal flexibility that can literally release the existing problem. The new paradigm of healing can thus be more focused, when working at this level, with change happening in a shorter period of time, sometimes vastly shorter or even instantaneous, than with traditional Western therapy. Change happens more quickly because the energy touches an essential level of being, which transcends the condensed consciousness that appears as a tangible manifestation of a feeling, emotion, or physical condition. Thoughts also can be experienced as patterned constellations of energy and, therefore, can be changed quickly by a change in the underlying, subtle energy formation.

Redefining Healing

In the Western psychological tradition, the notion of healing is a very vague one. Numerous clinical studies have been carried out in an attempt to define normalcy or mental health, and the findings often indicate that traits and behavior that are regarded as socially desirable end up being defined as mentally healthy or normal. We can see the obvious limitations with this system, especially if we happen to live in a deviant culture. Paramahansa Yogananda often said, "Environment is stronger than will power," and here we can see the full force of that statement. Do we, as autonomous individuals, want to be understood and defined totally on the basis of the majority that surrounds us? Perhaps we have other values that set us apart from our social-political-religious culture; are we then to be defined as deviant because of these differing attitudes and beliefs?

The spiritual path provides a unique perspective that redefines healing, in that the focus shifts away from "making things all right" to one of becoming more consciously aware of one's existence at all levels. A spiritual approach to healing focuses on the unfoldment of the soul, not the resolution of the symptoms. The soul's encasement in ignorance is the real problem, and the various symptoms, whether they be physical, mental, or emotional, are only the motivating factors that drive us to consider our soul's dilemma. For example, if someone comes in with a physical ailment, my primary concern is to use the symptom to help the person realize why they have that particular ailment, and the power that that disease can hold for them in the awakening of their soul. The paradox is that in the process of awakening to spiritual reality, symptoms often get resolved. The Bible teaches, "Seek ye first the kingdom of God, and all things shall be added unto you." This is the secret. Go directly to God and let God help. The nature of the Omnipresent One is such love and such perfection that many disorders, or states of dis-ease, melt away and dissolve in that presence.

A devotee of Paramahansa Yogananda tells a story that illustrates this effect. The devotee had been blessed with several personal meetings with the Master. Each time, Yogananda would ask him if he had any questions. Each time, the devotee was so immersed in the joy and love that emanated from Yogananda that he forgot whatever he had planned to discuss. Finally, he decided to write down some questions. Again he met with Yogananda, and when asked if he had any questions, he again replied, "Oh no, it is just so wonderful to be here with you." Yogananda replied, "I know you have some questions. You wrote them down and put them in your pocket. Take them out and tell me what they are."

Most of us are totally caught up in the limited definition of who we think we are. We identify with our physical bodies and think that's who we are, so we are afraid that if we were to die and lose this body, we would not exist. Many of us believe that we are our feelings, our emotions, and that our emotions are important because they define our identities. We also tend to believe that we are what we think, that our ideas about ourselves are, in fact, who we are. We lose sight of the deeper reality that our true nature is pure Truth, pure Spirit, pure Awareness. We, in truth, are Beings who exist in a realm that has no time and no space and no form. We are Beings of pure light and pure awareness. The ancient yogic teachings of Patanjali tell us that there are eight Divine qualities, which are as follows: Love, Wisdom, Light, Sound, Joy, Peace, Bliss, and Power. Often, people wonder how they can know if they are experiencing God. Paramahansa Yogananda says that the experience of the soul is ever-new, ever-existing, ever-conscious Joy. These are the qualities that we are attempting to become. In fact, we are already them, but we do not realize it, so the real work is in peeling off all the layers of delusion that keep us from recognizing these qualities as our true nature.

A New Theory of Normalcy

In the psychology of spirituality, a whole new definition of normalcy needs to be considered. Sacred healing is not concerned with acquiring the values and beliefs of our larger culture, for, indeed, as we look around and see what we are creating, one wonders about the sanity of such materialistic points of view, since this approach appears to be responsible for tremendous planetary damage. The spiritual notion of health is concerned more with balance, harmony, love, service, and heightened awareness. The truly healthy, spiritually-directed individual views all of life as an opportunity to work with reducing desires and attachments and to release the identifications of the little ego (ι) in order to merge back within that infinite Self, the soul. The truly spiritually-minded person knows that the only purpose for being here on Earth is to serve others and to return to that God-realized state.

From this perspective, all of life's trials and difficulties are seen as spiritual blessings, given in order to purify the self and live a life that expresses Divine love, joy, compassion, and harmony with all of nature. Through this type of practice, a sense of peace and serenity can be obtained, wherein life's difficulties do not create emotional dramas. As one becomes stabilized in soul consciousness, one becomes more able to truly love, because personal attachments and desires diminish.

As stated before, psychotherapy becomes a much different process within the context of spiritual consciousness. We all have emotional conflicts and identifications with aspects of our mothers and fathers. Many of us even have holes in our development, which make certain stress-filled situations more difficult. For example, if we have had a difficult early experience with feelings of abandonment, then separations often become very sensitive and filled with emotional reactions.

The perspective of spiritual consciousness allows us to identify with the eternal presence of our Spirit and not the transitory aspects of our body, mind, and/or emotions. Furthermore, this subtle shift gives us tremendous leverage toward changing our internal state. Clinical observation suggests that it is our identification with our problems that keeps them so solidified. It is as if our belief in them and our thoughts and feelings about them keep them in existence, and our identification with them makes us feel helpless and controlled by our inner conflicts and feelings. I have observed that it is much easier to engage in subtle energy work with those individuals who have achieved a certain level of spiritual consciousness than with others who have not, because the spiritually dedicated are often less identified with the symptoms. Spiritually awakened individuals know that they are not the body, not the emotions, and not the thoughts. They are more easily able to allow for the transformation of symptoms, because they do not hold those issues to be the essential definition of their Self.

Transforming the Therapist

Obviously, one must be able to discern among the various dense and subtle energy states if one is to work in this fashion. Familiarity with the subtle realms are a natural result of spiritual practice and meditation. They are gifts that one receives when one is focused upon God-realization. Nonetheless, it is important not to become driven by the desire to obtain these subtle powers but to gratefully and humbly accept such gifts as they do arise. It is not everyone's *dharma* (path or duty) to be a healer. Those of us who do share this path of service, however, can increase our ability to help others as we become more conscious of the subtle realms and deepen our attunement with God. Never forget, it is God doing the work through us.

The process of healing in this subtle fashion becomes a very sensitive and intimate internal experience. Often, during the work itself, the therapist may receive images, thought transmissions, bodily sensations, or a host of other impressions. There appears to be a direct relationship between our inner impressions and the actual mental, physical, and emotional experience of the other. When we have linked up at this deep level, we are in a unified state, and as our internal state changes, so does the state of our client. Thus, we have access to a rather subtle and personal feedback system, our intuition, to help us know what is happening inside our clients.

It is most important to mention again that deep states of healing happen *through* us; we do not direct them. This is crucially important to understand. God's grace actually does flow through us and directs us. We literally become the instrument, and the work flows through our very being. Our challenge is to learn how to open the way for this flow of energy. Our personal efforts are not what make this level of healing so powerful; in fact, the more we let go, and the less we do, the more actually happens.

The conscious therapist's intuitive ability to perceive what is to happen next, in each moment, becomes his or her greatest asset, because each moment is in truth orchestrated by a Divine hand, and if we can consciously perceive "the moment," then we can help to facilitate its manifestation.

We may very well feel, during the actual experience, in the moment, that a Divine consciousness is present and is offering a clearer, wiser, transforming possibility, and if we can perceive that

Divine possibility, we can help to support its expression and manifestation. Rather than busily and willfully doing what we want, and not listening and attuning to the Divine will, we need to proceed with greater receptivity to the Divine director. It is as if we are actors in a play and are in harmony with the director's inspiration and vision. If we listen and play our role well, bringing our own unique talents to the performance, then all our creative forces unfold to reveal the magic and wonder of the moment. However, if we just do what we want, based upon our own limited personal needs and desires, then we create chaos and disharmony. In fact, some suggest that our individual and planetary chaos is the result of our refusal or inability to clearly hear and attune ourselves to the Divine.

So, there is so little to do, and yet, so much to be done. We, in our little state of mind and our ego (ι), cannot possibly touch someone else with an infinite, all-knowing hand. Yet, when we make a little shift in consciousness and remember that we are the Infinite and that the Infinite resides within us, then all possibility emerges to help us discover our ultimate truth.

God, in whatever form we choose—father, mother, friend, beloved, *guru*, Jesus, Allah—dwells within each and every one of us. Our task, if we want to heal, is to attend to that Divine presence and offer ourselves in its service. Be aware, however, that this is no casual offering, for the path of healing is the spiritual path, and the process of purification and surrender is ruthless! The ego (ι) wants to live and hold on, and it will do anything it can to survive. The cosmic battle between the light and the dark, between good and evil, between the higher and lower natures, resides within us. All the power we can muster must be directed to our highest spiritual nature, if we are to survive as God-realized Beings. And, although we all are children of God, this is no game for children. It is a game for the courageous and the bold, the spiritual warrior whose ammunition is devotion for God.

The next chapter recounts the story of my personal awakening to spiritual dimensions and how this event impacted and began to become integrated into my psychotherapeutic process.

2

A Personal Account
of Awakening

THE MOMENT OF AWAKENING is different for everyone. Some come to an expanded state of awareness gradually, over time, through great disciplinary effort or as a result of intense devotional yearnings. Others experience a sudden and dramatic shift in their awareness, one that may include visions and powerful energetic forces moving through their bodies and their consciousness. Many individuals in the latter group find themselves in spiritual emergencies, because they are cast into new and unfamiliar territory without the inner experience and strength to understand what is happening and to see them through. My personal story is included here only as an example of the transformational process; however, bear in mind that spiritual awakening takes place in many different ways, always unique to the individual concerned.

This story is included here as a means of helping the reader understand, at least partially, such otherwise vague phrases as "expanded states of consciousness" and "subtle energy levels," as well as to give a glimpse into how subtle energy may manifest and be productively useful as a modality in the clinical psychotherapeutic context.

Encounter with Dr. Kübler-Ross

A dramatic and spontaneous awakening occurred within me in 1977, while I was attending an intensive retreat with Elisabeth Kübler-Ross, M.D., in Maui, Hawaii. I had no preparation for this experience and was not under the influence of any prescription or non-prescription drug, nor did I have any psychotic symptoms as the result of the experience. I share this story with the hope of explaining how the mystery of consciousness awakens and how we can be influenced by events and forces far beyond our current field of vision.

In 1977, I decided that I needed to address my personal fear of death. I was conditioned by my family to be afraid of death and therefore avoided any contact with family members who were seriously ill or injured. I entered individual psychotherapy to explore my feelings regarding this area and decided to work with children who were seriously ill. My first seriously ill patient was a three-year-old boy with a brain tumor. This child turned out to be one of my greatest teachers. Because of my involvement with him and others who were dying, I was inspired to go to a Holistic Health Association conference in San Diego to hear Dr. Elisabeth Kübler-Ross speak. That decision turned out to be one of the most momentous actions of my life. I, along with two thousand other people, became transfixed and elevated to a transcendent state of consciousness. For an hour I was spellbound and could see nothing but Elisabeth. Everyone and everything else receded into the background. The only thing that I was aware of was a beam of light illuminating Elisabeth while she told her story of working with dying people, of being in the concentration camps in Nazi Germany, and of her recent experiences with spiritual guides.

I felt moved in a way that I had never been moved before and knew that I must have a private moment to speak to her. After her presentation, she seemed to disappear instantly. I wondered where she could have gone, thinking perhaps she had crawled under the curtain behind the stage and quietly slipped away. However, I was somehow intuitively drawn to look down the aisle to my right, where

I saw two double-steel doors. I knew somehow that she was behind them, but I expected her to be surrounded by a horde of people. I opened those doors and instantly melted into the embrace of this small, loving woman, who gently reached up to hug me. I lost myself in her embrace. I had never experienced such love for another human being.

It was very shortly afterwards that I signed up for one of her workshops, "Life in Transition," which was to be held on the island of Maui in Hawaii. During that five-day experience, I watched as my perception of the universe was totally blown apart. I went to the workshop as a traditional psychologist, using theoretical constructs, empathy, and the rational mind. I left Maui with aspects of myself awakened that took nearly four years to integrate.

During the first two days of the workshop, various members told why they had come to Maui. I was somewhat taken aback at the levels of human suffering and pain that were being shared. Many had children who had just died or parents who were in the process of dying. One woman had even brought her three-year-old child, who had multiple birth defects and was being kept alive through intravenous feedings. His health was so poor that she carried oxygen with her, because he had difficulty breathing on his own. We all were aware that this little boy could die at any time, and we wondered if this was the place he would choose to leave his body.

Story after story unfolded, and I felt that I had nothing to share. My life hadn't been so traumatic—a little neurotic suffering here and there, a few suicidal desires, but it all seemed to be rather run-of-the-mill for the human experience, par for the course, so to speak. I began to realize that gradually over the course of my professional training and my own life, my heart had closed. I realized that this was the life-stuff with which I was working every day, and yet somehow I had become closed off to a deeper level of connection with human beings. In that moment, I felt my heart center begin to crack and open, as tears trickled down my face. From a deep place inside, I felt hopeful and relieved. I felt hopeful about the future and relieved that finally something was beginning to happen. I had become sterile, what with my clinical understanding and "professional sensitivity." I prayed that something could change to bring me closer to those around me. Perhaps, here in Maui, I could become alive once more and learn to live with Love and compassion.

The following morning I was distressed to find my throat so sore that I could barely swallow. One of the fellow participants, a physician, said that it looked like a strep throat and was happy to send me to the local pharmacy down the road to get some antibiotics. I was reluctant to take any medication, as I hoped that I could use the power of my own mind to heal my body. After all, I did believe in an integrated relationship between the mind and the body. I found myself somewhat desperately trying to visualize healing light coming into my throat, hoping to do something to relieve the pain so I could attend the morning session.

In the midst of this attempt at self-healing, I suddenly found myself transported into another time and space. It was something more than a vision, and yet not a dream, but a living, waking moment of being in another time and place. I found myself walking through a hallway of tiles and noticing row after row of little faucets coming out from the wall, and, as I looked up, I realized that they were showers. Judging by the height of the showers in relation to me, I must have been about six or seven years old. All of a sudden, I had a moment of realization that I was in the showers in Nazi Germany—the gas chamber. Far at the end of the showers, I saw a pile of bodies that were stacked and in decay. I realized that all the symptoms of my body seemed merely to be reflections of a deeper memory.

Then I was propelled further back into time, and I saw myself in the inner circle with Christ. Many thoughts ran through my mind: "Who could I have been?" I didn't know his name, but I remembered that there had been one disciple who betrayed Christ. Some deep, deep sense of guilt arose from my early childhood. I had been told constantly by my Catholic babysitter that the Jews had killed Christ. Since I was Jewish, I thought that perhaps it was me; perhaps I was the one who had betrayed the Christ. A moment of terror passed through my mind, and then another rapid shift in my consciousness, and I seemed to become the Christ energy. Now I thought that perhaps I was Christ, as I felt so merged into that essence. A part of my mind was watching all of these events, thinking, "This is crazy. I know that that thought is psychotic."

As all of these events were unfolding, layers upon layers of my consciousness witnessed these events. Part of me was thinking, "Aha! This must be psychosis. Far out! I'm a schizophrenic." Being a psychologist, I have always been intrigued with the states that people move through. I thought, "Here's a chance to really know what it is to be psychotic." Then another part of me was saying, "How can I be psychotic? There's too much rational ego here, discerning, comprehending, experiencing. If I am psychotic, I wouldn't be thinking about this. This must be something else." Fortunately, I had read the volumes by Carlos Castaneda, such as *The Teachings of Don Juan*, so I had some conceptual structure to reassure me that a mystical process was unfolding inside me. I let go of my concern about being psychotic and knew that the only way out was *through*. This was Wednesday. Monday I was supposed to be functioning in my office as a reasonable, healthy psychologist. I knew I had to keep moving—the only choice was ahead.

I desperately needed to speak to Elisabeth, because I knew she would understand. I quickly went to the central meeting hall, grabbed Elisabeth by the arm, and said, "I have to speak with you." I took her to a small alcove and revealed all these experiences. Then, looking at her, I said, "I feel like I have been with you before, that I was there with you at the time of Christ, and that I have been looking for you for a long, long time." She looked deeply into my eyes, into what I now know to be my soul, and said, "We were, and now we're here again to fight negativity." A place in my being then opened and went back through time and space, connecting to an energy, a place of Being, that brought me a sense of completion and tranquility that I had never known. Another place, a wound within me, healed instantaneously, from that one little moment and acknowledgment that we were one.

Prior to that moment, I often had felt a tremendous hole, a gap inside me. I would be driving around in my 280Z, longingly glancing at the women around me. My only understanding of this was a psychological one. I assumed that there was some deep, infantile aspect of my self that was longing to return to the womb or to recreate some symbiotic relationship to make me feel whole. The one moment with Elisabeth healed that place in me, and I never again felt that same sense of emptiness.

My strep throat was now totally healed. There was no pain. We returned to the main room, and I literally hid behind Elisabeth. I sat behind the corner of a couch, somewhat cautiously peering out at the rest of the group, because at this point, I felt so open and exposed that I could hardly stand the collective energy of their glances. As I was sitting there, I began to feel my leg vibrate, and I thought, "Ah! How interesting. This must be what *prana*[6] energy is." All during that morning session, Elisabeth stayed present with me, touching my hand, ever so gently. I found my mind opening and closing to receive her love. Much to my distress, I found myself feeling and saying inside, "Why don't you get your hand off me?" In that moment she withdrew. Could she read my thoughts? Then I would calm myself, become quiet and open, and then her hand would return. Opening, closing, she would withdraw and return. I felt a state of oneness with her that I had never experienced with another human being. As we concluded our morning session, I felt strongly that I had to stay with her. I and a few others followed her to her room. She announced that she was tired and needed to take a little nap. We all decided to nap as well. Suddenly, there was a knock at the door, an arriving visitor from Lahaina, who offered to do an "energy balancing" for Elisabeth. I had no idea what an "energy balancing" was, and I thought, "Boy, these nuts show up from all over the place." But I was trying to be gracious in my protection of Elisabeth, so I asked Elisabeth if she wanted the energy balancing. She said, "Of course, let her in."

By this time my sore throat had returned, and I thought, "Aha! Perhaps this is a psychic healer and I can get my throat cured." I did not want to act like I was greedy, so I tried to control my impulse to immediately grab her and say, "Heal me! Heal me!" When the moment was right, I somewhat casually asked if she could possibly heal my throat. She assured me that she could not guarantee that my throat would be healed, but she would balance my energy to the highest good. That sounded like a pretty good deal to me, so I readily agreed. She began to do a balancing of my chakras á la Brugh Joy. Once again, I found myself being teleported into another time and space. This time I immediately found myself lying on a table in a laboratory, again in Nazi Germany. Everything was so vivid. I found myself being tortured. Instruments were being shoved down my throat. A part of me was cognizant of my normal reality and wanted to scream, but that same part of me also said, "Come on now, keep it together. After all, there are a lot of people around here." So, I screamed inside. The torturing went on and on. Finally, they decided to leave me alone. I was so relieved and thankful to no longer be the victim that I did not even have a moment of compassion or concern for the woman who was next to be tortured.

Then my focus shifted to what seemed to be a human arm of pure light across my chest, as a beautiful smell of menthol filled the air. My body began to fill with white light, and my eyes began to flutter. I was elevated to a state of consciousness that I had never previously experienced. Once again, I found my throat healed.

These experiences provided deep revelations that affect me to this day. In one moment, I realized the oneness of the universe and saw our interconnectedness, like a circle or a sphere in which everything returned to its source. There was no action made in the universe that did not come back upon itself. I could see that even hatred and the desire for revenge that stems from terrible atrocities, like those of Nazi Germany, serve only to continue a negative cycle of energy. Violence does not stop violence; it only sustains it.

After these initial experiences, I found myself being changed, purified, transformed. Areas of negativity in me vanished—self-justified places of revenge were gone. I felt a place opening in me that included a sense of Love such as I had never known. I understood for the first time what Christ meant in his teachings about unconditional Love and "turning the other cheek." I now found myself saying things during my private discussions with other participants that I knew were wise. This new-found wisdom was a shock to me. Suddenly, I seemed to comprehend aspects of philosophy that I had tried to understand for years in graduate school but never could. I felt as though I had just completed a course in philosophy in an instant, and that now, ancient, eternal wisdom was available to me. A depth had opened for which I had longed for many years but had never been able to access. Previously, I felt as though I had a limited store of information and a total depletion of any deeper wisdom. Now, something within had been opened to a higher or deeper knowing. For the first time in my life, I felt like I actually had something to say that would be worthwhile.

The day wore on, and it was time for sleep. The next morning we were to go to Haleakala for sunrise, and I was feeling quite practical about getting a few hours' rest, since we were to awaken at four o'clock in the morning. Yet, it was impossible for me to close my eyes without experiencing a tremendous sense of dread and inner terror. All of my negative thoughts and feelings projected themselves into space and came back to me. I was afraid to walk out into the dark alone in order to go to the bathroom, because I felt that a presence lurked out there that would destroy me. Fortunately, I had a strong and fairly large bladder, so I could sustain the evening without having to venture into the dark. While I lay there in bed, whenever I closed my eyes, I began to feel a presence emerge. My heart started to pound and something would begin to overcome me. I seemed to see arrows and spears flying at me, as if I were under attack. Finally, I thought, "Enough is enough." I became so annoyed at all this that I said—and I'm not sure who I was speaking to, "Do what you want with my body. I'm leaving." In that instant, from some place deep within my consciousness, I saw a ball of brilliant white light emerge into the foreground. As it grew larger and larger, I found myself merging with this light, and as this light began to move away from my body, I looked back down and realized that the physical thing lying there (my physical body) was nothing. I actually imagined people coming and beating that body, taking picks and axes and chopping it into little bits and pieces, but it didn't affect me. There was nothing that anyone could do to that physical body in that moment that could have any impact on me. I was pure light, pure consciousness! Then, I immediately went to sleep.

I awoke the next morning with tremendous apprehension. I knew something very powerful was about to happen on Haleakala, but I did not know if I was going to meet God or Satan. A number of us piled into a small van, and we began to make our ascent to this most powerful crater. As we were moving, I felt some need to make conversation to assuage my anxiety, so I chatted with the woman sitting to my right. Pam was a sweet, sensitive, attractive young woman from Chicago who had spent some time studying psychic phenomena. As we moved farther and farther over the long, winding road up the slopes of Haleakala, I noticed that my throat, which had returned to its strep condition, was beginning to feel better and better. As we spoke, I began to hear a very faint but clear sound. I stopped talking for a moment, then asked Pam, "Do you hear that?" We listened, and sure enough, we both heard a choir of spirits, singing in high soprano. The blessings were beginning to unfold. The dark night of the soul was at last opening to the light of day.

Earlier in the workshop, we each had expressed what we wanted to finish up or leave during this time. I had stated that I wanted to be able to let go of my need to be so special and my feelings of omnipotence. They had felt like a burden to me. We finally arrived at the top of Haleakala, and I was standing around, feeling amazingly superinflated; after all, here I was, in a very close friendship with Elisabeth Kübler-Ross by now, plus having all these marvelous experiences, and I was thinking, "Boy, I'm pretty hot stuff." In that moment, through my inner spiritual vision, I saw a wave of energy seven feet high, in the form of a standing wave, coming directly at me. As this energy passed through me, I felt a change in my being that leveled me to the extreme opposite of my superinflated state. Now, I felt incredibly embarrassed for having been such a fool. I did not feel that I deserved even to stand on the same piece of earth with the other people present. They felt sacred and I so unworthy. I found it impossible to speak. I could only stand there and cry. As grace would have it, Elisabeth now showed up, and she started making small talk with me. I began to tell her about Pam and a thought I had had that they should meet each other. For, indeed, Pam had been so shy that she had not initiated any direct personal contact with Elisabeth.

Elisabeth was beginning to freeze from the biting chill of the early morning wind atop this 8,000-foot crater, so we decided to go inside a glass observatory for protection. I had been telling Elisabeth about Pam and how I felt that they should meet. As we walked inside, Elisabeth asked, "Where is this person you want me to meet?" Suddenly, standing right in front of me, was Pam. I looked into Pam's eyes, and there elapsed a moment of telepathic communication. All I said was, "She knows, I told her." Then, the two of them sat down for a delicate, time-honored exchange. A peaceful stillness settled around us. To this day, I cannot say for sure whether everyone in the room chose to stop talking, or if it was our state of consciousness alone that quieted us into this tranquility. We were surrounded by a bubble of eternal serenity, and a burst of sandalwood fragrance filled the air.

When they were finished talking, Pamela came to me and said, "How can I ever thank you for this? This has been the most wonderful moment of my life." I thought, "There's nothing to thank me for—I really haven't done anything." She reached out and touched my hand, and in that moment, a flow of electricity came from her and entered me. At this touch, every cell in my body began to flutter like a lotus petal. I was experiencing orgasms in my heart chakra. I felt as though I had been blessed, that I was in the presence of an angel. I was afraid to let go of her hand, for fear it would stop the experience. Instantly I fell in love.

At the end of the week, it was indeed a lesson in nonattachment to finally leave Elisabeth, Pam, and that sacred experience.

Two days after the Haleakala experience, I finally returned home, late on a Sunday night. I tried to figure out what I could do in my office Monday morning. How could I be a mere psychologist any longer? How could I merely talk to people about their personality problems? Suddenly aware of deeper levels of inner experience, being a psychologist now seemed to me to be so limiting and superficial. How could our traditional, limited forms of psychological guidance be of any lasting service to man and God?

Fortunately, I happened to have a series of albums by Ram Dass, and that night I chose to put one on. I listened to Ram Dass talk about *dharma* and the intimate balance of life energies. Our consciousness may transcend any of our particular actions or roles: garbage collector, doctor, teacher, mother, father, student; no matter, it is the attitude of service and the Love that we bring to each action and to each moment that matters. "No fame, no blame; just being, serving, loving, surrendering." I realized that it was my *dharma* to be in this role, and that to be an impeccable psychologist was a further fulfillment of my capacity to serve. What joy! I didn't have to give up everything I'd done, in order to be all that I am. I went to bed eager to explore what the next day would bring.

Some time during the first week of my return from Hawaii, I attended my personal weekly therapy session. Prior to my leaving, I had made plans to continue my postgraduate education and to apply to the local psychoanalytic training program in Los Angeles. At that time, I held the psychoanalytic perspective to be the pinnacle of professional success, and during the course of my graduate education had taken advantage of every opportunity to train and study with top people in that field. For example, during my graduate education I had been supervised by Hedda Bulgar, Ph.D., a Viennese-trained psychoanalyst, and I had three years of twice-a-week psychoanalytically-oriented psychotherapy with Joel Shor, Ph.D., who trained with Michael Balint, M.D. at the Tavistock Clinic in London. I had also been part of a brief supervision group with Albert Mason, M.D., who trained with Melanie Klein, M.D. in England. However, now, due to my experiences in Maui, I perceived a vast difference between a spiritual perspective that centers one's consciousness in the heart and looks to perceive the deeper, true Self of another, and the psychoanalytic perspective that values what one knows, one's store of information, and what an individual *does* or accomplishes over the deeper or spiritual aspects of the Self. Thus, upon returning to my therapist's office, I terminated therapy immediately and gave up all plans for any further psychoanalytic training.

Experiencing the Paradigm Shift in the Office

Then, back in my office in Beverly Hills, I wondered, "What will today bring me? How am I to manifest these new aspects in my Being?" After my typical breakfast in the coffee shop, consisting of two scrambled eggs, cottage cheese, a freshly-made bran muffin, and some hot water with lemon and honey, I was ready to start my day. The anticipated moment finally arrived, when my first patient pushed the button in the waiting room to announce his arrival.

I had been seeing John for approximately one year, although the intensity of our involvement had varied. John was referred to me initially because of a psychotic episode that left him vacillating between threatening to blow up one of the major supermarket chains and feeling totally blissed out and "one" with the cosmic order. He had been picked up by the police one day while strolling around the beach in a rather disheveled and disoriented state. John's main ambition in life was essentially to be able to return to his home and be taken care of by his mother. He had little desire to work, little desire to make friends, and little desire to do anything other than retreat to the safety of his maternal environment. He loved reading Superman comic books and watching soap operas on T.V.

This day, John came in, sat down, and began to relate the events of his week since we had last been together. I was aware immediately that something different was happening. As John continued to talk, I felt a strange pressure pushing in on me, forcing me deeper and deeper inside myself. I found it difficult even to keep my eyes open, as if somebody were trying to push me into a deeper and deeper state of sleep. As I observed this, I wondered, "Well, I know I've had a long, hard week, but I didn't think I was that tired," and then I thought, "Well, I just had breakfast. Maybe I'm just digesting my food, and my energy is going to my stomach." Then I thought, "No, that can't possibly be it." I then somehow shifted into a clairvoyant state and became aware of a stream of energy, some kind of force field, that was being emitted by John, forcing me more and more deeply into myself.

Thinking as a psychologist, I immediately began relating this effect to the nature of projection, speculating that projection could take the form of a flow of energy. I then thought, "Well, all I should have to do is to exert my will and be strong enough to send this stuff right back into John where it belongs." I sat up straight, took a deep breath, and pushed hard with my will, sending a stream of energy back towards John. In that instant, my consciousness cleared, with a breath of fresh air and a sense of clear light. Instantly, however, the penetrating voltage increased, as the flow of energy from John now became relentlessly stronger and stronger. This time I perceived it as a stream of energy that was much more concentrated, like a river flowing through space, coming directly at me.

So now I thought, "Well, I'll just be clever. I will create a 'magic shield' and direct the energy to the shield, so it will be deflected from me." I visualized a shield of light in my etheric hands, towards which all the energy was coming and then being deflected away. Once again, there was a momentary relief, but then the energy again came back towards me, even stronger. I now "saw" the energy as bricks flying through the air and began deflecting each brick with my astral hands. I figured, "It's about time to start talking about something." So, I began sharing what I was perceiving. I said, "John, I feel like you have many blocks against my seeing what's inside of you. Are you aware of how much energy you are putting into pushing me away?"

To my wonder and amazement, in that moment, everything cleared. John evidenced a level of his Being that I had never before experienced, and he suddenly opened in a way that was totally new to our relationship. "I know," he admitted. "I've been doing that all my life. I'm really afraid to have people get inside of me." This moment of clarity and honesty created the opportunity for us to explore and discuss John's real desire to have relationships with people, and that he did feel very lonely, but also felt such fear that it was impossible for him to initiate contacts. This day became the turning point for a new course of action for John, and we ended that session with a greater sense of connection and understanding. Obviously, this was no miracle cure, but it was the beginning for a much deeper, open, and honest exploration of what John's life was really about.

A few minutes later, my next patient arrived. Sally was a young woman of nineteen who had had a very serious eating disorder. She had been unwilling to allow herself to take in food. After each meal, she would feel inwardly driven to quickly vomit and empty herself of everything that was inside. Somehow, throughout all this, she still managed to digest enough calories to keep herself in a reasonably healthy physical condition. Also, Sally was having tremendous difficulties living at home. Her father was severely depressed and often threatened suicide. Her mother was having relationships with other men, and Sally was feeling caught in the middle, trying to keep peace in the family and support both of her parents. In fact, she was more of a parent to her parents than they were to her. Sally sat down on my couch and began to tell me about her week.

Again, to my utter amazement, I found my state of visual perception changing. I no longer was able to perceive the form of a human being sitting in front of me. I found myself propelled into a super-conscious state. All I could perceive before me was an egg-shaped, luminescent being. I saw only pure light, and from within this light, I heard a voice. Now, I can only imagine how I looked from Sally's point of view. Every now and then I would ground back into my physical body, and I would notice that Sally was looking at me rather strangely, probably wondering, "What is going on with this guy?"

Actually, while being propelled into this trance-like state, I really did not feel connected to her at the level at which she needed to feel connected with me. The entire session continued with my moving in and out of this state, and it became impossible for me to maintain contact with her on the physical/material plane. No matter what I did, I simply continued seeing this luminescent light and hearing the voice emanating from the light. It became obvious to me that I could not be of any further help to Sally, since the state I was being propelled into was not a state that she could relate to. She needed someone who could relate to her more mentally and emotionally and be more grounded physically than I could. That week she happened to be going for a medication consultation with a psychiatric colleague of mine. Fortunately, they made a nice connection and were able to continue treatment together.

From that time on, my work began to shift dramatically. I no longer listened only "with the third ear," nor attended only to transference reactions, nor looked at dreams simply as the inroad to the unconscious. Something new had opened for me, a direct perception of the deepest issues that confronted the client and myself in the therapeutic relationship. The soul's intuition had become my friend and companion.

That same first day, in the afternoon, a new patient arrived, a woman in her forties named June. As we began to discuss June's life, she told me of the many difficulties she had in relationships, the many difficulties that she had been having with her husband, and her general dissatisfaction with life and the world. As she continued to share, my intuitive perception once again revealed to me an energetic representation of the client: I began to see three planes of June's reality, literally floating in the space between us. Each of these three "horizons" symbolized a level of her consciousness. Her most apparent presentation to the world was as a rather hostile, obnoxious, sarcastic woman, who seemed to do everything she could to push people away. I was aware that if I allowed myself to attend only to that level of her manifestation, I quickly would be repelled and somewhat annoyed with her. Dropping down to the next horizon, I could see that the second level of her being consisted mostly of fear. Here was a fear of being hurt, a fear of being left, and a fear of what her anger might do. I realized that if I attended to that layer, then we would both be focused in fear, and attending to it thus might only serve to further magnify her discomfort. Dropping down yet another layer, I could see a soft, gentle, sensitive being with the desire to be treated lovingly, with respect and sensitivity. At this point, I began ignoring everything else she was saying and began to speak only to this deepest level. I merely shared with her what I saw and how everything else seemed to be only a means of protection to avoid the deepest level of her essential Self. As I watched, these horizons then began to move, and the deepest layer, which seemed at first to be at a distance, began to move in closer and closer, until finally it filled the space between us with a magnificent, gentle, heart energy. At this point, her entire being and presentation changed instantly. Once again, in a matter of minutes, I found myself in a most intimate and loving relationship with a client.

This first day back had been quite a teaching. Suddenly, the relationship between my inner life and the outer environment had become very clear. I had always known some relationship between my inner reality and the outer world, but never so clearly. Never had I seen it so dramatically and personally portrayed, as I watched the flow of energy streaming through space, seeing and realizing how my state of consciousness, how the quality of my Being, and how the very essence of my energy could literally touch and transform others. I realized then that all words were only as powerful as the energy and the consciousness that they contained, and that during therapy we could talk about anything at all—but what really mattered was the essence of the vibration, the openness of the Love, and the depth of the Truth that was held within the words expressed. The words spoken were no longer idle pieces of information that were teleported through space. My words clearly evidenced the embodiment of my

Being and the physical manifestation of my consciousness. They were the agents and containers of my healing energy. And this was true not only of words, but also of thoughts and feelings—all had form.

The ancient esoteric notion of thought-forms now became a living reality for me: thoughts have shape and form on a subtle plane, and they create our environment. The words that we share are only more concrete expressions of our innermost thoughts. Even more important, the thoughts that we entertain create energy as powerfully as the actions we make. I literally could observe single thoughts create new seeds of energy, new environments, new oceans to swim in—thoughts of Love, Peace, Harmony, and Oneness, creating an openness, an invitation, an environment of revelation and sharing.

On the other hand, I could clearly see how thoughts of judgment, criticism, or classification created only distance, duality, restriction, and a total flattening of the space in which we live. In other words, our quality of Being does make a difference: the very essence of our life creates our environment and is the instrument for our healing—light touching light, consciousness touching consciousness, ever playing, in a subtle dance of interweaving energies, gently magnetizing higher and higher vibrations, more and more light and more and more spaciousness, opening and opening to the Essence of our nature.

3

Awakening to Essence

U PON MY RETURN FROM HAWAII I was eager to find others who could help me integrate and understand the profound changes that had occurred in my consciousness. I sought out healers, meditation teachers, and anyone who was conscious of the subtle realms. The next major step in my development led me to a group of people who helped me realize aspects of my essential Self that had yet to be awakened.

In 1978, a dear friend of mine, Daisy, told me about a person in town who was doing bodywork. I knew that my body needed something, for I was feeling a constriction and blockage in my physical structure, and I knew that the flow of energy could not move on its own accord. I'd never actually had any kind of bodywork, and I had heard that Rolfing can be rather excruciating, so I was looking forward to what had been described to me as a more benign form of Rolfing—the Lomi school of bodywork. Daisy told me about a person in town who was quite good at this kind of bodywork and that I should go try him out. I made an appointment and went to a few sessions just to see what would happen.

David was a very gentle man who was a potter in addition to being a bodyworker. The strength in his hands was tremendous, and he seemed to feel no hesitation in applying that strength to my poor, frail body. I was glad that I had been meditating so long, for without that capacity, I'm not sure I could have successfully endured the pain. David informed me that a training program was upcoming in this form of bodywork that would last three months. Something deep within me knew that I was going to take this training, even though it seemed quite inconceivable at the time, since I was working full-time and this training program required a twenty-hour-a-week commitment. As it turned out, the commitment later became thirty hours, but they eased us into that level of involvement.

I met David's associate, Kathleen, in this form of bodywork, which was called Essential Integration. Kathleen lived in a little house in Malibu and greeted me with her wet hair wrapped in a towel. She was very bold, direct, and strikingly present in the moment. We spoke for awhile, and then she asked if she could look at my body to examine my alignment, posture, and structure. Since the training was in bodywork, I agreed to her request, even though I felt a little uncomfortable. After she completed her observations of me, we then made arrangements to meet for lunch to talk further about the training and myself. I was not sure whether I wanted to do the training or not, but I looked forward to the luncheon meeting.

Later, over the course of an hour-and-a-half at the Magic Pan in Beverly Hills, I was put through so many changes by the mobility and flexibility of Kathleen's consciousness, which totally overwhelmed me, that I became determined to take this training, just to be able to match her and feel her equal. I never before had experienced anyone playing my whole being like an instrument. I felt like I was a toy in her hands. She seemed to see right through me and push every button I had. One moment we were laughing; the next moment, I was on the verge of crying; the next moment she was talking to me as if we were lovers on a date—all of which left me very confused. I was sitting there, simply trying to understand what all this was about from the feeble aspects of my mind. "Presence"—she kept talking about "presence" and "being in the moment," "being here," "letting go." She was talking about letting go, and here I was, a Beverly Hills psychologist in a restaurant right around the corner from my office. I was thinking, "What does this woman expect from me? After all, these people may come and be my patients some day. I'm supposed to keep it together out here. She's telling me that consciousness can happen at any moment and that we should be there for it, regardless of our surroundings." I thought, "That's fine for her; what has she got to lose? She has no degree, no office, no credentials; she's got nothing to protect." I told her very clearly that I was open to doing this, but I would do it in my own time and that my own style was to go slowly, so just not to expect anything from me. Well, she quickly assured me that that was up to me, but I could change as quickly as I wanted.

Once the course began, the training schedule increased and intensified. My schedule was difficult, since I arrived at my office at eight in the morning to see one client from eight to nine, then drove across town from Beverly Hills to Santa Monica for class from nine to twelve, returned to my office by twelve-thirty, had lunch from twelve forty-five to one, saw five clients between one and six in the afternoon, ate dinner from six to six-thirty, then hopped back in my car to return to the classes, which ran from seven to ten at night. At times I was so exhausted that I could barely get out of my car in the evening to walk into the building for our class. What I kept discovering, to my utter amazement, was that if I ultimately could drag my exhausted body into our classroom, within ten minutes, some type of energy vortex happened that would give me such strength and vitality that I literally had trouble falling asleep by the time I arrived home at eleven o'clock at night.

I remember the first class experience. It felt as though I had entered a science fiction movie. All we did was close our eyes and share what we experienced on the inside when we tried to attune ourselves to another person. We began to see the relationship between our essential thought, our bodies, and our emotions. Something happened on a subtle energy level that propelled me into a state of consciousness that was an entirely new experience for me. Inner spaces were being awakened, giving me sudden and direct access to aspects of our consciousness that I had never even heard of. I asked myself, "What is this essential nature? What is this spark of our essence that exists throughout time and throughout space, and identifies us as our unique being? How does this essence get permeated into our physical bodies? How is it that our physical structures vary from one another and yet seem to contain a reflection of our very nature? How is it that we have different qualities of mind states, and that each of our minds seems to organize and perceive our experiences differently? Is it true that when we incarnate into physical manifestation, we bring with us certain aspects from other incarnations, certain aspects that are eternal, across time and space, that permeate every incarnation? Could it be that I actually was beginning to have some direct experience of the soul and to perceive how it is reflected on every level of our being?" I felt drawn more and more deeply into my own experience across time, across space, opening my mind, being released from the limitations and the identification with my mind, to have an appreciation and a direct experience of myself as something more than my mind, my body, or my emotions. This experience was a beginning of breaking away from the old identifications that kept me trapped into limited definitions of who I was or who I could be.

I began to experience a fluidity in my consciousness that allowed me to be anything in any moment, if the moment called for it. I began to see how I could change, without "doing" anything to change. Previously, the only way I knew how to change was to work at changing: talk about it, think about it, worry about it, emote about it, try, effort, do something, while trying equally hard not to keep being the way I was. A process was unfolding here, and a way of being that was entirely new to me. It obviously had something to do with letting go, opening, surrendering, and allowing some type of experience to come through me that would transform me as it passed. The key was trusting, being present, setting an intention, and just letting go. When I began to experience myself as consciousness, being present in each moment, and as greater energetic forces, which were moving through me, it became possible to ask for my next level of evolution to come to me. As I became less attached to my personal identity as emotions, ideas, and concepts, I found it possible to experience transformation without effort. This was a very new and exciting reality for me.

At the same time, this was not always an easy process for me, because I was still very identified with my mind. One evening our group was on retreat in Lake Arrowhead, and the two leaders, David and Kathleen, were helping one member with a problem. They were laughing and having such a good time, but I could see nothing changing for this individual. I, as a psychologist, looked for some insight, some emotional release, something that would give me a hint that this individual was touched by the experience. I was not shy, so I spoke up and told them what I thought. I was not aware of being especially rude or obnoxious. We took a break, after which the group resumed. One of the leaders informed me that David had been crying because my energy seemed to assault him. They asked me if I really wanted to learn anything or not, and they invited me to leave if I did not really want to learn. I was shocked. I told them, "I've never been thrown out of anything before." I felt bad and had no idea what I had done. I decided to apologize in the hopes of making peace, although I was not sure for what I was apologizing. I did say that I was sorry if I had hurt David.

Then, something miraculous happened, moments afterwards. I experienced an elevation to a different state of awareness, in which I could perceive subtle energy in a most profound way. My mind was incredibly still and my sense of clarity profound. I suddenly felt very close and connected to all those members present and felt a great sense of peace. In retrospect, it seems that my ego (ı) had to get hit a bit, in order for something of my Higher Self to emerge.

Thereafter, I began to learn how to become aware of my own experience without becoming lost in it. I began to see my consciousness as an aspect that was transcendent from my mind, my body, and my emotions. In this state of awareness, I could allow energy to move through me that literally could change my vibration like a harpist runs her fingers along her instrument. I began to feel the sense of how God can play us like a finely tuned instrument. When it's time to change, the symphony, orchestrated by his hand, passes through our lives.

Ever since my awakening in Hawaii, I had had a constant and clear capacity to perceive and to understand energy. At times, when a certain vibration would come in, my mind would try to understand it, and this would seem to push away the awareness. Only when I was willing to allow for an experience to be there, totally undefined, totally nonunderstood, with total willingness to be with it, consenting to be *in* an experience without any comprehension of it, would the experience stay. How could this be? How could change occur when the mind does not comprehend it, when the mind is not controlling? My psychological training always encouraged me to analyze, understand, and interpret our experiences. These all were very new experiences, which were to set the stage for more and more deepening and further profound awakenings.

Over time, I began to see personalities, bodies, minds, and emotions as plays of light. They all related in an intricate dance to create either harmony or imbalance. My work changed gradually from being a psychotherapist, focusing on emotions and mental states, to feeling more like a sensitive tuning instrument that was seeking only to bring other instruments into harmony. The work became a delicate touch here, a gentle opening there, a minor shift in order to rearrange a whole array of energies into an entirely new constellation. This process of healing felt like the subtle dance of a Tai Chi master, who by simple and gentle movements creates such leverage that a whole energy system becomes transformed.

I began to realize that any known "techniques" of healing really were distractions, for they focused on the wrong thing, for only the clarity of perception and the clarity of my own being allowed me to be more sensitive and more refined, in order to know those delicate points of balance. What good were a variety of techniques, without clarity and sensitivity in the moment?

My intuitive awareness became heightened in this group. Now I could perceive, via subtle, visionary, holographic images, a person's potential. In some cases, I could see an individual in the future when they had fulfilled that potential. It was certainly an interesting way to come to some kind of prognosis—based upon intuitive knowing.

During this two-year training experience, the group gave me the gift of reflecting my essential Self. Our training group consisted of seventeen individuals of varying age, profession, sex, and spiritual awareness. One evening, the group was exploring "being present," i.e., sustaining one's connection to the essential Self, and "staying in the moment," i.e., opening to the Divine plan as it unfolds consciously, second by second. The leaders had perceived that it was my "moment" to realize more consciously my essential Self. At the time, my intuitive perception had been heightened tremendously by the *kundalini*[7] experience in Hawaii with Elisabeth Kübler-Ross, but I understood little of the changes that had occurred within me. The trainers asked me to pay attention to my internal sensations and impressions as they energetically reflected my essential nature. They held the energy of my soul and magnified my experience through their fields. Their ability to consciously sustain a particular vibration allowed me to sit in that experience for fifteen minutes and openly discuss what was happening. I felt qualities of love, humor, sensitivity, compassion, joy, and light, which were all brought together in a unique way that was me. I felt lifted above my emotions and apart from my judgmental mind. I felt an appreciation and love for myself that I had never felt before and saw myself with a pure mind, while experiencing the reality of my essential nature in every cell of my Being. I was deeply and profoundly touched by the nature of my own Being. There was no pride, no ego inflation, no comparison with others—merely a state of wonder and value for my own Being, and how lovely that essential state was.

That moment helped me to value myself at the deepest level for what I was as a Being, clearly apart from anything I might ever have done or ever will do and helped me appreciate the subtle transformation process wherein one holds a conscious space for another's unfoldment. I now know the value of just existing and of sharing that state with others. I saw the value of being present, as by doing so, we share our wondrous Essence with each other and consciously offer and align our energy with the Universe. This event was a great personal inspiration to explore applying such processes to the psychotherapeutic setting and in passing on the awareness that simply being here, being present, is our gift—in merely showing up and saying, "I am here, God Bless Life!"

Thereafter, as time progressed, my office became my laboratory, even though I seemed to be venturing further and further afield from the traditional practice of psychotherapy and the majority of my esteemed Western colleagues. Each day, new experiences, new marvels of grace, new wonders were uncovered. I watched people integrate and change in ways that I never understood or believed possible. When working on my patients' physical structures, I saw fascia moving, muscles realigning, physical structures changing, and skeletal systems rearranging. As they physically changed, I saw openings within their consciousness that allowed for emotional releases, changes in mind states, and the awareness of reality. I had never encountered such integrated work. This clearly was the deepest, most profound work I had ever done. The body became a doorway to working with deep aspects of consciousness. Therapy became more than biographical; it was biological. Therapy moved to a deeper level, past the mere discussion of historical events to the transmutation of energy, consciousness, and cellular structure.

As years have progressed, I eventually refrained from doing any hands-on bodywork because of the difficulties with malpractice insurance and the problem with intensified transference problems. Now I find that I can be very helpful, even while remaining only at the level of subtle energy work and allowing others to do the deep structural work, if that appears to be needed. I found that it was too confusing for patients to shift from a traditional format of talking to one in which they were being touched. Plus, the boundaries issues were too complicated to manage. It is much easier to focus upon one style of treatment.

The Essential Integration bodywork training touched me in profound ways that I still carry in my heart. I became more present, more open, and much more conscious of subtle realms of healing.

Even still, I felt a lack in my soul. Something was missing. I felt some separation from God and some questioning in my heart. A well-known psychic in the Los Angeles area casually remarked to me, "Maybe you need a *guru*." I had no conception of a *guru* and did not even know where to begin with the hope of finding one. Little did I know how soon a *guru* would become a central part of my life. The next chapter reveals the story.

Finding My Guru

THE CONCEPT OF A *GURU* is poorly understood in the West. In recent history, we have witnessed spiritual teachers misuse their power and authority and place their disciples in harm's way. The result is often a fear and mistrust of those Beings who claim to offer help and guidance on the path towards spiritual enlightenment. Some great souls like the Dalai Lama and Mother Teresa, fortunately, provide a safer, more hopeful image.

A *guru* in the classical sense is a fully enlightened Being whose sole purpose is to help others find God-realization. They live to serve and uplift human consciousness from the delusion of duality and separation from God, and to help others find oneness and obtain spiritual liberation. The following is my account of the events that led me to Paramahansa Yogananda, founder of the Self-Realization Fellowship.

The Autobiography of a Yogi, by Paramahansa Yogananda, is a unique story of spiritual unfoldment and the life story of one of India's greatest spiritual teachers. This one book has touched millions around the world and has recently been recorded as read by Ben Kingsley as an audio book, published by the Self-Realization Fellowship.

Many years ago, in 1975, my friend and roommate, Jeff, gave me *The Autobiography* as a present. I had never heard of Paramahansa Yogananda and felt no great inspiration to read it. I was finishing my formal graduate training in psychology and was very busy with the demands of school and everyday life. Upon completion of my education, I began working, earning a good living, and continued to change my place of residence several times until I eventually settled in Topanga Canyon, just outside of Los Angeles and inland from Malibu. With each move, I diligently packed my belongings, including *The Autobiography*. Year after year, I carried this book from one home to another without ever opening its cover.

After the completion of my training with the Essential Integration bodywork, I still felt some spiritual lack and mental confusion, in spite of the wondrous things I had learned. One weekend in 1978, I was attending a weekend retreat with a local psychic and had a vision of an elephant spraying me with water. I wondered what it meant. She suggested that I might want to find a *guru*. What a novel idea! I had no knowledge of *gurus* and certainly had no clue as to finding one. I left, thinking, "What a strange idea." I put the thought out of my mind but did begin to explore various meditative traditions. I studied with the Kundalini Yoga students of Yogi Bhajan, chanted with the followers of Nicherin Shoshu Buddhism, and went to meetings with the Dalai Lama in the Tibetan Buddhist tradition. I found them all very interesting, some more inspiring than others, but nothing that called to me from the depths of my soul.

In the summer of 1979, I was grieving over the end of a relationship and felt devastated by another failed attempt at human connection. I had been married during graduate school, and like most of my classmates, became divorced during the program. I was young, immature, and totally absorbed in obtaining my doctoral degree. I was not good material for a devoted husband. The pain over the recent loss drove me inward. I spent hours each day looking for solace and comfort within my soul. My inner relationship with God provided a tender love and support that soothed my broken heart. During this time I remembered the book, *The Autobiography of a Yogi,* and felt moved to read it. Now, four years later, something prompted me to finally open the cover.

There is a familiar saying, "When the student is ready, the teacher will appear." Each soul has its own timing for awakening. Forces both seen and unseen proceed until the moment is right. Many unknown karmic events unfold until the fruit is ripe and ready to be picked. I read Yogananda's words with a spiritual hunger and thirst, and my soul's longing was quenched. Each word was imbued with a spiritual force that shot from the page. This book was not merely a story about some past events; it became a living, conscious reality that spoke to me. Paramahansa Yogananda was alive in these pages. The stories of the Great Masters in India ignited my soul with hope and inspiration. I became on fire with a desire to reach the exalted goal of Divine realization. I was tired of being trapped in ignorance and became determined to rise above the delusion of material reality and inspired to surrender more to God in every aspect of my life. The accounts of Mahavatar Babaji, the deathless Master who resides in the Himalayas, sparked a recognition of truth deep within my soul. I knew our true state to be Spirit, beyond the reach of death. I knew our consciousness to be far greater than the limited ideas of the mind. These Beings were real, and we are made of the same life force, the same consciousness. I was burning to speed up my spiritual development.

Chapter after chapter unfolded until I reached the section on *kriya yoga*. Yogananda explained how this ancient technique speeds up our spiritual development. The *kriya* technique, working with breath and the energy in the spine, provides a key to unlock the doors of Divine realization. *Kriya yoga*, a rocketship to the Divine! I was ready to take off! I thought, "This is what I am looking for."

My home in Topanga Canyon was about fifteen minutes from the Lake Shrine, one of the temples built by Yogananda. I closed the book, stopped crying, got dressed, and drove straight to the Lake Shrine. It was Sunday and I arrived between the ten o'clock and twelve o'clock services. The monk in residence, Brother Turyananda, was just coming out of the little windmill chapel as I was walking down the red brick path. We stopped face to face, and I said, "Where can I get *kriya yoga?*" He looked at me and after a long silence said, "Follow me and I will show you how to get the teachings."

There is a great esoteric discussion as to whether or not it is imperative to have a *guru* in the physical body. Some say "yes" and others say "no." Paramahansa Yogananda left his physical body in 1953. When he left, he told his closest disciples that it would only be after his death that people would truly realize who he is. A fully realized Master is omnipresent and is not limited in influence by the confines of the physical body. Brother Turyananda often told a story about a time that he met a particular enlightened Being and asked to become his disciple. Brother Turyananda said, "I want to follow you; my *guru* is dead!" The spiritual teacher responded, "Your *guru* is not dead, you're dead! You keep following Yogananda."

Yogananda said that the teachings will become the *guru* when he was no longer in the physical body. His words are permeated with his consciousness. When one reads the written words of an enlightened Being, a direct transmission of consciousness occurs. Yogananda, being an *Avatar,* one who is sent by God to help with the spiritual upliftment of humanity, is alive through his written words and within the inner realms of spiritual reality.

I personally find a greater motivation to turn inward since my *guru* is not readily available on the outside in a physical body. I believe there is a certain gift in moving beyond the physical form, because it helps me to deepen my inner connection with God and maintain an internal focus. So, back to the story.

Brother Turyananda told me about a three-year series of written lessons that are sent from the International Headquarters in Mt. Washington, Los Angeles. He advised me to take the lessons and, at the end of one year, if I chose to do so, I could apply for *kriya* initiation and receive the technique when I became a formal disciple of Paramahansa Yogananda. I felt content with this and left with the literature in hand.

Time passed quickly, and I received *kriya* initiation. This simple technique changed my life. Each time I did this advanced *pranayama* (yogic breathing) technique, the quality of my breath changed, the state of my consciousness changed, and my life changed. I never saw anything like it! For the first two weeks, I was being transformed every day. The rocket was lit and I was taking off. Each meditation took me deeper into spiritual realizations, and I became more peaceful, more loving, and more centered in God in all aspects of my life.

At that time, even with all my great experiences in meditation, I still had no idea regarding the depth of my relationship with Paramahansa Yogananda. Each year the Self-Realization Fellowship offers a worldwide convocation for the students. Various monks and nuns of the organization offer classes on meditation, yoga philosophy, and those who were direct disciples offer inspirational stories about their time spent with Yogananda. His presence becomes alive during this week. Three to six thousand people come together to meditate, and his Love and Joy permeate the air as the Bonaventure Hotel in Los Angeles becomes transformed into a shrine, a temple.

A few movies have been made about the early years when Yogananda was teaching. During my first convocation, I was enthralled with the power of a film, *The Lake Shrine Dedication*, and when his picture flashed upon the large screen, I felt my soul leap out to the screen, while something of Yogananda leaped off the screen to meet me halfway in midspace. I felt a transmission of information explaining how I had spent forty incarnations with him and that this was a continuation of that work. He was a living reality for me. His presence, his joy, his love caressed my soul and uplifted my consciousness. A Master of his stature is far beyond time and far beyond the limitations of physical, material reality.

Paramahansa Yogananda lives within my consciousness. My attempt at surrender and attunement are not motivated out of a desire to become a mindless robot, but from the knowledge and experience that his omnipresent spirit brings out the best in me. My attunement to my *guru* brings me closer to God. My surrender to God, to the Holy Spirit that guides us here on earth, blesses me with wisdom, clarity, love, joy, and the ability to serve others. When I am at my best, I am not there at all. I am the instrument through which the Divine is flowing.

My relationship with my *guru* deepens each year. I feel more and more connected as I learn to serve more selflessly. The *guru* can guide and protect us when we make the proper attunement. During the past earthquakes in Mexico City, the local meditation group of the SRF was miraculously spared from great harm. Buildings all over Mexico City were collapsing, but the building in which the center resided did not fall, even though buildings on the right and on the left were destroyed. Engineers examined the building and could not explain why it did not collapse as well.

God and *guru* are here to help us. I have seen the power of this love in even little ways. A number of years ago I was lecturing to a local hospice group in Nevada City, California. After the evening meeting, I left to find the director attempting to start her classic Mercedes. She kept turning the key, but the motor would not start. She explained, "I always have this problem and ultimately have to call my husband to come get me." She tried and tried with no success. She was about to give up and go inside to call her husband when I suggested she wait a moment. I closed my eyes and prayed, "Dear God, you created this entire universe. Surely you can fix this one little car." I suggested she try it once more. The car started up immediately.

I have had many, many experiences to prove without a doubt the omnipresence of this great Master. He has helped me and my patients in more ways than I can say. Many of the situations are too personal to share, and ultimately each one of us must have our own direct relationship with God, in whatever form we choose or find, in order to develop a solid faith that is based upon experience. The first step is to ask. Once we have invited God into our lives, then it all begins.

Given my profound revelations with an inner *guru*, I was very interested to travel to India and meet other teachers of great spiritual stature. I wanted to know what they actually looked like walking around on the Earth. My decision to go to India provided me with great teachings and a maturing of my spiritual life. The next chapter reveals that story.

India:
The Fire of Purification

ANY DISCUSSION THAT INCLUDES YOGA AND SPIRITUALITY would not be complete without a story about India. In 1980, I spent one month on a personal pilgrimage to many sacred ashrams in India. Although it is difficult to make definite plans when traveling in India, I did have several specific goals in mind. I wanted to have direct personal experience with those spiritual Beings who were reported to be fully God-Realized. I knew of three: Sathya Sai Baba, Sri Ananda Moyi Ma, and Charan Singh. I did not feel a great need to visit the historical sites of my own *guru*, because I was not interested in architecture; I wanted to personally contact and see with my own eyes this Divine state in earthly form. I may have been a little foolish, but I did not make any formal plans before my departure. I chose to put my trust in God, show up in India, and let the adventure take care of itself.

In real life, the transformational process unfolds through our earthly experiences. Ram Dass has said, "When I first hear someone wants to start on the spiritual path, I feel like telling them that if they are smart, they will run like hell the other way." He shared this sarcastic bit of wit because the spiritual path is not easy. A sincere devotee must give up many attachments in the world and go through many challenging experiences in order to transform the self. Transformation, in other words, is not an intellectual process.

In the ancient times we had the sacred temples and the pyramids with the mystery schools. When we entered for training, we went through whatever we had to in order to find realization of the infinite. Today, except for monastic orders, we have no schools; life itself is the great teacher. Once we decide that we want to be on the path, life will bring us the experiences we need. I hope these stories provide some insight into the nature of the transformational process.

My journey to India was not an easy one. I left at the time of a nationwide blizzard, and every step along the way I encountered delayed planes and misconnections. Two days after my departure, I finally arrived in New Delhi; however, my bag had landed in Bombay. I was told that my bag would arrive in a few days. After two days of waiting in a five-star hotel, eating Szechwan Chinese food, and listening to American rock and roll, my bag still had not arrived. I decided to take a short jaunt up north to Amritsar, to visit Charan Singh. I had known about him for years and heard stories that suggested he was a fully enlightened Master. Besides, I had not come to India for rest and luxury in a Western setting. I bought a blanket, shirt, and cotton pants, and decided to travel light, sort of a Western version of the Indian *sadhu*, or wandering monk. In spite of a nationwide train, airline, and bus strike, a *satsanghi* (devotee of Charan Singh) offered to take me to the Derah, Charan Singh's ashram, under the cover of darkness. We made the 100-kilometer round trip in his little three-wheeler motor scooter. We stayed for *darshan*, the opportunity to see the Master, heard a discourse in Hindi, and returned home. I was pleased to have made the journey, for at least I was out of the hotel, but I did not feel any great spiritual revelation from having been in this Master's presence. His blessings were yet to come.

The following morning, I became fully aware that I was dreaming. In this dream, I was totally conscious, and a woman was coming close to kiss me. I realized the symbolic meaning of her kiss. It was a test of my capacity to be open and receive love. I thought, "Are you kidding me? Of course I'm open to receiving love; I love it; come on, let me have it." The moment her lips touched mine, I began to cry, and through my sobs, she quietly spoke to me. She told me that an aspect of my heart had been closed for such a long time because of the damage received from emotional trauma earlier in my life. A special place in my heart had closed, which had never been reopened.

Ever so gently, an energy entered my consciousness and I felt a subtle shift in my heart. I also was aware of Charan Singh's holy presence in the background, blessing this sacred healing. I continued to sob and moved from dreaming to waking, never an instant separating the two. I sobbed some more, and then gently drifted back into sleep.

Upon awakening, I felt more open and softer on the inside. My heart was less guarded and less protected. I was grateful for the healing and felt reassured in the knowledge that I will receive those things that I need in life. I have often experienced a direct transmission of Divine energy when I am in need of help. These types of experiences have strengthened my faith in God's help for me in all aspects of my life.

It has been said, "God will give you what you need but not always what you want." My entire India journey was filled with many disappointments and obstacles in the fulfillment of my desires. It seemed that every time I had a desire, something was put in its way, which forced me to have to confront all my desires and attachments. Little things like comfort, baggage, information—all became obstacles woven together in an intricate dance to help me see the little places that I resisted, reacted, and closed my heart. Every moment, every day, became an opportunity to see myself and to learn how to let go, to surrender, and to be with the moment as it came to me, not as I wished it would be.

For example, when I returned to Delhi, I discovered that my bag still had not arrived from Bombay. I had arranged for confirmed airline tickets, starting from the north. If I had to fly south to retrieve my bag, these tickets would be useless. I found myself becoming enraged at the Indian airline agent because he could not find my bag. I realized I would have to fly to Bombay to get it, and suddenly imagined my traveling to Bombay and my bag simultaneously being flown to Delhi. I really lost it then and started shouting, "If I go to Bombay and my bag comes here, I am going to sue somebody." A small part of me was still calm, and I realized that I really was losing it. I was going nuts over these outer circumstances. I concluded that I could not continue to let these outer things affect me in such a manner. Once again, I was forced, in order to gain any peace of mind, to totally release any desires and expectations. So, now having regained my sanity, I let go of all my attachments to my confirmed tickets and made new arrangements to travel to Bombay. Upon arrival I went directly to customs and was reunited with my lost bag. During the customs search, the Indian officer became quite attached to my survival food. I had brought about twenty trail pack food bars to ensure having enough protein during my stay in India. This man began to harvest a number of them for his own private pantry. I said, "Don't be so greedy; I need these! Three is enough for you." I was willing to share but still felt the need to trust in my own resources. I was not ready to become a total renunciate and give up all my worldly supplies.

Sai Baba, Maker of Miracles

Now that I was in the south of India, I wanted to find Sai Baba. Of all the living spiritual masters in India, He has received considerable attention. I knew many of His devotees and had read several books about Him. In fact, while I was reading *The Holy Man and the Psychiatrist* (Sandweiss, 1975), a story by one of His devotees, I thought, "I wonder what it is like to live in His state of consciousness." My bedroom instantly filled with a golden light, and I was elevated to a state of being in which everything was Spirit. I felt no attachment to anything physical or material. Since Baba was so quick to respond to my thought, I wanted to see Him in person.

Finding Baba was no easy task. I went to Bangalore, only to discover that he had just left and gone to Madras. Once again letting go of my plans, I had to flow with this new direction. There also was an added note of adventure and need to trust in God, since I was informed that there were no hotel accommodations available anywhere in Madras because of the local international cricket tournament. By this time, I was too close to this holy Master to let a little thing like a hotel accommodation deter me. I put my trust in God, got on the airplane, and made my way to Madras. God's grace was with me, and once in Madras, I was able to find a very inexpensive yet clean little room close to the airport.

The trip to the hotel, however, was not without its tests as well. From the airport in Madras, two young boys driving a local taxi offered to take me to the nearby hotel. We arranged the price of forty rupees and began our journey. By this time it was about eleven o'clock at night as we made our way along the main road, and suddenly we turned off to the left. We entered a dirt road that went on and on, deeper and deeper into the darkness, presumably farther and farther away from any signs of civilization. After a few more minutes, we finally turned again and came to what appeared to be a dead end at a railroad crossing. The passing gate was closed. The driver quietly turned off his lights and his engine. There I was, sitting in the back seat in total darkness. My mind began to panic. I was sitting there with fifteen hundred dollars in travelers' checks and a few hundred dollars in rupees. I felt sure that my time had come. These people had taken me off to this dirt road only to rob me and perhaps kill me. I thought, "If I have to go, let me at least go thinking of God." Chanting OM at my spiritual eye, I tried to remember that this is only the physical body, and after all, how much pain could I endure before I would leave it? My heart was pounding right out of my chest! I could hardly imagine that I had come all the way to India just to die in a robbery. That instant, the gate began to rise, the engine was turned on, the lights lit, and we began our journey once again, further into the darkness. A sense of comic relief filled my consciousness as I laughed at my own paranoia. They finally deposited me, safe and sound, at the small but clean and comfortable hotel.

The manager of the hotel informed me that Sai Baba was to hold *darshan* at the Sundaram Temple that afternoon. I arrived an hour-and-a-half early, in the hopes of obtaining adequate seating. Three thousand people showed up for His *darshan* in Madras. Baba usually stays in Whitefield or Puttaparthi, so it was a special treat to the people of Madras to have access to His holy presence.

Despite the crowd of three thousand people, I was led to the very front row, right where Baba would pass by. We sat and chanted *bhajans* (devotional songs to God) for two hours, building energy and opening our hearts. The beautiful songs to God were chanted over and over again, with a devotion and sincerity not often encountered here in the West. Finally, the sacred moment arrived; we could feel Baba's presence just by the rising energy in the group. Suddenly, there was more light, a sense of expansion, and certainly more joy. The chanting picked up with the added fervor of this inner excitement. Off to the left, I could see Him coming. My first thought was of such gratitude to finally be in Baba's holy presence. I had come so far, and at last, my great desire was being fulfilled. He came closer and closer, working His way through the crowd, stopping, giving blessings, giving a gentle touch, and sharing His Divine energy. While it always is a blessing just to be in the presence of a Master, a direct look or a gentle touch provides an even deeper contact and a powerful exchange of energy. As Baba came closer and closer to me, I found myself totally speechless, in a state of bliss and appreciation for this tender moment. As He approached me, His eyes met mine, and He continued to look and to send waves of Love as He came closer and closer. His eyes stayed fixed to mine for two or three minutes as He walked by. It seemed like an eternity. As He passed on and moved down the row, I thought, "I should have touched His feet." I continued, with great compassion for my Western training:

"I am not trained to do this firsthand. My Western culture does not prepare me for such an experience, and certainly it was not out of disrespect that I did not do this. In fact, I wish I could have this opportunity for, indeed, I do feel a sense of devotion and respect for Your holy being."

At that moment, Baba was about thirty feet away; He turned around and made His way back, step-by-step, closer and closer, until finally He stopped in front of me. I gently leaned down and touched his feet.

Blessing after blessing continued to unravel from His holy presence during the week that I stayed at His ashram. Baba could read every little thought and every little desire that was in my consciousness. Often, He accepts written notes from people as a way to acknowledge inner communication. He suggests that if you write your thoughts down, it grounds them in this plane so He can hear them more readily, but of course He really does not need this, for He clearly demonstrates the capacity for omniscience and omnipresence.

It is very compelling to be in the presence of one such as He. We have a tendency to be drawn outside of ourselves and to forget that God is inside, within us all. Desire arises to be close to His physical body, and it's easy to forget that on the inner dimension, there is never a separation or a moment of aloneness. During my week's stay with Baba, I had one twenty-four-hour period in which every second I felt His presence. It was impossible to experience one egotistic or negative thought, for He was always there, lifting me up higher and higher in Love and Joy.

The week rolled on, and I would have moments of feeling perfectly content and so full that there were no desires and no longings, and then another wave of desire and longing would come. Knowing that I was in the presence of this Holy One, who, if anybody on the planet could, had the capacity to awaken me further and bring me closer to God, I found great longings for God-communion or cosmic consciousness stirring within me. I began to request in my notes for some blessing from Baba to awaken me to cosmic consciousness.

My time to leave was getting closer. I felt the inner direction to pursue other places on my journey, and yet no major flash of *samadhi* had occurred. Finally, on the last morning at Sundaram, I went to *darshan* with full-blown desires burning within me. It was as if I was a beggar, longing for His holy grace, and I could think of no way to coerce this God-Being into giving it. I knew that even if I had a temper tantrum on the ground, it would have no effect. I was powerless in that moment to make anything happen. I began to reflect on my state of agony and suffering and the intensity of my desire. Oh, how I longed for complete enlightenment, pleading, "Please, please, please, bring me closer, bring me closer." As my suffering increased, a sudden revelation unfolded within my con-sciousness. I realized that my attachment to enlightenment was the cause of my suffering, and that only by letting go of that attachment would I gain true contentment and inner peace. I realized, in that moment, that there was nothing I could do to make anything happen that was not already occurring. If I was to feel any freedom and any inner peace, I had to let go of this long-sought goal of cosmic consciousness.

In that moment of insight, a place opened within my Being, and I became quiet and silent in a way that I never before had known. At that moment, I completely accepted that even if it took me ten billion more incarnations to reach my goal, so be it. This was a profound and permanent shift in my consciousness that has remained with me to this day. Thereafter, though nothing had changed on the outside, I continued to meditate even more deeply than before. I continued to work, but with even greater joy and dedication than before. The only thing that had changed was me. No more urging, no more pressing, just letting be, letting each moment unfold as it must, and deepening to the joy of that moment. Nowhere to go, nothing to do, just to be with each moment, allowing its exquisiteness to take me deeper and deeper into the unfoldment of my life.

The paradox of life confronted me once more. "Nothing to do, nowhere to go," yet it was time to leave the ashram and go somewhere else. The inner Self had nowhere to go, but the body needed to move along. I became quiet and attempted to know intuitively what to do and where to go. Although I was not sure, I felt some pull to go north into the foothills of the Himalayas.

The Old Delhi Train Station

I left Sai Baba's ashram and flew to the northern part of the country. I arrived at the Old Delhi train station at six-thirty in the morning, preparing for my ride up to Rishikesh, in the foothills of the Himalayas. I was told that the "Dehra Dun Express" would arrive at seven-thirty and take me to Hardwar, and from Hardwar, it was only a short bus ride to Rishikesh. I bought my ticket by candlelight in the cold, predawn hours. Taking up my pack and blanket, I found what seemed to be a relatively clean place on the concrete pavement of the train's landing station. I was surrounded by a sea of humanity— children, families, businessmen—all quietly awaiting the early train. Sitting peacefully and quietly, I began to meditate. Eyes open, eyes closed, it made no difference, each moment feeling full and rich in the depths of its presence. An hour passed by quickly, and it was announced that the train would be approximately an hour and forty-five minutes late. "No matter," I thought, "just another forty-five minutes." Half an hour later, it was announced that the train would be two hours and forty-five minutes later. At this point, time had collapsed for me. Each moment was like a second and an eternity. All of existence permeated each breath. As dawn approached, I began to reflect on my surroundings, and I realized that I was probably in the most filthy place I'd ever been in my entire life. Children to the left of me were vomiting on the pavement; people to the right of me were urinating. Everyone seemed to use the open pavement as a place to spit up any mucus to be discharged. Here I was, all alone, after tremendous effort and output of energy, sitting in this physically wretched place. Once again, another revelation began to unfold. I realized that in the midst of all this, I felt wonderful. I felt so content and so full of peace. I was filled with God's presence and a deep sense of serenity.

I also knew in this instant why I had to make this trip alone. All my life I had been struggling to prove to myself that I, indeed, could master my environment, and a quality of independence and willfulness existed in me that came from this need to prove my independence. I suspect that there were many levels to this trait, perhaps some of them influences from past incarnations.

I certainly could see the roots of this characteristic in this current lifetime—having a very dominant mother who often did not allow me the opportunity to feel my own sense of worth and control. I could see the limitations that this aspect of my being had created for me in relationships and in working in groups. I knew that if I ever was to be totally open to another relationship, I would have to allow myself to be more open to receiving and surrendering to the oneness of the two. I also realized that the social consciousness in America was changing, with a new focus upon collective energies and less concern with our own individual, egotistic desires and attachments. I also felt, since having seen Baba, that there was no further need to press or to try and get something for myself in order to reach deeper and deeper states of enlightenment. Each moment was enough, and it was time for me to work more with others in a shared, collective effort. I felt my old sense of self beginning to dissolve and another space opening within me. I felt more expansive, more loving, more receptive, more whole, and a deep sense of serenity and joy permeated my entire being. Deep in my heart, I thanked God for the blessings after blessings that continued to unfold on this sacred journey.

My first stop off the train was in the ancient city of Hardwar. I found a room in a rather dirty hotel and spent the night. I awoke early at 5:00 a.m. to catch a bus to Rishikesh. During the forty-five-minute ride I became instantly ill. There are many things about the source and nature of disease that are not fully appreciated in the West, as karma and consciousness often play a significant role in creating illness. I believe I was given this illness in order to set the stage for some later events to unfold in a small ashram near the Ganges river. I was sitting in the back of the bus and the window was open. I was feeling quite fine when I noticed through my intuitive vision that some energy force was coming at me from outside. It came in through the window and entered my left ear. The second this energy entered my body, I developed a fever, a loss of energy, and some upper respiratory problems. This illness actually lasted throughout the remainder of my journey.

Rishikesh and Swami Premvarni

The bus finally arrived in Rishikesh, and I proceeded to the Shivananda Ashram, where I had made previous arrangements to stay. Two local residents grabbed my backpack and offered to help. As they began to put it on the ground, I saw that they were going to place it right in the middle of a fresh cow chip. I was unsuccessful in my attempt to stop them. Then, just as they dropped it into the dung, a beautiful butterfly flew right past my face. I felt the cosmos was showing me a paradox and mystery: that beauty and transformation arise out of the dung of our lives—a very profound teaching.

Mucus continued to flow from my body. Fevers, colds, coughs, loss of strength—my physical body was suffering but my spirit was still high. In retrospect, I believe I became ill in order to give me the opportunity to resolve some unfinished business with Swami Premvarni, a local yogi who has a small ashram in the jungle of Rishikesh on the other side of the Ganges River, across from the Shivananda Ashram. I had met this particular Swami a few years ago in America when I offered my home in Topanga Canyon to him so he would have a place in which to teach. He had stayed there for about a month until I actually had to escort him out and back to San Francisco. He was playing so many power and control games that he was driving everyone nuts. He came down with a cold as the result of his confusion with the air conditioning control. He turned the air conditioner on all night and gave himself quite a cold. When he left, he was feeling extremely ill. Now the tables were turned and I was feeling ill. I had no intention of contacting him because of the craziness he created in my home. But in my weakened condition, I reached out to him for help. He made me special food and kept me warm as he began to nurse me back to health. In the late hours of the evening we talked, and he apologized for his behavior. He was honest, direct, and took responsibility for his past actions. It was like a breath of fresh air between us. He confided that he had seen that we were brothers in a past life here in India. We talked, we laughed, and he offered to take me up into the caves and meet his friends who had been meditating for years. I do not believe that I would have made this opportunity to resolve our conflicts if I had not been feeling so poorly. Swami Premvarni asked me to remain in India indefinitely. He said, "You can be back in America in one day. How long did it take you to get here? You never know when you will be back. Please stay. I will arrange your visa and ticket." I was very torn. What was the right thing to do? I felt the energy of his desire pulling on me, and I could not feel clear enough to make a decision. By this time I was feeling stronger. I also had patients scheduled for the beginning of the month, and I simply did not know what to do.

I decided to take a walk to try and find some peace of mind, in order to find clarity regarding my decision. A local *sadhu* (wise man) lived on the banks of the Ganges river nearby, and I decided to go there. He was known as the "Cow Baba," because there were so many cows around him. I walked up to a small group of devotees surrounding him, and he asked me if I was English. I replied, "No, I'm from America." At that point he seemed to lose interest in me, and I thought, "Good, he doesn't have any need for me; maybe I can get clear if I sit here for a while." I sat down and began to meditate, hoping to withdraw my focus and find some inner guidance. A few feet away from me were some large burlap bags filled with carrots. We were all sitting upon a concrete slab a few feet above the sands of the Ganges. Cows began to jump up on the concrete in order to get the carrots, and mass pandemonium broke out. People started screaming, "Get the carrots, throw them to the cows, hurry, hurry!" I was compelled to help, so I started flinging carrots to the wild cows. All hell broke loose and the cows ran amok after the carrots and all over my Birkenstock sandals, which I had left on the sand.

This was too much for me. I thought, "I can't take it anymore; I'm leaving this place. I'm going home." As I left, the *sadhu* gave me an apple that he had blessed. I have no idea what blessing he placed on the apple, but I was so disgusted with all the chaos that I walked over to one of the cows and said, "Here, maybe this will help you get enlightened." I threw the apple to the cow as I left!

Krishna's Temple

I hired a taxi and drove back to Delhi along the sacred banks of the holy Ganges. With six more days until my international flight, I had a chance to visit the holy city of Benares. Unfortunately, no plane reservations could be had until another day or two, so I took a quick jaunt down to Agra, visited the Taj Mahal, and stopped in Vrindaban to receive Krishna's holy blessings. A few minutes in Krishna's sacred temple left me in a state of tranquility and bliss that lasted for two hours. During that time, all the flu-like symptoms that had troubled me totally disappeared. I finally returned to Delhi for my short trip to Benares.

Benares

As soon as I stepped off the plane at Benares, I was touched by the vibration of this holy city. A softness and a peace permeated the ether here that was different from any of the other cities I had visited. The weather was warmer, and certainly the place was much cleaner than Delhi. I felt that God was being so nice to me, giving me a place to rest and heal myself for my journey home. I was fortunate to find a room in the local Taj, a five-star hotel. I sat down to have a wonderful meal to rebuild my strength. As always is the case, I needed to confirm my return flight back and was fortunate enough to have a gentleman offer to do this for me. An hour had not passed when this kindly man returned, saying, "I think you should come to the airline office."

I looked up, "Problem?"

He looked down, "Problem! No ticket! You should come to the office." Well, without further ado or finishing my lunch, I was off to the office.

I thought, "I haven't even been here two hours, and already it's starting up again. Does the difficulty of traveling in India never cease?" I finally made it to the nearby Indian airline office, via a short bicycle ride, and was told that on my date of departure, no plane tickets were available. I informed them that my international flight was to leave in three days, and that I needed to return to Delhi. They assured me that the day I had planned to depart was totally impossible, since a large tour had fully reserved the plane. They suggested two possibilities: either I go tomorrow with the hopes of getting on the plane (I was number twenty-six on a standby list, and they told me that my chances were fifty-fifty), or take a twelve-hour, all-night train ride back to Delhi, which would leave the following day as well.

Certainly, neither of these two options seemed very desirable, for I had just lost my wonderful, restful time in the holy city of Benares. I decided to play it safe and try for the one o'clock flight on the following day. If I were to miss that flight, then I still would have time to catch the train and make my way back home. I took advantage of my short stay in Benares that afternoon to visit the ashram of Ananda Moyi Ma, one of the highest living saints in India, and to visit the holy Ganges.

Ananda Moyi Ma

Ma's ashram was located on the banks of the Ganges. She was very close to leaving her body at that time and was lying, near death, in a small village hundreds of miles away. In spite of her physical absence, her presence permeated this ashram. My heart was filled with Love and devotion. Once again the omnipresence of the Great Ones was being demonstrated. I was greeted by a lovely man who ran the ashram, and he was kind enough to spend a few hours with me to share some stories about his life with Ananda Moyi Ma. We spoke about healing, and he told me about a man who would often approach Ma and plead, "Ma, please heal me. I know you can take away my sickness." Month after month he would approach her with his plea. Finally after many months she did heal him and freed him from all disease. Afterwards, she confided in my new friend, "I really have mixed feelings about taking away his disease. It gave him such motivation to do spiritual practice, I am afraid he will try less now that he is well." It is true that many of us do become more highly motivated only when we are suffering.

As we gazed into the nearby Ganges, he continued with another story about Ma's greatness. He shared a cherished memory. "I remember one day when we were sitting here and Ma walked down these steps to bathe in the Ganges. I saw her walk down into the river and dissolve into Light as she went under the water. She was gone for half an hour. She just dissolved into particles of Light! After that time, she just walked out and came up the steps."

My brief time in that ashram has left a lasting impression on me. His sincerity and devotion to his *guru* touched me, and his stories confirmed my deepest knowing that we are far more than these physical bodies. Consciousness, Light: this is our true nature.

India's Purifying Power

My short stay in the sacred city of Benares had come to a close. I needed to attend to the trials of transportation. Since I still felt quite exhausted and feverish, I slept in and arrived at the airport by about eleven-thirty. There I was informed that the airplane would be three hours late. Another moment of despair sunk in, as I now realized that I could not catch the train if the airplane was totally full. I was not sure what to do. Because of my poor physical condition, I was very reluctant to take the twelve-hour train. I decided to wait and hope for the best. I found myself a comfortable little corner, wrapped myself in my blanket, and sat quietly meditating, watching my breath, and feeling my fever rise higher and higher.

Hour after hour, I waited. The plane was delayed even longer, and I felt a rage welling up within me. This trip had been a grueling one on the physical plane: fevers, exhaustion, poor food, dirty and uncomfortable places to sleep, and many plans unable to be completed. Frustrations had followed frustrations and still continued to arise. As I sat contemplating and experiencing these woes, I began to feel more and more annoyed. I had come to India under the delusion that because I devoted so much of my life to God, I would be supported on the physical plane. I assumed that if God really loved me, and because of my love for God, I would make plane connections, train connections, and be able to see all of the saints and shrines that I wanted to see. As I sat there feeling trepidation over the possibility of missing my airplane, and resentment about possibly having to take some grueling, all-night train ride while suffering from fever, I became more and more enraged at God. I felt that my entire life had been a constant test of letting go and surrendering: letting go of relationships, concepts, personal desires, and possessions. This journey was no exception, and I had come to the end of my rope. I totally forgot all the blessings I had received. In that moment of rage, I looked to God and said, "Okay, God, this is it. I've asked for very little in my life, and right now the only thing I want is for You to get me on this airplane. If You have any love for me at all, You will get me on this airplane, and if You don't, then screw You; forget it; our relationship is over!"

I was feeling so physically weak and exhausted that I actually could not imagine surviving a twelve-hour train ride. In the midst of my physical suffering, I had reduced myself to a rage toward God in which I was willing and determined to sever my beloved relationship because of the discomforts with the physical body. Moreover, when the plane finally arrived and I was given a seat, I did not even feel a moment of appreciation. On the contrary, I felt extremely self-righteous and that God and I were square—we could continue on from that point.

Two weeks after I returned home from India, I found myself experiencing a subtle depression, though I was not sure why. Then, in conversation with a friend, it suddenly occurred to me what had happened in India. At the outset, I had dedicated that trip to God, vowing to trust my intuition and do only what God wanted. Now, I suddenly realized that by the end of the trip, I had told God to screw off! I couldn't believe the lack of faith, the lack of loyalty, and the lack of trust that I had expressed—on account of mere comfort for my physical body, I had been willing to forego my love and devotion for God. On the one hand, I was deeply disturbed at my own limitations, but I also was deeply grateful that this teaching came to me so early in my life. I was still alive and not in the throes of suffering either from a terminal illness or from physical disasters around me. I remembered Christ's suffering on the cross and His capacity nevertheless to be one with the Father. Oh, how easy it is for us to forget who we really are in the pull of this physical/material plane.

An Interview with Swami Satchidananda

Several years after this trip to India, from 1983 through 1986, I was involved in citizen diplomacy efforts between the United States and the Soviet Union. I founded a non-profit organization, Projects for Planetary Peace, which brought Soviet and American citizens together in both countries and worked with the Soviet Peace Committee. One great boon resulting from this work was the people I met. Swami Satchidananda, the founder of Integral Yoga, was very supportive of many groups in this effort. I interviewed *Gurudev* (a more affectionate term for him) about his beliefs, and one aspect of our discussion focused upon his experience with surrendering. He is a living example of one who has fully dedicated his life to God and service, and has been rewarded with more than he could ever have gained as a businessman. He shares some personal insights regarding selflessness and surrendering:

Ron Mann: Projects for Planetary Peace believes that in order to find peace in the world, individuals have to open their hearts. The more we share and serve others, then the less we fight.

Gurudev: There's no need, no need. . . . When you begin to give more, they would want you to be in good shape so that you can give even more. So it is the other people who take care of you, because they want you to be there. A simple example is: if a tree is giving a lot of fruits to you, would you neglect the tree?

Ron Mann: No, I'd take good care of it.

Gurudev: You will take more care. Because that is the one that gives more fruit. You will put more nourishment, give more water, protect it from any animals. Why? Because if you don't do that, you will lose all the fruits. In the same way, if you are a tree laden with fruits, and if the public is going to enjoy the fruits of your existence, it's their business to take care of you. You don't even have to worry about your personal care. I see this in my very own life. I don't have to bother about myself at all. My food, my clothing, my shelter, my travels, whatever. It is all taken care of. They are more careful, they take more interest.

For example, (while I am here) in Los Angeles from San Francisco, they (his students) brought a lot of things here for my stay, to make it comfortable. It's not that I have an order that wherever I go all people should bring all these things and put them here. They want to take care of me. Because if they lose me, they lose that benefit.

People can live like that. If it can happen to me, it can happen to you and to everybody. But the thing is, most people don't believe in that. Our egos don't allow us: "I must take care of myself first." That's very wrong. If the car runs well, won't you take care of it? If your horse draws your cart well, won't you take care of it? They're all there to serve others, and the others take care of them. Why can't that happen to people?

Ron Mann: It sounds like what you're saying, too, is that if we all make a conscious choice to simplify our lives, want less, then we will have our basic needs taken care of, and we'll probably get more.

Gurudev: It's not even want less: want nothing. Then you get everything. Then at the time, all you have to do is say, I don't want any more. I don't want any more. Please don't dump everything on me. It's too much for me; I cannot handle it. We should learn to say that: "I don't want."

Ron Mann: I know what you're saying is true. All we have to do is to go through the tests and survive. (Here is where most of us become terrified at the prospect of starving, becoming homeless, dying, etc.)

Gurudev: Of course that's it. In the beginning, God will want to test you, to see how sincere you are, how serious you are. So, for something you may not get anything in return. You may even be starving; you may be totally ignored, neglected. But still be convinced of this truth: "No matter what happens, I'm not going to search for anything; I'm not going to ask anything."

In fact, there was a time in India when I was traveling all over the country, simply roaming like a wandering fellow, a mendicant, with two principles: not to have even a cent in my pocket (because I never had a pocket), and not to ask anything from anybody. No money to buy, no mouth to ask. Not even food. If I was thirsty, I would look in some public place and find tap water or river water and drink it. If I was hungry, I would wait until somebody came and asked me. Certainly, I starved for a number of days. Then, gradually, it started opening up. After some time, wherever I went, food was abundantly around me. People used to pile up fruits around me. I distributed fruits to everybody. In fact, in one railway station I was simply sitting there. I knew that I could just wait on the platform. The ticket examiner would come and say, "Sadhu, you want to go somewhere?"

"Yes."

"Okay, this train goes to Benares. Would you like to go?"

"All right."

He took me, made a place for me, had me sit there, and he brought me food at every station. When I sat on the platform, people brought fruit—piles of fruit all around. Then I kept distributing to all the people and passengers waiting there. But that happened only after several weeks of no food at all. That's what happens. God tests to see how sincere you are, how honest you are. Otherwise, sometimes you may think, "Ahh, that's a good trick. If I say I don't want anything, I can get everything." No. Don't keep anything for yourself. Even your life is not your own. It's given to you to use for others. There was a great sage who gave even his bones for a public use.

Conclusion

The value of any pilgrimage is that it provides the opportunity to purify one's ego (ι), because the intention of the spiritual journey is to move closer to God. Since the only obstacle to our full liberation is our own ego (ι) consciousness, a spiritual journey draws the fire of purification. This story and the wise counsel of Swami Satchidananda demonstrate that spiritual development is not an intellectual exercise. The individual becomes fully engaged at every level of being and is tested throughout the process. Each successful victory opens the way for greater spiritual expansion and awareness. Life, then, becomes the great teacher and provides fantastic opportunities for growth and development. We need only to develop better skills at surrendering and allowing Spirit to purify our hearts and transform our consciousness. Our ability to open to the transformational process is largely determined by our conception of and attachment to the "self," and it is easier to surrender when the mind offers little resistance and we are not attempting to hold onto parts of the self that need to be transformed.

The next chapter compares different theories regarding the self and suggests the benefits that result from a spiritual perspective.

6

Comparative Theories
of the Self

THE UNDERLYING BELIEF regarding an individual's core identity marks one of the greatest distinctions between Western psychological thought and spiritually-oriented psychotherapies. In comparison to the Western view, sacred psychotherapy embraces a much larger conception of the self and a much broader view of life's essential purpose. Let's take a look at these differences, as a means of delving further into the aspects of subtle energy or consciousness that constitute the Self in spiritual terms.

Western Conception

The traditional Western psychological position regards the self as a psychological-biological-behavioral system that exists within a specific time-space continuum. The self is defined by one's ability to think, organize, synthesize, feel, and act. All of these functions are limited to the existence of the physical body and officially begin at birth and ultimately end when the body no longer exists. Thus, the definition of life is defined as the interval between birth and death, and life's purpose is to live a happy and fulfilling life as defined by conventional Western standards. Typically, then, a good life is one in which you make a lot of money, are successful at work, get married at least once, and bear and raise healthy and happy children.

Object Relations Theory

Western personality theorists suggest that our personality develops as the result of biological processes and/or social conditioning. One theory, known as object relations theory, is clinically a very useful explanation of personality development. Object relations theory suggests that we have various aspects of personality that have evolved from our earliest human contact, and that the different parts of our psyche result from a process of internalization, in which aspects of our parents and siblings have become absorbed into our own psychological world of the inner self. Once these qualities have entered into our private inner kingdom, they reside at different levels of the psyche. Some qualities, which are experienced as thoughts and feelings, become internalized but not integrated into our personal identity. These kinds of thoughts and feelings may be experienced as attacking and negative forces within us. We may not actually feel like these thoughts; they seem alien in some way, but they clearly reside within us. In this case, we have not identified with these negative forces, but through the natural process of personality development, we have absorbed them into our psyche. Thus, they are internalized, but not fully integrated.

On the other hand, a deeper degree of internalization results when we more fully identify with our parental models. Various qualities *become* the self, and we actually feel like "this constitutes me." When we feel completely in agreement with various thoughts and feelings that may have originally been imposed from without, i.e., aspects of mother or father , whether positive or negative, then we have internalized and identified with those aspects of the other to such a degree that we experience these as our actual self. Environment, as one can see, plays a very powerful part in personality development. The infantile psyche is like a sponge that absorbs the external world of thoughts, emotions, and behavior. The child may fully internalize what is observed, as well as the direct verbal messages that he or she receives.

A pathological result occurs when negative qualities of the other have been internalized to the degree that we feel there is something bad, shameful, damaged, or wrong about ourselves. This process can result either from direct statements that have been made towards us or from observing and absorbing others' behaviors and attitudes.

The Biochemical View

A less psychological and more superficial theory of human behavior lies in the purely biological explanation of existence. In this construct, all thoughts, feelings, and actions are regarded as the result of complex chemical interactions in the brain. This type of biological explanation holds no value for the notion of the unconscious or psychodynamic forces within an individual. While the use of psychotropic medication can be very helpful to individuals, this purely biological view of human existence does not help to explain life's ultimate mysteries.

Summary

In summary, then, our personality, the definition of the self by Western standards, comes into being as a mixture of genetic factors psychodynamic forces, and social conditioning. The strength of the personality or self is determined by the degree of integration between the various aspects within the self. A well-functioning person exhibits an inner life that is supportive, adaptive to life's challenges, and is able to confront outer threats and difficulties with positive, creative, and functional behaviors. Problems are not denied, avoided, repressed, or attacked. Problem-solving is directed towards positive solutions that provide for learning and "win-win situations."

While the Western model of psychotherapy provides valuable assistance in resolving personality problems, it is not designed to address the Sacred and awaken the essential Self or soul. Many individuals never realize soul consciousness because they have not done the difficult work of distinguishing the difference between their conditioned personality, mind, and emotions and their deeper spiritual nature. The essential Self is typically discovered through a careful, persistent, and disciplined process of concentration, introspection, meditation, and discernment. Often, it takes another, "conscious" or enlightened individual to help us recognize the conditioned aspects of our personality and also serve as a vehicle to reflect our own divine nature or essential Self.

Spiritual View of the Self

The mystical view of the self, in contrast, moves beyond the limited notions of the psychobiological, space-time bound individual. Many individuals in this country and abroad are having direct experiences of consciousness that cannot be explained by traditional psychological or biological theories. Spontaneous healings of serious illness, direct perception of spiritual realities, and near-death experiences are forcing people to look for different answers and for more complete explanations regarding the nature of the Self.

Returning to the metaphor of the master music-stand maker, the true Self is the music stand, encased within the tree trunk. The spiritually conscious view of the self moves beyond the trunk, or form, to explore the inner essential core. Diagram 1 on page 86 may be helpful in this discussion.

In the spiritual or metaphysical view of the self, the essential Self or soul exists within each of us. The soul has consciousness that continues throughout eternity, and this consciousness is not bound by time and space. Life, as consciousness, began before we were born and continues after the death of the physical body. Consciousness moves through the illusion of time from one incarnation to another, adopting the form of the current physical body. However, the essential nature of the Self, as defined by Sankhya[8] philosophy, is "Sat, Chit, Ananda," or Consciousness or "Being," Intelligence or Awareness, and Bliss. It is suggested that our essential nature is created in this Divine image and that the soul is an individualized aspect of the Divine, just as a wave is an individual aspect of the ocean. The soul rises out of the Divine substance, eventually to return to complete union. The soul, being a part of the Divine, contains the Divine essence of Love, Peace, Joy, Bliss, Light, Wisdom, and Energy. In this mystical understanding of the Self, the soul is always good, and it is only one's separation from or nonrecognition of the essential reality that creates evil. Thus, there are no "bad" souls, and "evil" exists in people only to the degree that they have lost connection with the Truth of their Divine nature. Just as a dark room loses its darkness when a light is turned on, an individual can lose his or her dark, evil qualities when the light of the soul is uncovered. The conscience, in this sense, is regarded as a vehicle for Divine thought to reach human consciousness. Those who have not developed their connection with this internal moral conscience find themselves adrift without the inner guiding force to behave well and help others. The darker elements of the self have taken over to promote the lower tendencies of greed, selfishness, lust, and hatred.

The mystical view of the self perceives the apparent reality of the body, mind, and emotions as encasements around the soul. An individual loses his or her direct experience of the soul to the degree that he or she identifies with the outer, transitory aspects of the self. Object relations theory provides a useful parallel model regarding internalization and identification. If we apply this frame of reference at a metaphysical level, an individual is caught in "delusion" or ignorance, i.e., an incomplete recognition of the soul, only to the degree that he or she completely identifies with the outer, transitory aspects of manifestation, confusing these for the true Self. Sankhya yoga philosophy refers to the condensation of consciousness from God-consciousness to material reality. So, in a way, the outer forms and substances of the mind, body, and emotions have been absorbed from outside as they were first created by God. Metaphysically speaking, then, object relations theory may be applied to the enlightenment process in that through attuning or focusing on the Divine or

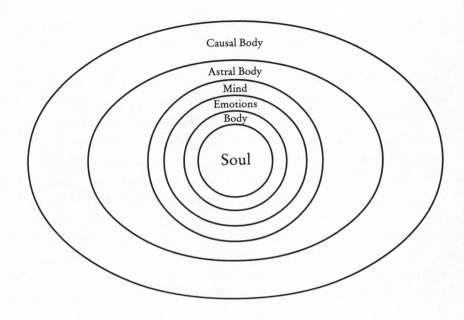

Diagram 1

Soul: The individualized aspect of Spirit that is by nature ever-existing, ever-conscious, ever-new joy. The soul is encased in the physical body, the astral body, and the causal body until it reaches full liberation.

Body: The physical vehicle for the soul.

Emotions: The emotional system that relates to the expression of the personality.

Mind: The mental, intellectual aspect of the self. The yogic system actually addresses two qualities of mind: *buddhi* and *manas*. *Buddhi* refers to the discriminative intelligence that is relatively more intuitive in nature, and *manas* refers to the quality of mind that is in turn more related to sense consciousness.

Astral Body: An energy body of subtle consciousness directly above the physical. The astral realm mainly consists of energy and light.

Causal Body: The subtle body beyond the astral and consisting of thought.

any higher value or aspect of the Divine, one gradually internalizes, and ultimately fully integrates, Higher or Divine Awareness into the Self.

Our true, deeper Self or soul must be carefully perceived through a precise process of discernment that results either from a spontaneous spiritual awakening or through the quiet, ongoing, self-reflective discipline that occurs through meditative practices, which are of great value in reaching this goal. A successful meditative practice allows one to interiorize consciousness and attune to the finer, subtler realms where very delicate and refined perceptions are possible. This progressive state of awareness can be likened to moving through a cloud or a mist until a region of inner light and clarity has been revealed. In this region, information is imparted in a holographic-like manner, in which images and symbols are imbued with meaning and direct knowledge is automatically absorbed into awareness. The Self, in this context, has access to a much greater field of experience and wisdom than in ordinary mental or emotional realms, because it has direct access to higher dimensions of existence that are not limited by time and space, the highest of which is the Changeless Absolute. If all thought is energy, and if energy cannot be destroyed, then all Universal Wisdom permeates creation.

The soul or the Self, as Divine consciousness, can attune itself with these higher realities in order to become aligned with the Cosmic Will. Synchronicity, harmony, Divine guidance, and grace all flow from the same great well of Spirit. Another reward of inner illumination is the key to life's mysteries: solutions for life's problems, directions for life's actions, and an understanding of life's purpose all reside in this great cosmic sea. The soul is the doorway, and one's treasure lies within!

The *Chakra* System

The Sanskrit word, *chakra*, means wheel. The *chakras* are spinning vortices of conscious or subtle energy. Each *chakra* corresponds to various physical glands or organs and is imbued with different states of awareness. A detailed description of the *chakra* system is warranted because it provides a useful way to conceive of human consciousness from an esoteric-developmental perspective. The *chakra* centers are located along the spine and correspond with different levels of awareness or states of consciousness. Each *chakra* also has an astral sound. As each center becomes activated and open, the consciousness of the individual changes. Meditation, *asana* (posture), and *prana-yama* (breathing) techniques are designed to stimulate these subtle energy centers, activating them and thereby transforming consciousness. The various *chakras* are generally described as follows:

Muladhara **Center**: This *chakra* is referred to as the first *chakra* and is located at the base of the spine, in the coccyx. The energy in this first *chakra* is related to the earth and survival instincts. The concept of "being grounded" is also related to this energy center. It is often said that we should have our "head in the clouds and our feet firmly planted on the earth." The earth energy that can be contacted through this center allows an individual to keep the consciousness centered in the body, even though powerful energies may be flowing through that consciousness. In intensive spiritual practices that open up the higher centers, it is easy to feel "spaced out" and disoriented. A solid sense of being grounded strengthens an individual's ability to work with these strong spiritual forces. The astral sound associated with the *Muladhara* or root *chakra* is that of a bumblebee.

Svadhishthana **Center**: Commonly known as the second *chakra*, this center is located a few inches below the navel and tends to be physically related to the ovary and prostate glands. The energy in this center is related to sexuality, procreation, and the life-creative principle. The energy in this center can lead to physical reproduction or be transmuted for other creative purposes. The astral sound associated with this *chakra* is that of a flute.

Manipura **Center**: Commonly known as the third *chakra*, this is located around the solar plexus and relates to personal power. The consciousness expressed from this center tends to be egoic (ı). The astral sound is that of a harp.

These first three *chakras* typically represent the activated state of consciousness for most members of Western civilization, in that their major focus is upon money (survival), sex, and power. Thus, not surprisingly, Western psychological thought also tends to focus mainly upon these issues.

Anahata **Center:** The heart center, located in the center of the chest, is typically referred to as the fourth *chakra* and is physically related to the heart. Unconditional Love is the quality associated with this *chakra*. The activation of this center marks a dramatic change in consciousness, because of its sense of expansion beyond the personal to include all of humanity and, even further, all of creation. Consciousness at this level shifts beyond personal love to an impersonal Love that is all-inclusive. At this level, limited personal identification and individual boundaries and concerns begin to dissolve into a greater, more expanded feeling of Love. The astral sound for this center is like the sound of a church bell.

Vishuddha **Center:** This fifth center is commonly referred to as the throat center and physically affects the thyroid and thymus glands. The qualities of communication and expression are related to this energy. An experience of expansion is also associated with the opening of the throat *chakra*. The fifth and second *chakras* are related, in that the life-creative energy can be drawn up the spine and transformed into creative expression. The astral sound of the fifth *chakra* is like the wind.

Ajna **Center:** This *chakra*, located at the point between the eyebrows, is physically related to the pineal and pituitary glands. This center is commonly called the sixth *chakra* and known as the spiritual eye. It is regarded as the seat of spiritual consciousness, and the corresponding astral sound is *Om*. Many Eastern meditative traditions direct the student to focus the attention at this center. A subtle shift in consciousness occurs when the physical and mental gaze is fixed at this center, as one's awareness is drawn up into the superconscious realm.

Sahasrara **Center:** The seventh *chakra* is located at the crown of the head and serves as a doorway into transpersonal realms. Individuals who have very open crown *chakras* tend to see visions and appear very light and airy.

Practical Implications for Spiritual Consciousness

Understanding and internalizing an expanded definition of the Self allows for a more profound understanding of life's mysteries and tragedies. From the expanded perspective of consciousness, life's purpose becomes much greater than wealth, happiness, marriage, and children, and the scope of life moves far beyond the limited notions of this earthly reality, as death does not touch the soul, and neither does birth define it.

The conventional Western definition of the self can only explain life's circumstances as being based upon genetics, family dynamics, social conditioning, and good or bad luck. When life is viewed from this perspective alone, it is easy to understand the rise in teenage violence and gang killings. When someone feels trapped by financial and social conditions with no hope of improving life, then despair and violence are a common result. The harsh reality of the physical/material plane often provides little substance in terms of purpose and meaning, and, regardless of one's social or economic position, fulfillment of physical desires often leads to a sense of emptiness and a feeling that some deeper need still remains untouched. Furthermore, without a greater purpose or guiding principles, why wouldn't one seek to live for oneself alone and try to get as much as possible, even at the expense of others? Fortunately, life does not have to be reduced to such a despairing reality, and sometimes it is one's very despair and disillusionment with the ups and downs of physical/material life that eventually causes one to seek spiritual answers.

On the other hand, expanded spiritual awareness thrusts one deeply into purpose and meaning. Divine awareness allows one to comprehend that life is a school in which we learn valuable lessons, typically through difficult circumstances. We are drawn into each life because of unfilled desires and unfinished lessons along the path towards God-realization. Eventually, we come into the knowing that God is Love and we learn that our greatest fulfillment results when we align with that Love and serve others. Unconditional Love, Compassion, Truth, and Service to humanity become important values for those who have been touched by the Divine hand and have awakened to their essential spiritual Self. A higher set of morals and ethical standards is encoded in the soul as part of its essence, but humans are not always able to live up to these lofty standards because of their ignorance and limited awareness. However, underneath the dross, these values are inherent and the goals are clear. Life then becomes known as an opportunity to reach perfection and to obtain a stable state of God-consciousness. This earthly show is recognized for the limited delusion that it is, and the greater spiritual reality of astral and causal existence is revealed. Ultimately, the advanced soul learns to transcend the limits of the physical body as his or her consciousness becomes stabilized in the Divine. In the end, death becomes a transition out of the confinements of the earthly dream into the subtle astral and causal realms.

Going back to Diagram 1, the astral and casual aspects of the self are represented as surrounding the mind, emotions, physical body, and soul. The astral body is an energy body that surrounds the denser aspects of the self, a "light body" that becomes our identified form when we leave the physical body. The astral plane is a subtler level of reality, in which energy and light are the substances of creation, for physical matter as we know it on earth does not exist on the astral plane. Vibratory rates determine different levels on the astral plane. Thus, one's consciousness at death determines the vibratory realm of astral existence. The causal realm is an even higher vibratory level, composed of thought. This last realm before final immersion into the Cosmic Sea also has lessons for learning and areas for development.

Yogic philosophy suggests that life on earth allows us an opportunity to complete all desires, until our only desire becomes God-union or Self-realization. Meditation and other yogic practices allow us to internalize our consciousness and concentrate our life force energy into the spine and brain. This stimulates the subtle energy centers and channels and eventually reveals the Truth of our real nature and allows us to perceive the joy and bliss that is our soul. These deep, transcendental states reveal the illusory quality of the physical world and the ultimate power that consciousness has over the physical, material plane. Yogic philosophy explains that we are not helpless victims in a senseless and chaotic world. Karma, or activity and its consequences, or cause and effect, is a universal, cosmic, mathematical law that directs life's experiences. However, since all of creation is a flow of consciousness and energy and therefore can be changed by consciousness, higher levels of spiritual evolution can free us from the mistakes of our past and end the cycle of birth, death, and suffering. Eventually, we become free from the limited identification with our physical body and move on to the higher spiritual realms.

Spiritual development is not a random process. The ancient yoga system actually provides a well-developed, scientific process for interested seekers. Advanced yogic techniques of meditation and life force control allow us to accelerate our spiritual development and transmute our karma. The next chapter provides a detailed explanation of this ancient, spiritual process.

Yoga: A Scientific Method for God-Realization

OGA, THE SCIENTIFIC PRACTICE that leads to the exalted state of cosmic consciousness, has often been reduced here in the West to learning a set of physical postures. All too often the term yoga is understood only to be the practice of *asana*, or *hatha yoga*, the physical exercises that are a part of the greater system of *raja yoga* as taught by the sage Patanjali.[9]

A complete discussion regarding yoga and its philosophical roots and practices is well beyond the scope of this book. The most definitive source on the science of yoga can be found elsewhere in other texts.[10] However, I do want to address those aspects of yoga that are essential to the psychotherapy process. First of all, the *asanas* or exercises taught in *hatha yoga* are in fact designed to prepare the body for meditation. One is considered to be a master of *asana* if one can sit for three hours without moving a muscle. But let us consider the entire system of yoga as developed by the sage Patanjali. It consists of eight steps that lead to Self-realization. They are as follows:

Yama and *Niyama* (right behavior and action)
Asana (physical postures)
Pranayama (life force energy control through the breath)
Pratyahara (internalization of the mind and the senses)
Dharana (concentration)
Dhyana (contemplation)
Samadhi (immersion into the object of contemplation).

Yama and *Niyama*

First there are the *yamas* and *niyamas*, the dos and don'ts of behavior, something like the Ten Commandments. Their basic underlying belief is that one has to learn to behave correctly as an initial step on the path towards Self-realization. The *yamas* and *niyamas* set the foundation for our spiritual life. The *yamas* are: nonviolence, nonlying, nonstealing, nonsensuality, and nonattachment. The *niyamas* are: cleanliness, contentment, austerity, self-study, and devotion to the Supreme Lord.

It makes good sense to teach basic moral values as part of a system that is designed to awaken the reality that we are all part of the same cosmic source. If we are all the same, then it makes little sense to steal from yourself, to kill yourself, or to lie to yourself. Integrity and right action become important qualities in any system of personal development, and to progress spiritually it becomes essential to align oneself with the highest of values and principles so that one's actions become a reflection and expression of that great truth. We become hypocrites when we talk about a level of awareness and a level of spiritual attainment but do not live it from day to day.

The world has seen many examples of such hypocrisy. A great soul has said that "one's true spirituality is tested in the light of day."[11] The foundation of yoga begins with the teaching that it is important to behave correctly. A deep esoteric necessity lies in the reality that as one meditates on a regular basis, one develops great spiritual power and energy. This energy flows according to the consciousness of the individual, and if the individual has not developed a sound basis of right action and moral behavior, then great misuse and harm can result from this power, so inner transformation is necessary.

Psychotherapy actually plays a very important part in this first step. It is impossible for a yogi to fake a level of development. Whatever unresolved issues that exist in one's personal psychology will rise to the surface like a skin diver who is out of air. Typically, issues of sexuality and power are the most common forms of abuse in America, and "great swamis" who have acquired large followings are found to be less than immune to these temptations and less than perfected in their actions regarding sex, money, and power. Consciousness wants to perfect itself, and it will necessarily bring forward all of one's shadow aspects on the path towards Self-realization. We need mirrors to see ourselves clearly, and if we rise to a level where we perceive that we have no equal or more advanced soul to function in that capacity, then life itself will become the mirror, and in a public arena. Several well-known swamis in America during the 1980s lost some or all degree of respect as their shadow material was played out across the mass media channels in this country. Even today, in 1997, some dramas are still being played out in the courts, as hurt and outraged devotees sue over their perceived damages. We in America have been very naive in our ability to discriminate between enlightened beings and nonenlightened beings. We have frequently assumed that a man of renunciation and apparent spiritual power was perfectly safe as a teacher, and many of us entered blindly into a *guru*-disciple relationship. We gave our trust and matured through the process of deception, and in the process we have learned a great many painful lessons. The *guru*-disciple relationship is a sacred one and does serve the spiritual seeker, but the *guru* must be a perfected being, and these great souls are naturally extremely rare.

The *guru* is a teacher, a spiritual preceptor, and functions as a mirror to help us see ourselves. If one has the good karma, the accumulated merit from past goodness, to have a fully enlightened being as one's *guru*, then the *guru* also serves to speed up one's evolution by lifting some of one's karma and helping with one's attunement to God. Subtle, vibratory forces are at work that help and hinder each person's spiritual progress. The true *guru* is a Divinely sent messenger to speed one's journey homeward. While the *guru* can help our progress, we still must make an enormous personal effort, and our desire, actions, and the use of our free will determines our progress.

Asana

Asana becomes the next step in the yogic process. The physical postures or *asanas* allow one to stretch the spine, which allows for the subtle currents of energy to flow freely during *pranayama* and meditation practice. The postures also allow for tension that has been stored in the body to be released, which explains why this practice has become so popular and useful in stress-reduction programs. When *asanas* are taught correctly, in combination with the breath, the student begins to experience how breath affects the physical body: tension and chronic muscle contractions begin to dissolve as one consciously breathes into the source of discomfort. The student begins to experience that there is something beyond the mind and the body, which he can access through this practice. *Asana* practice prepares the student for meditation, both mentally and physically. The mind begins to be drawn within as the focus of the breath is placed upon the body and the flow of energy within the body. The body becomes relaxed, and the flow of subtle energy is enhanced.

The *asana* system also relates to recent findings in mind-body medicine. Clinical observation with those patients receiving body-work reveals that repressed memories and strong emotions are released when physical blocks in deep tissue are released. The unconscious also resides in the body. Specific systems of modified *hatha yoga* practice such as Phoenix Rising Yoga Therapy,[12] use the power of *asana* to help release deep emotional conflicts. The body often provides a quicker path for emotional release and personal transformation than traditional psychotherapy techniques that focus mainly upon emotional and conceptual levels.

Pranayama

Pranayama is the scientific practice of controlling the life-force energy through the direction and use of the breath. Advanced forms of *pranayama*, such as *kriya yoga*, work to cleanse the body of venous blood, so that the heart and lungs do not have to work so hard. Breath controls the flow of energy. Three subtle currents run along the astral spine: the *ida*, on the left, comes upward as one inhales, the *pingala*, on the right side of the astral spine, goes downward upon the exhale, and the *sushumna* is in the center of the spine. Advanced *pranayama* practice focuses the breath in the center of the spine in order to draw life force energy away from the outer senses into the higher centers of the spine and brain. Simply holding the breath will not achieve these results.

In deep states of meditation, once the heart has been stopped, it is possible to stop breathing for extended periods of time and cause no harm to the brain or any organs of the physical body. The body can be sustained on subtle energy during these altered states of consciousness.

Pratyahara

Pratyahara, or internalization, is reached when the consciousness has been successfully redirected inward, away from the linear, rational mind and the senses. The previous techniques help to achieve this state, wherein the life-force energy has been withdrawn away from the outer senses of awareness into the deeper regions of the spine and brain. As the life-force energy is redirected inward, consciousness can move into the superconscious realms.

Dharana

Next comes *dharana*, or concentration. *Mantra* (repetition of sacred formulae, names of God, or prayers) becomes useful in this process because it allows one to focus upon a single-pointed object, in this case a sacred sound that carries a vibration of holiness. Various Sanskrit *mantras* hold this power to fix the awareness on the sound and thought of the Divine. As one develops the capacity to stay focused upon the breath and the *mantra,* then the distracting thoughts of the mind recede into the background of consciousness. This process allows one to observe the contents of the mind and the field of emotions that come and go across the screen of awareness. This practice deepens the awareness that one is not the body, mind, or emotions. One becomes more stabilized as the observer of pure consciousness.

This practice develops an inner strength that is laser-like in its focus. Deep concentration allows one to stay focused on the subtle aspects of consciousness and to avoid the pull of passing creations of mind and emotions. Then, the reality that we exist within a dream becomes clearer and clearer.

The great scriptures say that we are the product of God's dream, yet we tend to take our own reality so seriously and regard the contents of our mind as the living Truth. We have evolved to the extent that we do not take our nightly dreams as absolute reality, yet we take our daily dreams so much more so. Once the student moves into *dharana,* the reality of the mind's creation becomes as tangible as the movies on the big screen. We observe our mind creating the images and realities that we hold so dear. We watch the dramas and stories emerging and dissolving into the void from which they come. Thus, the student's ability to concentrate becomes the tool for emerging more deeply into true consciousness and exploring the illusion of reality. The process of perfected concentration leaves us clear to identify with the Being that is observing the inner movie. The macro melts into the micro, and the micro expands into the macro. Reality begins to emerge and collapse, and we watch as we become identified and lost in the illusion and then re-emerge to the Truth of our awareness, which is pure and eternal.

Dhyana

Dhyana, the process of contemplation, takes us even more deeply into the Divine, for we become That which we contemplate. There is an old story of a disciple who was sent into a room and instructed by his master to meditate on a water buffalo. Three days later, his master came to him and asked the disciple to follow him out of the room. The student protested that he could not get through the doors because his horns were too big!

Once we have developed the capacity to concentrate and focus, then we choose the object of desire: the Divine. Some individuals need a personification of the Divine and therefore choose to focus upon a *guru*, such as Jesus, Buddha, or some other holy figure. Others relate to the impersonal and experience God as Light, Love, Bliss, or Peace. The adept student keeps a steady bead on the Divine. God becomes the polestar of the mind. The attention does not waver and the focus remains clear: God, God, God. These inner callings tug at the Divine heartstrings to capture a Divine response. Peace, Love, Joy, and Bliss open to the quiet and stillness within that is saturated with the individual's sincere devotion.

Samadhi

The ultimate purpose for the spiritual aspirant is to obtain final liberation from the limitations of delusion. As the student experiences deeper meditative states, he or she can encounter different degrees of Divine perception. Just as the dreaming person believes the dream material to be real, the spiritually ignorant individual beholds the cosmic dream, the physical/material world, as the ultimate reality, whereas the spiritually awakened individual begins to behold the levels of creation behind the outer apparent reality. Paramahansa Yogananda describes the various states of this ecstasy, *samadhi*, in his interpretation of the *Bhagavad Gita:*

> The first stage of Divine ecstasy *(savikalpa samadhi)* gives the yogi the experience of God-union, in which no memory is present of

the phenomenal universe. When he returns to mortal consciousness, he finds it hard to retain his Divine realization. By further practice of *kriya yoga*, the devotee is able to experience God-union even during the wakeful state of activities in the world. He has then achieved the "half-awake" ecstatic state, in which with open eyes he consciously sees the world around him as the Divine dream.

By development, however, the devotee is able to remain in continuous ecstasy with open or closed eyes *(nirvikalpa samadhi);* he learns to commingle his consciousness fully in the Lord and also to produce from that consciousness the dream of the cosmos. In this state he can choose to remain awake in God, without viewing the dream of creation, or he can remain in the "half-awake" blissful state, realizing the cosmos as a varied dream. When *nirvikalpa samadhi* is attained, the yogi no longer perceives the "actuality" of the world as does the ordinary man.

Modern science has discovered that the various material elements are nothing more than differently vibrating atoms. The universe is a cosmic motion picture of dancing atoms, which in turn are energy-sparks—not matter at all, but vibratory waves.[13]

The ultimate value of yogic practices and meditation are to achieve this true perception of reality and to stabilize one's consciousness within the Divine vibrations. This shift in the basic "ground of being" provides a dramatic change in one's life and one's relationships with others. All of life becomes an extension of the Divine and sacred for that reason. And while the deeper states of meditation do result in profound degrees of Peace, Love, and Joy, the ultimate purpose is far deeper than just the attainment of these heightened states of consciousness: the *samadhi* experience transforms the individual's consciousness and nature of Being beyond the limitations of the dualistic worldly delusion.

The aim of this brief introduction into the path of yoga is to clarify that meditation is more than riding a bike and running for a mile or two. Meditation appears to be so misunderstood here in the West. It is a common occurrence to hear someone say, "Oh, yes, I meditate—every morning with my morning coffee or while I am jogging." The great liberating benefits from spiritual practice, including avoidance of tremendous suffering, are lost in this superficial understanding, which ignores the splendors of the interior spiritual life.

Kriya Yoga

Paramahansa Yogananda explained that it is eventually possible for an individual to obtain final liberation in the normal course of development if that person continues to live a good life, serve others, and love God—but that in the normal course of evolution, it will take one million years to achieve this spiritual freedom. *Kriya yoga*, an advanced *pranayama* technique, provides a way to dramatically accelerate the slower, normal process of evolution. *Kriya yoga* has been handed down over the last one hundred years through a lineage of fully realized spiritual Masters. This technique, which activates the subtle life-force energy in the spine, is explained by Swami Sri Yukteswar, Paramahansa Yogananda's *guru*, in the following way:

One year of life spent on earth is determined by the twelve-month cycle and the revolution of the earth around the sun. The *kriya* technique, which uses the breath and the flow of energy within the spine, is said to be equivalent to one year of spiritual development for each *kriya* that is properly performed. Thus, one complete breath which moves up and down the spine is equal to one year of time spent on earth. Therefore, by *kriya yoga* practice, the devotee can speed up spiritual progress immensely. With the help of this process, it may be possible for one to achieve final liberation within one to three lifetimes. Once again, we can see the difference between the notion that meditation is only a practice that promotes relaxation and stress reduction, and the understanding that yogic meditation is a way to obtain spiritual liberation and freedom from the cycle of birth and death. The true roots and functions of yoga and meditation are much greater and the results much more far-reaching than most individuals understand.

Comparison of
Yogic Cosmology with
Western Psychology

EASTERN YOGIC PERSPECTIVES regarding the origin and nature of human consciousness differ greatly from Western psychological perspectives. Yogic philosophy suggests that all of creation emanates from the light of God, with God's light becoming transformed into thought, energy, and matter.[14] The Western perspective assumes a mere biochemical origin, from which higher life forms have evolved via the biological evolutionary process. In the Western view, human consciousness appears to be the result of complex biochemical processes that result in thought and awareness. Volumes have been written on both subjects; it is not my intention to review all that literature. However, I do want to once again focus upon those key aspects in yoga philosophy from the *Bhagavad Gita* that relate to the topic of psychotherapy and healing.

Yogic Cosmology of Consciousness

Yogic philosophy suggests that human consciousness is a reflection of Divine consciousness and that God created two forces:

attraction and repulsion. The force of attraction, which is love, works to bring us back into the Divine realization of our true nature: being one with God-consciousness. That state is described as love, joy, bliss, peace, and ecstasy. The individualized soul, or *purusha,* is an aspect of God that is manifesting in creation. The soul perceives all creation as a unified, interconnecting web of light and energy, and the ultimate goal of life is to return to this absolute reality.

The force of repulsion creates the delusion that we are separate from God, that we exist solely in a physical/material reality. The subtle elements or energies descend into denser realms of creation and manifest as the illusion of individuality or separate existence. Within the *purusha,* or soul, *chitta* (inner consciousness) exists. The *chitta* is a spark of love that has descended into the heart, creating the force of existence in the Self and functioning as a tuning fork for the Soul's final mergence into light. Therefore, love is the external force of attraction that frees us from delusion, while devotion turns our limited love toward the Divine love so we can re-emerge into the light.

This *chitta* force further condenses into two elements: *buddhi* and *manas. Buddhi* is the higher vibratory manifestation of the two, holds the power to perceive truth and wisdom, and is attuned to the subtle element of truth eternal: Love. *Manas* is the downward expression of this force as it descends into physical manifestation: mind. The mind is connected to the physical senses and relates to the physical brain. Since grosser elements express at this level, the result is an outward experience of separation and individual identity.

The *ahamkara* or ego (ι) is the collection of those elements that include the *manas* and result in the experience of individual identity, apart from any spiritual reality. We can see the problem here with conceiving of the mind as the instrument of discernment, because the mind, *manas,* can perceive only the grosser elements in physical/material reality. On the other hand, the *buddhi,* or intellect, contains the faculty for perception of Truth, because of its access to subtle realms that transcend the delusion of isolation and separation, and it is the premier instrument for discrimination of the real from the unreal. Many spiritual traditions speak of the heart-mind. This intuitive function of the *chitta*, or heart, allows for direct, intuitive know-ing, or accessing a higher state of mind than that of *manas*. Informa-tion received from this level reaches the consciousness as impressions and "knowing," while the *manas*, or mind, has no involvement with this process. Furthermore, linear, rational thought is a function of *manas*, not *buddhi*. *Buddhi*, the intellect, is able to access knowledge from a higher eternal source wherein all information exists. This higher vibratory library is known as the *akashic* records.

Returning to the process of descent in density, consciousness continues to condense from *manas* into the five organs of the senses (smell, taste, sight, touch, and hearing) and into the five organs of actions (excretion, generation, motion (feet), manual skill (hands), and speech). The force of repulsion works to perpetuate the delusion of physical/material reality and the separation from God-conscious-ness. This repulsive force is very strong and creates the belief that true fulfillment is the result of sense gratification. The more one focuses upon physical, sensual, and material pleasure as a way to find meaning and fulfillment, the more this self-perpetuating cycle of delusion is sustained. Within this aspect of the whole, each action, each infusion of energy into mind and the senses, moves the individual awareness further and further away from the Divine consciousness of true perfection—the higher center in the heart.

Once again the reader is referred to *The Holy Science* for a more detailed discussion of the process. This overview is presented here to suggest that in yogic theory, consciousness unfolds throughout all aspects of creation, with no separation between the mind, body, and spirit, and with the understanding that everything in creation is essentially energy manifesting as a continuum of subtle to gross forms of expression. Perhaps it is easier to understand Patanjali's *raja yoga* in this light, as a process in which the experience of the self is transformed back into the essential realization of Spirit, and wherein the gross identification of the self, as mind, body, and emotions, which most people mistake for their real Self, becomes transmuted as the experience of soul consciousness becomes fixed and grounded into one's awareness.

Western Psychology

If we give any credence to the yogic cosmology, then the Western psychological perspective appears to be very limited, because it considers only the realm of *manas*, or mind, which manifests solely within the illusory realm of physical/material reality. Western psychological thought provides no understanding for the meaning of life other than to work, love, have sex, make money, and be happy. Many individuals who follow this advice find that they have successfully completed the first two tasks, work and loving relationships, but they still feel unfulfilled and hence, never truly happy. Western thought gives paramount importance to the ego(ι), the aspect of the self that experiences itself as separate from God, and provides no understanding and explanation of the soul. While various transpersonal authors attempt to speak to the spiritual aspects of the Self, our society generally remains fixed in the identification with sense objects and sensory pleasures, with physical/material reality as the accepted truth of existence. Television reflects this mainstream thought, which in turn drives the American commercial market. Hundreds if not thousands of hours are spent watching violence, death, and murder—with a significant amount of the violence portrayed as being directed at women. Furthermore, children spend hundreds and thousands of hours playing video games that reiterate main themes of death, violence, and destruction. By these indications, the collective force of Western consciousness is being directed downward and away from the light. Therefore, is it any wonder that our streets are filled with violence and that many are not safe to walk in their own neighborhoods after the sun goes down?

In the face of these and all other pathological symptoms of the society, the toolbox of Western psychological thought relies almost solely upon the hope of the ego's (ψ) ability to function effectively. Let's review the Western psychological definition of ego: *The ego is a hypothetical construct for those functions of thinking, perceiving, organizing, and integrating reality.* To the credit of Western psychology, considerable effort has been directed at helping people to live more effectively within the human realm. Psychological understanding of human personality development has improved child-rearing practices, added more skills for interpersonal and organizational communication, helped families achieve greater intimacy, and helped individuals resolve emotional conflicts that lead to anxiety and depression. Also, Western psychological approaches have made significant contributions in understanding and addressing some of the important problems in living.

Besides those who subscribe to the biological view, which suggests that all emotion and behavior can ultimately be explained on the basis of neurochemistry, many Western psychologists recognize psychodynamic forces as being at work within the psyche, wherein unconscious forces are assumed to affect conscious mental processes and behavior. From this point of view, it is assumed that the body can be a repository of unconscious material, hence psychosomatic problems. Still others adopt a cognitive view and assume that most feelings are the result of the way an individual frames his or her reality, wherein one's thinking and concepts become the major focus of attention and explanation. While all of these perspectives appear to be valid to some relative degree, they remain focused, from a yogic perspective, on only the gross aspects of existence, while the nature of subtle energy and the evolutionary journey of the soul is not even considered. The Western goal and directive is to adjust and adapt to one's environment, and questions concerning the overall meaning of one's particular predicament are not considered.

In spite of its limited cosmic perspective, traditional Western psychotherapy does offer the basic promise to help individuals find relief from fear, pain, emotional suffering, and to regain hope. In most situations this promise is fulfilled, and many Americans report that they have been helped by psychotherapy.[15] In fact, longer term treatment was reported to be more helpful than short-term methods. However, as humanity continues to evolve, the social pressure for more enlightened health care will no doubt increase. Individuals will not be satisfied with approaches that treat them as mechanical objects, separate from their feelings, thoughts, and spiritual needs. A higher promise in health care could offer an understanding of the purpose of life, our place in the cosmic drama, practical techniques for finding Joy and Bliss—rather than drugs and alcohol, which serve as poor substitutes, and ways to deepen one's relationship with the Divine.

Given that traditional psychological approaches do not allow for the inclusion and understanding of spiritual realities, can traditional Western psychological methods actually address the healing of the whole person when these parts are ignored? Individuals are seeking healing systems that speak to all levels of the awareness, and in my view it is impossible to find wholeness without realizing the spiritual unity that is inherent in one's own being. As a psychologist, I suggest that we collectively broaden our definition of the "self" to include our spiritual nature as well.

The incredible escalation of violence in America, especially among children, is frightening, but it is no wonder that our society is becoming so violent when we lack collectively shared spiritual principles and experiences that can provide a rationale for a different perspective. Despite increasing interest in spirituality, the wisdom that is gained and shared from direct experience of the deeper mysteries of life remains largely outside of the mainstream of visible American culture. Ironically, the original inhabitants of this country, Native Americans, do have a strong spiritual tradition to help provide meaning and continuity to their lives. Furthermore, although America is a melting pot that contains deep and wonderful traditions from all parts of the globe, the Western rational, scientific tradition ironically does not allow for the embrace of transcendental, mystical approaches to life.

Now, however, the nature of our collective understanding of subtle energies and consciousness is expanding as more individuals are awakening spiritually and the planet moves to a higher level of consciousness. The current evolutionary cycle, according to ancient yogic calculations, places us in a time period in which human consciousness can more easily experience energy and the subtle realms[16] than has been possible in some other eras. The evolutionary process allows for a profound integration of yogic wisdom and Western approaches, and the integration of these two cosmologies can foster a quantum leap in the quality of health care and healing in our culture. Balanced, well-integrated, complementary approaches that draw upon the best resources from both traditions will allow for a more profound involvement with our patients and result in spiritual advancement along with physical or emotional healing.

A quantum shift in perspective allows for new understanding and explanations regarding the nature of reality and our place in the cosmos. The next chapter speaks to these issues.

9

The Cosmic Dream

"WHY ARE WE HERE?" and "What is life all about?" are important questions that speak to the heart of yogic philosophy. Let us consider further the nature of reality according to yogic philosophy, in an attempt to answer the questions that confront us and shed light on the nature of difficulties that we encounter in this life. According to yogic philosophy, we are all playing out our parts in a cosmic drama, a cosmic dream, and this is how it all began:

In the beginning, there was God, and God wished to experience Itself and share Its experience with others. God created the universe with a thought. The thought was condensed into light or energy, and the energy was condensed into matter. Hence, the three planes of creation: causal, astral, and physical. Creation is like a great motion picture, in which the cosmic dream is created and sustained by God's thought and light, which projects outward from the Mind of the Infinite. Two great forces affect the cosmic play: the force of attraction, which is Love; and the force of repulsion, which is *maya*, delusion, or Satan. The greater force, Love, functions as a gentle current, constantly pulling us back into the source, the Infinite. We are all being pulled by this Love.

The opposite force, delusion, creates resistance. *Maya* attempts to keep us from our final destiny, the remembrance of our God-consciousness. *Maya* creates the false sense of separation from the infinite. *Maya* creates the darkness, the despair, and the hopelessness that results when we experience ourselves as being separate and isolated. The loneliness and meaninglessness become too much to bear, so we turn to drugs, alcohol, sex, and any sense stimulation to fill the void and give us a false sense of joy and fulfillment. *Maya* seduces us into believing that false or temporary worldly power will provide meaning and purpose to our lives. Under the influence of this illusion, we do harm to one another, steal from each other, abuse each other, and believe that we can actually advance in life at the expense of others. This delusion speaks to our deepest fears and calls forth our lowest nature.

Love, however, works to counteract this tragic drama. Divine Love comes in the form of Enlightened Ones, awakened Masters such as Jesus Christ, Buddha, Ramana Maharshi, Ananda Moyi Ma, Paramahansa Yogananda, and Beings such as Mother Theresa, to uplift our consciousness and remind us of a deeper Truth. God's infinite hand touches us in the stillness of our minds and fills our hearts with compassion and tenderness and speaks to every cell of our Being. God's Love uplifts our consciousness to rise above the delusion of this limited, physical/material reality, and we perceive the unity of all creation and the joy that results from serving and loving God. We see the path out of the darkness and are given the inspiration and inner spiritual strength needed to overcome our shortcomings.

The pull of delusion is so strong, however, that we easily become identified with our senses and physical/material reality and lose awareness of ourselves as Beings of Light and Energy. We forget our connection to the Divine and lose our attunement with the Divine Will. We begin to go our own way and become lost in the forest of our own desires. Desire leads to desire, and we move further and further away from the Divine. We frantically attempt to find happiness outside of ourselves in human love, material acquisition, or sense pleasure. The more we try these false paths, the further we go from the true source that can free us. Each action that stems from our egoic (ı) desires creates karma. Our unfulfilled desires become magnets that pull us back into yet another incarnation, yet another birth. We are ultimately freed from this cycle when all desires melt into the one desire to love and serve God.

The Law of Karma

The Universe was established with mathematical precision. The law of karma is that formula: for every action there is an equal and opposite reaction. "What ye sow, so shall ye reap." The illusion of reality is that we live in a linear universe, whereas in fact, we live in an interconnected, united sphere of consciousness, in which we are affected by everything we do. Our thoughts and our actions create forces that affect us. Ultimately, however, we are here on earth to learn about Love and this state of unity, so we are continually brought back to confront those beings and situations that hold the seeds to our greater understanding. We go round and round until we unlock the secret to life's mystery.

As long as we resist surrendering to the moment, project disowned parts of ourselves onto others, act from fear, react with hatred, and create separation through judgment and blame, we will continue to cycle through this earthly drama. A great movie, *Groundhog Day*, depicts this truth. The main character, a very selfish, self-centered, egoic individual, finds himself trapped in a little town in America, replaying the same day of his life, for eternity. After many days or mini-"lifetimes" of satisfying only his own needs and desires, he begins gradually to help the members of that community. Eventually, his day or "life" becomes devoted to serving and helping others. He becomes recognized as the "saint" of the town. When his life finally becomes an expression of love, he becomes free from the circle of endless repetition.

Life *is* a school in which we are learning, and we are destined to repeat the same class until we have learned the course material. Recurring dreams are another analogy of this life-after-life process.

The psychological phenomenon of a recurrent dream is an attempt of the unconscious to resolve some conflict. Yet, it is but a dream within a dream. In truth, we are all dreaming, and God is dreaming us.

What About Problems and Difficulties?

Contrary to popular belief, God does not punish us with misfortune. So many people do not understand this fact. God is a Being of Love. God's nature is love, light, bliss, joy, ecstasy, peace, and energy. God is not a vicious and revengeful creature who is trying to punish us for our "sins." Rather, our problems are the result of our own past actions. Sin, in this light, is any action that is not in alignment with God's will. Negative karma is created when we act in ways that are against the will of God. Obviously, one must meditate deeply to develop one's *buddhi*, the discriminating faculty of the intellect, and the spiritual attunement to know and do the will of God. Many people are so completely focused upon their own needs and desires that they never take the time to turn inward and attune to the Divine for guidance and direction. Again, our difficulties and tragedies are the result of our own actions. We simply and necessarily draw to us those circumstances that we need to complete our learning and neutralize the seeds of our past actions, i.e., our karma. God is ever-present and His Grace does transcend the law of karma. So, through sincere prayer and devotion we can draw upon the limitless supply of Divine Grace, which will help us through the most difficult of times.

The cosmic drama is not only being played out in this physical realm, for karma is created on every level: physical, astral, and causal, and we continue to learn and complete our karma after we leave this physical dimension. The astral play consists of Beings of light and energy bodies, and our state of consciousness at the time of our death determines where we go on the astral plane. The various levels or "places" in the astral plane are determined by vibratory rates of consciousness. Thus, "heaven" and "hell" reside within our consciousness, and we attract to us that which we are. However, we continue to grow and evolve spiritually on all levels, no matter what our state of consciousness, until we finally are free from even the causal realm, a realm of pure thought, and return to the Infinite Cosmic Sea of Bliss. All are headed "Home."

The individualized Self or soul is that aspect of God that is expressing itself in creation, and we all have that spark within us. In some it shines more brightly than in others. As one gains greater attunement to soul consciousness and learns to express it in daily life, then the Divine spark becomes integrated and manifested through every aspect of one's Being: mind, body, and personality. This Divine integration and expression is present in those who demonstrate a perfect balance of masculine and feminine qualities, in those who carry and express a certain sense of grace and refinement, in those who radiate light and goodness, and in those whose speech rings of Truth so loudly that the vibration from their words sends chills up the spine and almost stops one's breath from the profundity of their wisdom.

Once we awaken from the cosmic dream, a larger reality becomes available, and the psychotherapy process opens to new possibilities. The eternal journey of the soul becomes a legitimate concern, and the trials and tribulations of this one lifetime can be placed in proper context within the greater unfolding process. The next chapter turns to the heart of yogic philosophy, which is found in the *Bhagavad Gita*, and discusses the potential for this broader perspective in psychotherapy.

The *Bhagavad Gita*

Ancient Wisdom
Applied to Modern Psychotherapy

T HE *BHAGAVAD GITA* is considered to be one of the most sacred texts in Vedanta philosophy. It is part of the great epic story, the *Mahabharata*, as told by the sage Vyasa. The *Mahabharata* uses the conflict between two royal families and the great battle fought for wealth and power as a vehicle to explain symbolically the evolution of consciousness and the inner battle of each individual to obtain God-consciousness. Krishna, considered to be the Divine manifestation of God, provides counsel to Arjuna, who does not want to enter battle. The wisdom of this discourse has been passed down for centuries and provides individuals with knowledge to understand the deepest purpose of life.

Some of the principles discussed in the *Gita* can be very useful in a psychotherapeutic context. Many translations of the *Bhagavad Gita* exist. I have chosen to quote extensively from the translation by Paramahansa Yogananda[17] because of his profound wisdom and personal level of spiritual development. By all standards, he is considered to be a fully illumined Master, and his entire story can be found in his book, *The Autobiography of a Yogi*.[18] In his introduction to the *Bhagavad Gita*, Yogananda discusses his relationship with his guru, Swami Sri Yukteswar, and the method that his guru used to enlighten him about the inner meanings of the various verses. Sri Yukteswar instructed Yogananda to meditate for hours on a verse, until he obtained direct intuitive perception and understanding of the verse. In this way, he learned to attune his consciousness to the source from which these ancient teachings flowed. His translation and extensive discussion of the text provide a clarity and depth of wisdom that I have found unparalleled. The following excerpts from the *Gita* and discussion will focus on those elements that have direct clinical application.

Beyond Pain and Pleasure

> *O Flower among Men (Arjuna)! He who cannot*
> *be ruffled by these (contacts of the senses with their objects),*
> *who is calm and even-minded during pain and pleasure,*
> *he alone is fit to attain everlastingness!*
> Chapter 2, Verse 15

Most of the patients who come for professional help are driven out of a desire to end pain and suffering. Happy people do not seek out psychotherapy! Western methods are very useful in helping individuals learn better skills for introspection, stronger ego (ψ) functions, and an ability to adapt more effectively to one's environment. The focus is typically on learning how to become more skillful in fulfilling desires and learning how to cope with those frustrating times when personal needs and desires cannot be fulfilled. This latter area is most often addressed by learning greater tolerance for frustration through sublimation and imagination. The realm of therapeutic focus, however, remains, in spiritual terms, within the context of duality and the realm of delusion that perpetuates the cycle of birth and death. An actual end to suffering cannot be hoped for at this level of manifestation because pleasure and pain are inherently a part of the human experience. Yogananda offers insight into this fact:

> The basic principle of creation is duality. If one knows pleasure he must know pain. One who cognizes heat must cognize cold also. If creation had manifested only heat or only cold, only sorrow or only pleasure, human beings would not be the irritated victims of the pranks of duality. But then, what would life be like in a monotone existence? Some contact is necessary; it is man's response to dualities that causes his trouble. So long as one is slavishly influenced by the dualities, he lives under the domination of the changeful phenomenal world.[19]

While the traditional Western approach may help us become more comfortable and perhaps more effective in this dualistic state, it cannot provide us with the wisdom and technology to rise above the inherent limitations and restrictions of a dualistic world. On the other hand, ancient yogic wisdom and technology provide the hope and actual methods to stabilize one's consciousness above the fickle fates found in the delusionary expression of dualistic reality. Whereas Western approaches are very interested in one's feelings and wants, the yogic perspective suggests, "Man's egoistic (ι) feelings, expressing as likes and dislikes, are entirely responsible for the bondage of the soul to the body and earthly environment."[20] It is through yogic meditation that one learns to withdraw the life force energy away from the outer senses and into the spine, resulting in a neutralization of the waves of emotions and a stabilization of one's consciousness in peace and serenity. A commonly held misconception about this relatively detached state of being is that a person will become cold and aloof, uncaring about others and the world's problems. However, there is no basis for this concern, because experience shows us that those devoted souls who have achieved states of divine bliss and peace are actually more involved in helping others than those who have not.

In fact, one's ability and desire for service increases as one is touched by the Divine experience. We are made in the image of God, and our soul is an individualized spark of Omnipresent Spirit. God loves and cares about all Beings, and that love and care is encoded in our soul as well. Those individuals who touch God within feel a great desire to serve others and furthermore do so. I suggest that they are actually more adept in this service than others can be, because their consciousness is more stabilized in the heart, the center of unconditional Love, and their acts of service are purer, less self-centered, and less emotional or based on the likes and dislikes of the personality. For example, Mother Theresa was given the Divine message to serve the most disenfranchised of all humanity. She has done so consistently and selflessly all her life. It is difficult to describe, but the actual state of awareness that can be achieved allows for a steady, stable, clear presence that sees past all surface appearances to the Truth in a moment. This heart-centered being and knowing allows one to stay present and open in all circumstances.

In contrast, fear, preference, desire, and ambition all function to deter one from the connection with the moment and to push one off in scattered directions. However, when one's consciousness is stabilized in the soul, a peace and clarity exist within the Self that is similar to being in a high, mountain-granite lake with perfectly still, crystal clear water. The peace and clarity of the water allow one to see hundreds of feet to the very bottom of the lake. This pristine environment, so far from the noise and pollution of the city, is filled with a presence that touches the heart of one's soul. In this silence, wisdom saturates the air. The healing presence of love permeates every cell. The busy chatter of the mind stops, the longing for unfilled desires, like an unquenchable thirst, has been finally and totally fulfilled, and one's inner clarity and direct knowing is beyond words.

Most of us spend our lives as though a dozen stones have been tossed into the lake, and the many resulting ripples cloud our vision and disrupt our peace. We cannot see clearly because the waves of emotion and desire have caused too much inner commotion.

The Essential Nature of the Self

> *This Self is never born nor does it ever perish; nor having*
> *come into existence will it again cease to be. It is birthless,*
> *eternal, changeless, ever-same (unaffected by the usual processes*
> *associated with time). It is not slain when the body is killed.*
> Chapter 2, Verse 20

The "It" in this verse refers to the Self or the soul, suggesting that consciousness is eternal and transcendent of the body, mind, and emotions.

> Spirit is ever-existing, ever-conscious, ever-new, omnipresent Joy; the soul is the individualized reflection of ever-existing, ever-conscious, ever-new Joy, confined within the body of each and every being.[21]

This verse provides insight into the eternal aspect of the Self that cannot be harmed by any outer circumstance, even death. Most individuals struggle with great existential anxiety regarding their condition. How is my health? Can I go to work in order to make enough money to support myself and my family? Will I lose my job and become homeless? Is this illness going to kill me? What am I doing with my life?

Western psychotherapeutic approaches typically deal with the surface manifestation of these questions. The real, authentic self, within psychological terms, as discussed by Fairbairn,[22] Winnicot,[23] Guntrip,[24] and Masterson,[25] is at best the integrated ego (ψ), effectively and authentically interacting with internal psychological structures or objects and the outer world of people and organizational structures. The self is still conceived of as separate and alone, except for a well-established social network of friends and family. However, experience shows most of us that even the best of friends and family cannot be counted on, one hundred percent of the time. Then, in the end, when death comes, according to Western psychological perspectives, all awareness ends and the "It" stops. A rather cold and frightening prospect!

The value of knowing that the true Self exists throughout eternity is that it can help to reduce the mind's reaction to the earthly drama that we must all experience. When our personal trials and tribulations can be seen in a greater context, the fear of annihilation disappears in the face of this great wisdom and the direct experience of our deeper nature. Mere intellectual understanding is not sufficient to reach this goal.

Direct experience as the result of spiritual awakening provides answers to the grand questions regarding life's direction and purpose: if we continue to exist as consciousness, throughout eternity, merely changing forms from one incarnation to another, then what does this one particular lifetime have to offer in that greater perspective? In this light, the question rightfully emerges: what have we been doing before that is affecting us now? From the spiritual perspective, our limited time here on earth becomes both a very sacred place in time, because it is the only moment in which we will manifest in this particular state, and a little less dramatic because we hold a larger perspective about existence. Our personal drama becomes slightly less inflated when viewed as a part of the cosmic drama, and death obviously loses its terror since death becomes only a transformation from one state of Being into another. A caterpillar undoubtedly does not experience a major existential crisis and resulting anxiety disorder with possible post-traumatic stress symptoms as it weaves its cocoon and prepares to change form, ultimately surrendering unto one death to be reborn anew as an exotic butterfly. Western psychological thought, taken alone, does not provide this expanded context for understanding life's opportunities.

Many people are so confused: why is this happening to me? What did I ever do to deserve this? God must really hate me. I have everything I want and I still feel empty and unfulfilled; what is wrong with me? Realization of the Self allows for intuitive perception and understanding of life's many mysteries. These questions, which arise from ignorance and blindness regarding the eternal nature of our soul, the laws of karma, and the illusion of time and space, fall away when consciousness expands to embrace the unity and perfection that is inherent in Omnipresent Spirit. Yogananda eloquently states:

> The soul, in essence the reflection of Spirit, never undergoes the pangs of birth nor the throes of death. Nor having once been projected from the womb of immortal Spirit will Prince Soul, on return to Spirit, lose its individuality; having entered the portals of nativity, its existence will never cease. In all its bodily births, the Spirit-soul never felt birth; it exists everlastingly, untouched by the maya-magic fingers of change. It is ever the same—now, past, future—as it has always been ageless, unchanged, since its immemorial beginnings. The deathless soul dwelling in the destructible body is ever constant through all cycles of bodily disintegrations; it does not taste death, even when the body quaffs that fatal cup of hemlock.[26]

The Road to Joy

> *Equalizing (by even-mindedness) happiness and sorrow,*
> *profit and loss, triumph and failure—so encounter thou*
> *the battle! Thus thou wilt not acquire sin.*
> Chapter 2, Verse 38

This one verse may be the most useful for all clinical work and basic human living. Krishna counsels Arjuna to rise above the delusion of duality in which pleasure, happiness, outer worldly gain, fame, success, and even health, are seen as superior to pain, sadness, poverty, blame, failure, and disease. Sin in this context means acting against God's will. Creating karma based upon the attempt to fulfill personal desire only perpetuates the cycle of reincarnation.

This verse opens the way for an exploration of happiness and joy. Everyone wants to be happy. Americans spend a lot of time and money in an attempt to be happy. We buy lots of toys and go lots of places and even exchange lots of partners in an attempt to be happy. The difficulty is that happiness is a result of the ego (ı) obtaining some object of desire. Since happiness is part of duality, unhappiness is quick to follow when that object of desire changes or is lost. Worse yet, it is the nature of the mind that one desire leads to another without end. Thus, it becomes ultimately impossible to fulfill all the mind's desires, as long as the source of those desires rests in duality. One cannot know what happiness is without sadness or pain. Just as light is known as the opposite of darkness, all aspects in duality have their counterpart.

Dualistic reality creates a yo-yo effect between pleasure and pain. If the life focus becomes directed towards obtaining pleasure and happiness, then tremendous consciousness energy must be directed at "what do 'I' want and how do 'I' obtain it?" Ignorance, or sin, here, is the misdirection of the will from the Divine will toward the fulfillment of personal desire. Unfilled desires become the magnet that draw us back into another incarnation. Joy, on the other hand, is feeling good without any particular external reason. Joy, which many people have never actually experienced, is based upon an inner reality. One of the qualities of the soul is joy. When one learns to internalize the focus of one's attention and to withdraw the life force energy away from the outer senses, then one's inherent joy is discovered.

Since joy is not a result of personal ego (ı) fulfillment, joy can be felt even in the most apparently unusual circumstances. For example, a friend of mine once told me that while she was having a stillbirth, she felt an overpowering sense of God's presence and a great inner joy. The paradox here is that both situations can occur simultaneously. The outer life situation may be very difficult, but an inner sense of joy can simultaneously exist that actually provides strength to survive the outer challenge.

Nine years ago my younger brother tragically died in a drug-related accident. I was struck by the paradox of feeling a tremendous amount of personal grief and sadness over his loss, while simultaneously feeling a very clear inner connection with him and knowing that he was fine and actually feeling well on another plane of existence.

Yogananda explains this verse in the following manner:

> A basic principle of yoga is that practicing mental equilibrium neutralizes the effects of delusion. Without the involvement of the emotions of the dreamer reacting to the sensations and incidents of a dream, the dream loses its significance—and especially its hurtful effects. Similarly, the cosmic dream of life loses its delusive power to affect the yogi, who with unruffled inner calmness and even-mindedness views the dream of life without emotional involvement. This advice of the Gita enables the yogi to keep himself aloof from the agitation and sting caused by the clash of the opposites sporting on the mental screen of his consciousness, even while he perceives and enacts his part in the dream drama.
>
> An evenminded individual is like a mirror of discretion that reflects the true nature and appearances of favorable and unfavorable events; thus he holds himself in readiness to act wisely and properly without being misled by emotional distortions.[27]

Bad Luck or Karma?

> *The ultimate wisdom of Sankhya I have explained to thee.*
> *But now thou must hear about the wisdom of Yoga, equipped with*
> *which, O Partha (Arjuna), thou shalt shatter the bonds of karma.*
> Chapter 2, Verse 39

This verse provides great clinical help, in that it provides a ray of hope in the most desperate and despairing situations. Nowhere does Western psychological thought provide a technology for changing what appears to be one's bad fate or continued bad luck. So many times clinicians hear patients bemoan their fate and life patterns that seem to trap them in unbearable and unrewarding circumstances. Individuals will say, "I feel like there is some invisible wall keeping me from getting what I want." They are perfectly correct, and that wall is their karma.

Karmic forces have been created from past desires and actions from this lifetime and previous incarnations. Just because we do not have conscious memory of those times, events, choices, actions, and desires does not mean that we are free from their effects. The universe is mathematically structured, and it is we who have created the difficult circumstances in our lives. God is not punishing us. We live in a difficult realm, earth, because the forces of delusion are so strong. It is difficult to know what is the "right" choice. The mystery is being able to discern the truth and then having the courage and ability to act in accordance with our inner knowing.

We are not cursed by our karma, nor are we trapped by it. God's Grace transcends the law of karma, and we can draw Grace to us through our devotion and sincere love of God. We must remember that karma is consciousness manifesting in physical/material reality, and that consciousness is energy. Yoga is a scientific method to transmute energy from lower levels of manifestation, delusion, to higher levels of expression, God-consciousness, and the system of *kriya yoga* is specifically designed to speed up one's spiritual evolution and provide the devotee with the tools and inner spiritual help, in the form of the *guru*, to overcome all obstacles of delusions. Meditation, devotion, and prayer are tools that can be used to break the bonds of karma and free one from continued suffering.

It is true that we have created some very difficult circumstances for ourselves here on earth. However, it is not true that we are doomed to suffer in those circumstances. Life is ultimately God's dream, and yoga is a technology for us to awaken consciously from the dream and change the picture. Suicidal despair is often the result of too much pain and the loss of hope, but once hope is reestablished, then new strength emerges to confront life's difficulties.

While this message of inspiration may seem very hopeful, it still falls short to many Western ears that require more precise information regarding this process. It is far from sufficient merely to explain that a law such as karma exists and that it can be overcome. Esoteric literature is filled with volumes of mumbo-gumbo regarding the esoteric structure of the universe. The Sankhya-yoga philosophy,

which is explained with unparalleled clarity by Paramahansa Yogananda in his discourse on verse thirty-nine of the *Gita*, offers the
reader a credible and meaningful explanation. Although it is a bit
lengthy, it is worthwhile to quote because of its unique explicitness.

I find this information especially helpful because it offers a clear
conceptual scheme for the process whereby spirit becomes matter.
God in the unmanifested realm condenses into form to create physi-
cal/material reality.

> *Prakriti* is the creative power of God (bringing forth all phe-
> nomena), the aspect of Spirit as creative Mother Nature—Pure
> Nature or Holy Ghost. As such, it is imbued with the seed of
> twenty-four attributes, the workings of which give birth to all
> manifestation. From *Prakriti* evolve *chitta* (intelligent conscious-
> ness, the power of feeling—the basic mental consciousness—
> Sankhya's *Mahatattva*), inherent in which are *ahamkara* (ego);
> *buddhi* (discriminative intelligence); and *manas* (sense mind). From
> *chitta*, polarized by *manas* and *buddhi*, arise five causal creative
> principles *(panchatattvas)* that are the quintessence and root causes
> of the remaining twenty evolutes of creation. These causal prin-
> ciples are acted upon by the three *gunas*, or qualities, of Nature
> *(sattva, rajas,* and *tamas)* and become manifested as the *jnanendriyas*
> (five instruments of sense perception); the *karmendriyas* (five in-
> struments of action); the *mahabhutas* (or *mahatattvas:* earth, water,
> fire, air, and ether—the five subtle vibratory "elements" or individu-
> alized forces [motions] of the Cosmic Creative Vibration); the five
> *pranas* (five instruments of life force empowering circulation, crys-
> tallization, assimilation, metabolism, and elimination). The *pranas*,
> together with the five subtle vibratory elements, inform all matter in
> solid, liquid, fiery, gaseous, and etheric form.[28]

Although the specific Sanskrit terms may be complicated, the
important point to remember is that we are the manifestation of
God's thought. The entire universe is a result of Divine consciousness manifesting from finer realms of pure spirit to the denser world
of material reality. This esoteric truth, when united with the transfor-

Sankhya Philosphy

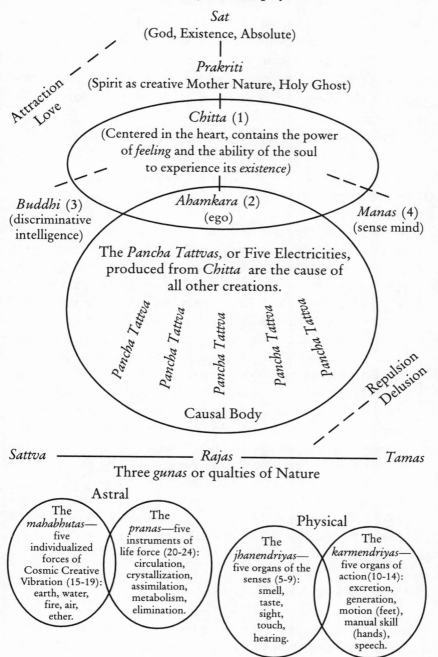

Sat
(God, Existence, Absolute)

Prakriti
(Spirit as creative Mother Nature, Holy Ghost)

Attraction
Love

Chitta (1)
(Centered in the heart, contains the power
of *feeling* and the ability of the soul
to experience its *existence*)

Buddhi (3)
(discriminative
intelligence)

Ahamkara (2)
(ego)

Manas (4)
(sense mind)

The *Pancha Tattvas*, or Five Electricities,
produced from *Chitta* are the cause of
all other creations.

Pancha Tattva

Pancha Tattva

Pancha Tattva

Pancha Tattva

Pancha Tattva

Repulsion
Delusion

Causal Body

Sattva —————— *Rajas* —————— *Tamas*
Three *gunas* or qualties of Nature

Astral

The *mahabhutas*—
five individualized
forces of
Cosmic Creative
Vibration (15-19):
earth, water,
fire, air,
ether.

The *pranas*—five
instruments of
life force (20-24):
circulation,
crystallization,
assimilation,
metabolism,
elimination.

Physical

The *jhanendriyas*—
five organs of the
senses (5-9):
smell,
taste,
sight,
touch,
hearing.

The *karmendriyas*—
five organs of
action (10-14):
excretion,
generation,
motion (feet),
manual skill
(hands),
speech.

mational power of spiritual practice and yoga meditation, provides the technology to change and improve our life condition. The process of yoga is about the transmutation of energy. Since all of creation is essentially energy, we can change our lives when we change our consciousness. The higher yoga techniques, such as *kriya yoga,* provide the technology to work on the subtle realms to improve our life circumstance.

The process of Self-realization thereby unfolds as the yogi is able to transmute consciousness back into its subtle beginnings. Yogananda's clarity and ability to articulate this sublime process continues to be very helpful here:

> By ascent of the consciousness through the subtle centers of life and spiritual awakening in the spine, the yogi learns the inner science of changing the consciousness of gross matter into the consciousness of its primordial principles. He resolves the five vibratory elements along with their manifestation of the five senses, five organs of action, and five life forces from grosser to finer principles; changing the consciousness of vibratory earth into the consciousness of vibratory water; the consciousness of water into that of vibratory fire; the consciousness of fire into that of vibratory air; the consciousness of air into that of vibratory ether; the consciousness of ether into that of mind (sense consciousness or *manas);* the consciousness of mind into that of discrimination *(buddhi);* the consciousness of discrimination into that of ego *(ahamkara);* the consciousness of ego into that of feeling *(chitta).* By thus dissolving the twenty-four principles successively into one another, the yogi then merges the consciousness of feeling into that of the primordial cosmic vibratory force *(Aum),* and the consciousness of *Aum* into Spirit. He thereby reaches the Ultimate Unity—the One from whom has sprung the many.[29]

Yogananda continues to explain:

> Self-realization consists in experiencing the different states of intuitive consciousness attained by meditation that lead to this

ultimate union. . . . The devotee who knows the art of yoga, experiencing the pure joy of meditation, does not further involve himself in new desire and new karma. And by yogic techniques the cosmic energy "cauterizes" the brain-cell grooves in which past tendencies are hidden. Yoga practice therefore not only prevents the formation of new karma-making desire, but also scientifically frees the devotee from impending karma (nearly ripe fruits of past actions).[30]

And finally:

Different individuals have different "fates." The sense-enslaved man is guided largely by his habits of the past; his free will is meager. He is permeated with desires (whether able or not to fulfill them). A spiritual man, on the other hand, has freed himself from all worldly desires springing from past-life seeds, and has thus redeemed from bondage his free will. The ordinary man eclipses his free will with dark shadows of the past. The spiritual man, ever watchful for freedom, safeguards it by meditation. When the will is free, it vibrates in harmony with the Infinite. Man's will is then God's will.[31]

The clinical hope offered here is that we are not "doomed" by our fate and that we do have the power to change the course of our lives, not only through our behavior, but also through esoteric practices that can access the deeper energy or consciousness that may reside at the very root of our difficulties. Hope is the greatest empowerment for energizing the spirit. Individuals give up when all hope is lost. A little ray of hope can ignite tremendous effort to strive for victory.

One great value in this yogic perspective is that it places the real battle within one's own consciousness and provides the tools to overcome great difficulties. We cannot change others nor the world; however, we can change ourselves. These principles and techniques provide the actual way for such success. I am suggesting that when we ignore the presence of these powerful, karmic, subtle forces, we limit the amount of healing that is possible. We blindly fight to overcome outer problems when the roots to the cure are hidden deep within us. Combining the ancient esoteric wisdom of yoga practice with the modern tools and skills of a conscious psychotherapist results in a powerful force for change and healing.

On a devotional note, Yogananda has said that we should look to God to help us in every aspect of our lives. We did not create the world and this reality. When life becomes truly difficult and we seem to be at the end of our rope, when we have run out of all hope and have no more answers or solutions to our problems, this is the time to turn to God in the silence of meditation and the depth of our hearts.

Talk to God and say, " I did not create this world. It is your dream, your delusion that I am caught in. I have done everything I can to solve this problem. I am helpless. I know that I have created this situation, but I did so out of ignorance. Free me from my darkness, free me from this ignorance, from this delusion. Awaken me to your Truth and Wisdom. Through your Grace, change me and my circumstance. You created this entire universe. You can certainly change this little situation in me."

Do not think that you have to live life alone. You cannot! Delusion is too strong, and you will never make it on your own. Turn to God for help and learn to develop a healthy dependency on God's inner Wisdom and Grace. The Bible says, "Ask and you shall receive." Just be sure you have put out one hundred percent effort on your part. God helps those who help themselves. Don't be too proud to ask and receive the help you deserve. Also remember, God works through others to help you. Do not expect to experience some miraculous manifestation or beatific vision, for God works in simple ways to help us.

There is a great story about a man who was caught in a flood and was sitting on the top of his house waiting for God to rescue him. The water was beginning to enter his house when the fire department came by and offered to evacuate him. He said, "Oh no, I trust that God will save me." The firemen left and the water continued to rise. Now the water was halfway up his house, and a rescue crew in a boat came by and offered to take him to dry land. The man replied to their offer," Oh, no, I do not need your help. I trust in the Lord and know that he will rescue me." Off they went, and finally the water had risen to the very top of the roof and the man was almost covered by the rising river. At this point a police helicopter came down and the rescue crew shouted, "Grab the rope, and we will pull you to safety." The man once again responded, "Oh no, thank you, but I trust in God and know that through His grace I will be saved." In a few minutes the water had risen over his head, and he drowned. The man died, and when he went to Heaven, the first thing he said when he got there was, "How could you do this to me? All my life I trusted in you and counted on you to save me. I had perfect faith, and you let me drown in that lousy flood. Why didn't you save me?" God replied, "What do you mean? I did everything I could to save you. First I sent the fire department with their truck, then I sent the rescue crew with a boat, and finally I tried to lift you off your roof with a helicopter, but you kept refusing all the help I sent!"

Action Without Action

Thy human right is for activity only, never for the resultant fruit of actions. Do not consider thyself the creator of the fruits of thy activities; neither allow thyself attachment to inactivity.
Chapter 2, Verse 47

Once again Krishna is imparting great wisdom to Arjuna that is beyond any concept of Western psychology. Krishna is saying that in order to obtain true joy and fulfillment and to spiritualize one's life, the focus should be on serving God and not on the reward, or fruit, of one's actions. In Western approaches, successful accomplishments are often viewed as helpful stepping stones to enhanced self-esteem. Many psychological systems are aimed at enhancing ego (ψ) functions. The methodology aims to identify personal desires and goals for worldly success. All too often we see patients whose sense of self is overdetermined by the opinion of others regarding their actions and performance. These individuals, with a low sense of self-worth, a poor sense of self-direction, and a high level of uncertainty and unhappiness, are misdirected in their focus. They have not discovered the joy and elevated sense of self that results when they forget about the results from their personal accomplishments and focus upon serving God in whatever manner they can.

In fact, we serve God by serving humanity. Many years ago I participated in a workshop at Esalen in Big Sur, California. During the first meeting, the leaders asked for volunteers to help in the kitchen. Initially, I thought, "I am paying a lot of money for this weekend and I am tired. I am not going to volunteer. I want to be taken care of." I watched a few people offer to help, even those who had established Esalen, and I felt a little ashamed of my attitude. I reluctantly volunteered to help. Later that night I spent one half-hour busing tables in the dining room. That brief period of time was the highlight of my retreat. I felt more joy and a greater sense of inner peace than at any other time during the entire workshop. The time I spent in the mineral baths soaking and taking in the magnificent view of the Pacific Ocean was nothing compared to the few minutes I spent picking up dirty dishes! I learned a great lesson during that weekend.

Many individuals are very lost in this life. They have no sense of direction and no sense of purpose. They have no intuitive connection to their soul purpose and how they can serve God in this lifetime. No matter what they do, successful or not, they feel as though something is missing. The wisdom of the *Gita* suggests that we should not look to the results of what we do, but rather, and more important, attempt to intuitively align ourselves with the Divine will through deep meditation.

The soul is not concerned with the reward, but rather the attunement to the will of God. When the motive is to serve and we allow the Divine will to flow through our consciousness, then great joy results, with no additional karma being developed. Krishna warns here also that nonaction is not an acceptable escape to this dilemma. We are here to learn and to grow. We must act. No action is action. We accomplish nothing when we refuse to act. The highest action, however, is when the action is in the service of God.

A major limitation of Western psychology is that it is not based upon an ancient system of wisdom. Western psychotherapy was designed solely for the remediation of disease states. The entire diagnostic nomenclature system of DSM-IV[32] is disease-based and developed by the medical community. Insurance companies do not want to fund prevention and the improvement in quality of life. The United States actually does not have a "Health Care System," but rather a "Disease Care System."

Psychotherapy, when freed from this focus on pathology, can offer much more to patients than merely attending to temporary disease states. A few key spiritual principles, put into action, can do much to strengthen one's state of mind and lift one's spirits, and an enlightened psychotherapist can help to guide and educate individuals by sharing ancient secrets for successful living.

Developing an Inner Life

He whose consciousness is not shaken by anxiety under afflictions
nor by attachment to happiness under favorable circumstances;
he who is free from worldly loves, fears,
and angers—he is called a muni of steady discrimination.
Chapter 2, Verse 56

This section provides yet another profound paradigm shift for the Western mind. Traditional psychological Western thought looks to the world and the satisfaction of one's desires as the measure of happiness and success; therefore, much of Western psychology is directed at helping individuals to be more successful in their worldly strivings. However, this ancient perspective again suggests that a greater level of wisdom is achieved when one rises above the outer circumstances of one's life and anchors the experience of Self within the consciousness of the soul.

As previously discussed, happiness, anger, and fear are personal reactions that result when worldly desires are fulfilled or frustrated. Many of the complaints that are commonly heard in professional offices stem from anger, anxiety, and hurt—over unfilled desires for love, nurturance, human understanding, and personal success. Besides, clinical observation has revealed that many disease processes are closely related to emotional factors, and the physical body becomes the symbolic screen on which anxieties, anger, and fear are projected. The ancient yogic verse quoted above suggests that wisdom, the power of discrimination, results when the consciousness is fixed on the identity of the soul. The soul-level experience of Peace, Joy, and Bliss allow one to be relatively untouched by the ups and downs of worldly fulfillment, and a greater sense of personal emotional tranquillity results when the outer fulfillment of needs and desires becomes secondary to the inner reality, in which a steady flow of Peace and Love prevail. One's inner reality can remain untouched when the consciousness is withdrawn from the outer senses. This change of perspective offers a tremendous paradigm shift for many individuals and may be easily integrated into a cognitive approach to psychotherapy.

The Inner Light of Wisdom

When the yogi, like a tortoise withdrawing its limbs,
can fully retire his senses from the objects of perception,
his wisdom manifests steadiness.
Chapter 2, Verse 58

The esoteric wisdom of yoga practice is revealed in this section. When the yogi is able to fully withdraw the life force energy, through an advanced *pranayama* technique such as *kriya yoga*, then the consciousness becomes stabilized into the superconscious. Many students of yogic meditation can touch higher states of awareness, but it is very difficult to stabilize and sustain this state of consciousness, and our Western models do not provide even an ounce of help to guide us in the right direction. Western approaches take us only as far as emotions and the mind and do not provide the spiritually advanced technology that allows us to withdraw the life force energy and redirect this subtle current into the higher centers of the brain, which results in the emergence of a profound clarity and depth of wisdom.

Most of us find life to be very difficult and confusing. We are given many tests and sometimes just do not know which is the best way to turn. Without a deeper connection to our Self and the resulting clarity that comes from the power of discrimination, it is very difficult to choose wisely. Yoga practice and yogic meditation provide a suitable methodology to access the profound inner resources that can light the way during times of darkness.

The Royal Path of Peace

That person realizes peace who, relinquishing all desires,
exists without craving and is unidentified
with the mortal ego and its sense of "mine-ness."
Chapter 2, Verse 71

Krishna strikes to the heart of the issue in this verse. This concept of the "mortal ego" provides the distinction between Western psychology and Eastern yogic philosophy. Western thought, going as far back as "I think, therefore I am!" (Descartes), is based upon this individual sense of identity, as separate from God. A yogic position might be, "I don't think, therefore I am!" More specifically, when the yogi internalizes the consciousness and withdraws the life force energy away from the outer senses and into the spine, then the rational or sense mind, *manas*, is transcended and the intuitive mind is accessed. In this state, there is no experience of thinking. Knowing through direct intuitive perception results, but not from an act of volition. This type of intuitive wisdom results when consciousness is no longer identified with the ego (ι). A perfect state of receptivity is required, in which the awareness is actively present but totally without desire for any specific result.

The sense of "I" is the major point of distinction between these two positions. The "I" who wants fulfillment of various desires and perceives the world in a dualistic sense that divides things into "mine" and "yours," is subject to great swings between elation and despair. The yogi who has gone deeply into the Self and developed the one desire to express the will of God, however, finds a great, undisturbed peace.

While yogic practices provide the technology to access this state of consciousness, it is our individual will and intention that sets us on this spiritual path. As little as one simple thought, when highly charged with will power, can change our entire life and magnetize to us all the experiences that we need in order to psychologically mature and spiritually evolve.

The blending and integration of Western psychological approaches with a mature and enlightened view that comprehends the underlying source from which peace of mind springs can provide a more balanced system of psychological health care than is currently being offered across the country today. Deep meditation and communion with God is the best stress-reducing technique available. The state of peace that comes from deep meditation also carries a presence that emanates from the very soul and can heal both the physical and emotional body of many disorders.

Spiritualize Dependency

With heart absorbed in Me, and by My grace,
thou shalt overcome all impediments; but
if through egotism thou wilt not heed Me,
thou shalt meet destruction.
Chapter 18, Verse 58

The essential theme of the *Gita* continues in this verse: it is possible to reach the height of Divine consciousness through the sincere practice of yoga, or union with God. Many individuals who struggle with psychological problems have great conflict over their dependency needs. It comes as no surprise to find that an individual is afraid or just feels it is plain hopeless to rely upon another, whether that be a human or Divine source, when their early life experience has been with parents who lacked sensitivity, empathy, and responsiveness to their needs. Often one's early pattern with the mother and father becomes projected onto one's relationship with God. These individuals, who tend to be counterdependent, are adverse to inviting Spirit into their lives. They have learned to rely upon their own limited resources and unfortunately do not appropriately reach out to others for support and nurturance. If Mommy and Daddy would not help, then why should God? Their heightened sense of independence is actually a reaction formation against their underlying unmet dependency needs. When this psychological posture becomes the template for one's relationship with God, then much is lost. The great spiritual traditions all speak to turning to God and asking for help and seeking protection in that relationship. This section of the *Gita* speaks to this reality.

Life is very difficult, and when we try to solve our greatest challenges alone, we often do not succeed. The Alcoholics Anonymous program may be a good example of this truth. Alcoholics who conscientiously "work" the program have a far better success rate for staying sober than those who attempt to proceed outside the program. Turning to God and asking for help is a key element in the twelve-step approach. God's Grace is a very real and tangible experience for those who have thus been touched. Some unseen yet powerful force enters one's life, personal burdens are lifted, and life's circumstances dramatically change. Devotion, "with heart absorbed in Me," is the force that draws God's response. Devotion is loving attention turned towards the Divine. God's response, as the experience of Grace, holds infinite power to heal mind, body, and emotions.

Those who have not learned to invite this Divine force into their lives cut themselves off from a power so great, so loving, and so wise, and often remain helpless to find a way through their greatest trials and difficulties. The egotism (ι) referred to in this section is the personal belief that "I" do not need help. The Bible says, "Ask and you shall receive." This is an ancient principle. We do have free will, and it is up to us to ask. A healthy dependency upon the Divine can strengthen us and free us from burdens that are far too great for us to challenge alone.

In summary, the wisdom of the *Gita* provides the key to unlock the door that hides life's mysteries. The nature of spiritual reality is explained, along with the transcendental impact on those who learn to incorporate spiritual truths into their lives. The change in consciousness is dramatic when a choice is made to align one's will with God and consciously strive to be an instrument of the Divine will. This shift in consciousness opens new possibilities in the realms of healing. The spiritually awakened individual has access to subtle realms of energy that inherently contain profound healing potential, and that spiritual consciousness creates an energetic environment that can directly transform others. The next chapter discusses consciousness within the context of a psychotherapeutic relationship, specifically, with the therapist as an instrument of healing.

The Dynamics of
Subtle Energy

WHEN ONE READS THE LITERATURE in transpersonal psychology, one important aspect in the psychotherapeutic process receives less attention than it deserves—the effect of the consciousness of the therapist on the patient. Various authors have explored the impact of belief systems on doctor-patient relationships, but an amazing gap exists in addressing the impact of consciousness itself, i.e., the dynamics of subtle energy, between the therapist and the client. Traditional discussions on countertransference provide a good starting point in considering the impact of the therapist's feelings on the patient, but little is understood about the actual effect of consciousness in the process. I wonder if this area is overlooked because it is so esoteric in nature that it is almost impossible to document scientifically. Clearly, this subtle interaction merits thorough exploration and discussion.

Transmission and Attunement

It is well known among health care professionals that we model ways of being that affect our patients. As mentioned previously, patients are sensitive to and influenced by *who we are,* and this truth is much greater than any intellectual precept that we can share. Therefore, spiritual realities must be integrated into our lives and resonate in our consciousness to have any real, positive impact. It is very common to hear individuals speak about spiritual teachings from an intellectual perspective. However, the power of truth consists of direct experience, and spiritual knowledge is acquired through some form of transmission that is beyond and more subtle than words alone. Individuals can feel and intuitively perceive the truth of our Being and the extent of our realization, whereas words and ideas alone are insufficient to help people change. The upshot of this line of reasoning is that we can help others to transform only to the extent that we have evolved ourselves. It is typical in psychoanalytic circles to expect that the psychoanalyst undergo a full analysis before he or she may presume to successfully treat others. This basic model rests on firm ground. In the Sacred Healing model, the therapist is to embody what he or she hopes to teach. In fact, continuous spiritual practice is a necessity to activate the forces that facilitate profound healing and heightened clinical intuitive insight.

For those who practice yoga, it is common at some point to begin to experience a sense of a greater, expanded energy within one's consciousness. As one deepens yogic practice and gains an ability to become stabilized in the present, sustaining a connection to soul consciousness, a tangible result occurs in the form of a strengthened magnetic field or aura. This heightened subtle energy, which is often referred to as *shakti* or *prana* in the yogic system, can be transmitted to others and can have a profound and uplifting effect on them. Spiritual devotees flock to the presence of a Master because of this phenomenon. The stronger energetic field of the Master influences others, attuning them to the Master's higher level of consciousness. This transmission of *shakti* helps to awaken higher states of awareness in those who are able to receive this attunement, these subtle blessings.

Heightened states of awareness allow one to perceive this subtle energy flowing throughout all creation. Also, every individual thing can be perceived as a unique vibration. In other words, everything in nature has its own vibratory signature. As one becomes adept at sensing and perceiving this subtle energy, one develops the ability to discern essential truths. For example, intuition might be understood as an ability to attune to energy patterns and read the information that is encoded within them. Since thought is energy, as one learns to attune one's consciousness to subtle energy, then direct, intuitive knowing can emerge.

Marcel Vogel, a great scientist who worked for IBM, studied luminescence and crystals. He hypothesized that the ancient pyramids that had no hieroglyphics held information in their quartz crystal structures. He believed that the ancients knew how to place thought into quartz crystals and subsequently retrieve it through telepathic means. The great yogis are able to tune their thoughts and direct them like radio waves. Although we cannot visually perceive radio and TV waves, we know that they exist. The great yogis have developed their subtle abilities for perception and transmission within these spiritual/energetic realms. New discoveries in modern physics address consciousness and the underlying truth that everything is energy.[33] Under close scrutiny, all matter becomes apparent as wave patterns that interconnect in a space-time continuum. We live in a pulsating, conscious web of energy. The practice of yogic meditation opens our consciousness to this reality and reveals the illusory nature of our limited, physical/material reality.

The practice of yoga may open this direct experience of subtle energy and increase its flow in those who practice regularly. One aspect of "God" is Energy, and cosmic energy is very powerful. In fact, many stories have been passed down from fully enlightened masters, who warn their devotees that they must prepare themselves for the experience of cosmic consciousness, because the force of that energy is so great that they would be damaged by its power if they were to receive it prematurely, as in the example cited previously of running a million watts through a one-hundred-watt light bulb. This energy has inherent intelligence and can shift aspects of manifestation on every level of Being: physical, mental, emotional, and spiritual. From this point of view, then, the state of one's Being becomes a very tangible element in the healing process. It is not only what one knows from an intellectual standpoint that is essential, but also the inner state of realization that one has achieved, because one cannot impart a level of teaching that one has not already experienced and realized.

At the very least, the healer must have awakened his or her awareness of subtle energy flow, have some personal experience with it to be able to understand its effects and manifestations, and be able to guide and counsel the patient regarding this level of work. Also, new perceptions and expressions may unfold for the therapist in the process of working with the patient. A healer does not necessarily have to experience everything prior to the patient, but he or she must know how to access the state of communion with the Divine, where all is possible. This expanded state of awareness allows for the direct transmission of experience to another via the subtle current or *shakti* (universal power or energy). Many teachers in the West have read many books on consciousness and spiritual development and become well-versed in various texts, but a large percentage of them have no personal direct experience of what they teach. They can speak only to the mental faculties and have no capacity to actually transform others through their presence. On the other hand, the simple and great teachers in India may have read very little, but their wisdom is profound. The deep states of *samadhi* (balanced, unruffled bliss or perfect awareness of consciousness) open the inner knowing and the consciousness to the eternal wisdom of the cosmic library, in which all information and knowledge is stored. The true teacher has gone within and personally explored this cosmic terrain, and therefore is qualified to help others on their journey.

Siddhic Powers

It is well-known in yogic circles that intense yoga practice results in certain powers called *siddhis*. These *siddhis* can range from such impractical talents as manifesting fragrances in the air, being able to defy gravity while in meditation, and psychic powers to see into the future, to profound gifts to heal others of serious disease or transmit enlightenment experiences. These types of spiritually-induced powers make for very interesting stories and stretch the limits of one's mind beyond the confines of physical/material reality. However, the yogic teachings warn against the inherent dangers of these powers. Due to the powerful pull of delusion, the ego (ι) may mistakenly assume that the individual has obtained a high degree of spiritual advancement when these *siddhis* appear. Paramahansa Yogananda counsels that the best measure of one's spiritual development is the depth of one's relationship with God. These various *siddhic* powers are not the goal and should not be interpreted as such. All great wise teachers warn students against becoming attached to these abilities. These subtle powers exist and are the result of one's consciousness becoming more finely attuned with spiritual states. The powers belong to the subtle realms, in which thought and energy are potent, tangible realities.

The Effect of *Shakti*

Shakti, which is power, light, or life force energy that can be transmitted from one individual to another, is also relevant to our discussion. This exchange can be directed by the will. An individual who has accessed his or her cosmic Self becomes aware that the self is a multidimensional energy body that extends well beyond the physical body. In fact, some studies, have shown that consciousness is able to have a tangible effect across space.[34] Esoteric teachings state that the energetic effect of consciousness moves across time as well. Paramahansa Yogananda said that an individual on a spiritual path who meditates regularly will help seven generations in his or her family, both in the future and the past.

Thus, the direct perception of subtle energy fields opens a new and fascinating reality that can positively change a person's life. Until now, this notion of an energetic reality has been relatively untouched by Western psychology, since Western psychotherapeutic practices on the whole regard the therapist and patient as separate, isolated individuals who can be connected only through the process of empathy and compassion. Yet, many systems of healing, such as acupuncture, therapeutic touch, and Reiki, address this subtle yet powerful force. Surely it is sensible to integrate this realm of subtle energy work into the psychotherapeutic process.

Energy Fields and Currents

One's consciousness may be viewed as an expanded field of light which emanates out from the various energy centers, or *chakras,* that exist along the spine.[35]

Furthermore, the spiritual Self *is* light and energy. The higher Self or soul is housed within the physical body, and aspects of it emanate outward from the physical body. The potential energetic power in the Self is enormous; Paramahansa Yogananda has said that there is enough energy in each of us to light an entire city. This energetic force can be controlled and directed by the will, which is located in the *ajna* center, the *chakra* at the point between the eyebrows. Many meditative traditions direct the student to concentrate attention at the *ajna chakra,* since it is regarded as the center of spiritual consciousness. A well-known esoteric principle is: "The stronger the will, the stronger the flow of energy." Deep meditative practice involving concentration on the spiritual eye results in greater focus, increased will power, and eventually a realization of the Higher Self, with the resulting conscious experience of subtle energetic realities.

Clairvoyants can perceive visually or sense kinesthetically this expanded field of energy. Our field flows around us and can be used either for very positive and healing functions or for negative, life-draining purposes. For example, one can consciously choose to send out light to others that will have a positive impact upon them, or one can choose, consciously or unconsciously, to link into other people's energy and suck on their life force. Those individuals who have been damaged as children and feel very emotionally deprived may be unconsciously pulling life force away from others in an attempt to fill the emotional and spiritual void in their own existence.

Most people have seen the wave-like patterns that emanate off the pavement on a hot day. The subtle currents of flowing consciousness and life force are similar to those patterns. Some see these fields as colors, while others sense them as vibrational qualities. Just as each radio band has its own frequency, everything in nature has a unique vibrational quality that can be sensed by adepts. Imagine existing in a field of light in which each individual radiates at different frequencies and emanates different patterns, depending upon his or her level of spiritual development and current mental, physical, and emotional condition. All the information about each of us resides in this energetic pattern. There are no secrets, no boundaries, no lies in this realm of truth, because everything radiates its nature in this essential state of Being. Perception at this level of reality is no mystery once the intuitive channel is awakened. In this state, one perceives information because one's consciousness is impacted by the surrounding consciousness, i.e., energy fields.

This effect can be illustrated by the story about a student who asks his master, "Master, how is it that you always know what I am thinking?" The Master replies, "It is very simple. When we are together, I hear someone thinking, and I know it is you." In other words, there is no way to separate our essential energy from our grosser manifestation as thoughts, feelings, and physicality: they are inherently connected, and we are more or less like an open book to those whose consciousness is attuned to the finer, subtle realms.

So we exist in this interconnected field of light or energy, with each individual vibrating according to his or her own level of development, and every aspect of each of us encoded in this energy. Yogic philosophy, as we have shown, explains that consciousness condenses into form and describes how the elements of consciousness are expressed, from the more subtle realms to the grosser realms of

physical/material reality. (See page 125.) Modern physics has come to
the same conclusion, and the reader can refer to that literature for a
very interesting discussion about these same issues from a different
perspective.[36]

The Subtle Nervous System

How is our individual existence encoded in this energy? First of
all, in addition to the *chakra* centers, within our astral spine are subtle
energy currents that hold our past tendencies, or *samskaras*. These
impressions influence our behavior and are the blueprint for many of
our habits. Also, there are *nadis*, which compose the nervous system
in the astral body. To review, three main *nadis* exist in the astral spine,
the *ida*, *pingala*, and *sushumna*. The *ida* is the positive current,
corresponding to the in-breath, and the *pingala* is the negative current, corresponding to the out-breath. These two currents feed into
the *sushumna*, which is located in the center of the astral spine. This
subtle nervous system controls the gross nervous system of the
physical body. Even the waves of thought and emotion that cease-
lessly arise and subside in consciousness are described as subtle
energetic forces called *vrittis*. The practice of yoga is designed to
neutralize these waves of thought and emotion.

We are, in essence, Light and Energy, and our thoughts, emotions, and physical being are reflected in this energetic reality. As
such, physical disease is both a biochemical problem that manifests in
cells, tissues, and organs and an imbalance of energy at a spiritual
level. Imagine building a house. Once the house is built, it takes quite
a bit of work to move a wall if you do not like the design. However,
it is much easier to change that wall on the blueprint, which will result
in a new wall placement once the house is built. The amazing truth
about our reality is that there is no difference between our blueprint
and our physical manifestation. The astral body[37] carries a blueprint
for our perfect expression, and once that blueprint has been touched
or changed, then the gross expressions of our being are changed as

well. For example, touching the astral nervous system influences the physical nervous system. So, how can this happen?

The Process of Transformation

Most of us are familiar with studies in entrainment, in which two different heart cells can be placed in a laboratory dish, next to each other. In a few hours, the cells will be beating in exactly the same rhythm. A room full of grandfather clocks will come into synchronous rhythm in the same way. Leave them alone, and after a few hours the pendulums all swing together.

In the same way, the subtle power of *shakti* affects others, and it can be consciously or unconsciously used to help or hurt others. A higher use of this power occurs when an individual consciously holds a particular vibration that is spiritually uplifting. An energetic frequency that is attuned to spiritual vibrations of Love, Joy, and Bliss will uplift others. We are all interconnected. Each individual can consciously choose to be receptive and learn to attune his or her own consciousness to particular vibrations. A spiritual Master might advise, "See good, do good, be good. Recognize God in all things." This is also the essence of the verse from the *Bhagavad Gita* (Ch. 4, 24), "The one who sees Brahman in every action, becomes Brahman," and the point behind spiritual practices such as repetition of sacred names or formulae, or meditation on the Divine. When we constantly contemplate, or "tune ourselves" to higher values, we become more like that upon which we are focusing. Thus, we can learn to resonate at higher frequencies. Spiritual practice is designed to transform our consciousness to resonate at the highest frequency of God-consciousness. It is simply a process of osmosis, in which one state of Being resonates with another to fine-tune consciousness to specific frequencies.

Darshan, which literally means receiving the blessing of having the vision of or seeing the Divine, but which is also often used to refer to being in the presence of the Divine, is a common and powerful yogic practice. The devotee may make a long pilgrimage to the holy site or to sit at the feet of the master in order to be in that Divine Presence. However, the receiving of *darshan* can result from the simple act of opening one's consciousness to the blessings of the Divine in order to speed up one's spiritual progress. Transformation does result from the direct transmission of spiritual energy.

True spiritual development is a process of transformation. It is not a process of accumulated information that one obtains by reading books. One can be extremely knowledgeable and informed, yet definitely not enlightened, because a significant difference exists between information and wisdom. Transformation requires an actual evolutionary, developmental process, in which consciousness is systematically changed to resonate at higher frequencies. This process can affect physical structures. The body, at cellular levels, must become accustomed to sustaining increasingly higher vibratory rates, and the mind must be brought firmly under control in order to open to higher realities and to stabilize and develop the pure, discriminative intellect.

In summary, as one internalizes consciousness and awakens to the reality of the Higher Self, a new perception of subtle energy emerges. The Self is perceived as a being of light and energy. Deepening spiritual practices strengthen the will, and one learns to consciously allow energy to flow according to the Divine Will. One learns how to attune with others and resonate this life force energy at any level of manifestation: mind, body, emotion, and spirit. The conscious psychotherapist uses intuitive perception to understand the patient's underlying core or essential problems and consciously holds higher vibratory patterns on behalf of the patient that can tangibly affect the consciousness, i.e., subtle energy patterns, of the patient.

Silence also becomes an important medium in this process, because Spirit more easily manifests in an environment where the disrupting mental currents of confusion are stilled and life force energy is calmly directed within. A pristine inner life is created as one learns to embrace the silent sound of Spirit. The silence invites God's

Grace and creates an opportunity for the therapist to delicately engage the subtle energetic realms.

The process of sacred psychotherapy moves beyond the mind and emotions, as subtle energetic reality becomes a legitimate field of investigation and change. A conscious psychotherapist learns to perceive the Higher Self in others and holds that energetic pattern in his or her consciousness in order to magnetize the patient to their own true Self. The spiritually conscious psychotherapist becomes a mirror, not only reflecting the truth of the patient's inner nature but also a tangible, magnetic, energetic impression, which helps to entrain and reawaken the patient to his or her essential Self.

Sexuality and Suble Energy

The relationship between sexuality and spirituality has been misunderstood by many. I often hear individuals reporting that they believe sex leading to orgasm will inhibit their spiritual development. It is important to remember that the ancient spiritual techniques are designed to internalize consciousness away from the outer senses into the deeper channels of the spine and brain. The theory is that the ego's identification with sense reality is what keeps the individual trapped in the delusion of physical/material reality. As one transmutes the life force energy, through meditation and *pranayama* techniques, the consciousness becomes more refined to the subtle elements of the superconscious.

The physical act of sex, with the culmination of orgasm, requires the expenditure of tremendous energy and is obviously very stimulating to the nervous system. When the identification is with the physical body, the delusion of the ego's separate existence, then the sexual act is reduced only to the fulfillment of physical desire, i.e., lust, and the consciousness is drawn down to a more base level of existence.

It is possible, however, to raise the sexual act to a higher level and honor the spirit in this most sacred union. The two elements needed are love and an awareness of energy. First of all, love creates a state of consciousness in which a union is experienced. The other becomes honored and valued and is not regarded as a "thing" or only as an "object" for the fulfillment of desire. Love breeds selflessness. In the loving, physical union of two individuals it is possible to transcend one's limited identification of self, i.e., the ego, and experience the transcendental aspect of the soul. When both individuals can touch in this state, then love-making is raised to a higher, spiritual plane.

We must remember that spiritual practice is designed to transmute consciousness, so while the act of love-making may have opened the door to a shared spiritual state, the consciousness of each individual may not have become stabilized in the superconscious through this method. The second element is energy. The subtle life force, *prana,* is the element that serves to activate higher levels of awareness. The ability to move this subtle current up the physical and astral spine, through the various chakras, ultimately leads to expanded states of spiritual awareness. One becomes stabilized in higher spiritual states as one learns to consciously withdraw the life force energy into the astral spine and brain. It is possible to use the intense energy between the male and female elements of the psyche in order to ignite the flow of energy.

In this practice, one learns to attune to the subtle energetic currents that flow through consciousness and withdraw the energy into the deeper channels. Thus, the physical merging of a man and woman can be used to activate a powerful energetic force that becomes elevated to a finer, more subtle level. This is actually the practice of Tantra Yoga. Tantra is about uniting the masculine and feminine aspects of the self in the interior of one's consciousness. Having sex is not a practice in higher Tantra teachings. Just looking at a member of the opposite sex can ignite this powerful energy. Physical orgasm, from this perspective, only dissipates the energy this activates.

Ultimately, one's identification with the body and physical/ material reality affects the consciousness in everyday life. It is my experience that one can make love and not be drawn into body identification when the consciousness is stabilized in the higher centers. However, since the sexual act does occur at the physical level, it is only a question of time before the consciousness will be drawn back into body consciousness, if continued sexual activity occurs without the balancing of spiritual practice. Thus, it may seem like a balancing act, depending upon the consciousness of each individual. Each person needs to assess his/her strength in maintaining a higher spiritual consciousness that transcends body consciousness: keep having sex without any spiritual practice and your consciousness will probably come back into the body. There is nothing wrong with the body, but if you are attempting to stabilize into soul consciousness and ultimately achieve liberation from the cycle of birth and death, then body consciousness is counterproductive to the final goal.

One final thought on this matter is a word of reasonable advice. You cannot force yourself to be something you are not. The sexual force is very powerful in nature, and if we attempt to deny our sexual needs in the service of spiritual awakening, then we may become very frustrated, short-tempered, and even perverted. Spiritual practice helps one to evolve through an organic process that results in a natural shift in one's sexual needs and desires. Each individual must honestly assess his/her needs and honor the reality of their current level of existence.

Impact of Soul-Consciousness

As one can appreciate, the direct experience of the soul results in some major shifts of thought, perception, feeling, and behavior. The Divine experience quickly shows us that we are not isolated, separate individuals. Inherent in Divinity is a sense of unity and oneness, as the true Self feels neither separation anxiety nor abandonment. Since Spirit is omnipresent, we actually can feel the Divine energy within us and around us. I have seen grieving parents who have recently lost a child find great solace and comfort through inner, spiritual contact with their departed child. Although the psychological sense of loss and resulting grief cannot be quickly removed, since it is a normal part of our human experience to feel loss, a deep sense of comfort, strength, and meaning does emerge, however, from this spiritual awareness.

The direct knowing of our Divine nature helps provide an inner strength to sustain us during the trials and tribulations of everyday life. Contrary to what some mental health people might say, spiritual beliefs are not a denial of reality and a crutch or defense against life. In fact, spiritual awareness is probably a truer perception of reality than the delusion of the physical, material plane! Unfortunately, those who have not experienced this transcendental state have no way to comprehend or appreciate its power and beauty. For example, a psychiatrist and colleague recently shared with me his theory that Jesus was a manic-depressive, because he had delusions of grandeur and pressured speech!

A clearer perception of reality results when consciousness becomes stabilized in the soul, and a capacity emerges that allows one to perceive subtle energy emanating from all creation. Clairvoyant vision, i.e., clear sight, is simply the ability to perceive the finer elements of creation. It is just the same as being able to see the TV frequencies without the aid of a TV set. As such, intuitive knowing is simply the ability to perceive directly the subtle vibrations that are around us in our daily lives.

These changes in perception result in greater wisdom. A Divine order to life actually exists, and the mystery is to find that deep direction and develop the faith to follow it. The mind can be filled with great ideas, but Wisdom comes from the heart and soul. The soul, in the superconscious state, can access all answers and solutions to every problem. There is truly nothing new in creation. God has thought it all. The answers to life's mysteries and problems await us within. This fact is actually quite comforting for those who find life confusing and difficult, for it is indeed possible to know what to do and how to make the right choices.

Again, the great paradox that unfolds from knowledge of the reality of the soul is that as one learns to *do* less, one can *accomplish* more. Contrary to Western psychological thought, which suggests that we must be very busy and thinking and planning in order to accomplish and achieve success, the spiritually wise and awakened being knows that subtle spiritual forces control and direct all of creation. Thought, when conceived in a spiritually conscious state, emanates subtle energy that draws experiences into manifestation.

The challenge and opportunity for the awakened soul lies in drawing upon the deeper inner forces and realities and integrating that level of awareness into everyday life, with the result that each day becomes a mystery and an adventure. Furthermore, since the soul is accessed through a process of letting go, one learns to solve problems and live life with less effort. Strength evolves from the will, from the ability to discern, and from faith and confidence.

The soul remains untouched by earthly trials and tribulations. One's ability to retreat into the sanctuary of the soul allows for self-healing and self-nurturing, because the soul's very nature is love, peace, and joy—all very healing qualities.

Nevertheless, the soul enters into various situations for the spiritual process of God-realization. Our problems are not created by a hateful and vengeful God! God is Love. Rather, the effects of our past actions are like ripples on a clear lake that eventually find the shores of our current circumstances, and each action we make sets out patterns of energy that create "good" or "bad" results. Karma is simply action and reaction, the results of our past actions that are now being experienced, for our personal desires dictate our actions, creating karma. The only relief is to dedicate all our actions to God, for only actions performed for God are without karma. Only when we have surrendered our will into the Divine will are we freed from karma-making consciousness.

Thus, awareness of the truth of the soul and the laws of karma allows us to be less reactive and less emotional over the ups and downs of everyday life. Unfortunately, each time we react emotionally to an event, we create more karma and additional reactions that must in turn be experienced through time as they naturally run their course. Think about the times you became upset when someone you love did a certain thing you did not like. Typically, one reaction on our part sets off the other person in a particular reaction, and then it takes some time to work through the process. As you learn more about yourself, you may be able to predict your reactions and how long it takes you to complete them, but it is not enough just to stop there. The individual centered in the soul gains a sense of balance, peace, and serenity that allows him or her to be involved in life and yet be less affected by it. The truth of the soul expresses a loving, stable quality that results in a balanced and gentle state of detachment.

I have seen individuals gain hope and renewed strength from a single moment of direct soul contact. The impact of a moment of Divine communion can be more powerful and more healing than months of psychotherapy. Yet, when spiritual consciousness is combined with psychotherapy, then the healing environment may be optimized, as the powerful realms of spiritual awareness can be accessed to consciously support the deepest healing of the mind, emotions, and body. The next chapter shares some stories of remarkable healing in this vein.

The Grace of Healing

T HIS CHAPTER PROVIDES SOME EXAMPLES that illustrate the points made in the discussion of healing, subtle energy, and Divine intervention, and indicate the range in applications of Sacred Psychotherapy. The following are all people and experiences that I know personally or have seen professionally. I like these stories because they stretch the limits of the mind. Some are anecdotal, and others have been documented by medical doctors and laboratory reports, but all these people have been helped in ways that traditional Western medicine and psychotherapy cannot provide. These experiences always inspire me to deepen my relationship with God, because I believe it is that great Source who is doing the healing, and all great and wondrous outcomes must be attributed to the Divine. Though greatly motivated to help people, I have found that I am much better at helping others when I let God do the work through me.

Autism: A Disease of the Soul?

Mary asked me if I would see her seven-year-old daughter, Jenny, disclosing that Jenny was mentally retarded. I did not know what I could do to help her but agreed to see her nonetheless. A few days later, Mary and Jenny arrived at my office. After taking one look at Jenny, I instantly knew that she was autistic, for I had never seen any child with so many classic autistic behaviors. I had worked with many preschool children at the Thalians Family and Child Study Center at Cedar's Sinai Hospital who had been diagnosed as Atypical Ego Development because they displayed many autistic-like features. Jenny was out of a textbook. She did not make any eye contact; in fact, her eyes were crossed. She looked at her fingers as she moved them up in front of her eyes. She had no language and was unable to make any purposeful action. I spoke with Mary for twenty minutes and discovered that she knew that her daughter was not retarded but autistic. She had not wanted to tell me, for fear that I would not see her. At that moment, I did not know what I could do with this child in the twenty minutes that were left for the appointment. I thought that perhaps if I had four years, three times a week, I *might* be able to help her. Mary was only temporarily staying at a local meditation retreat, and she would not be around for three years.

I wondered what Jenny would do with some creative play. Would she relate at all to the outside world? I took her into my sand tray area to observe what she would do with all the little miniature figures. She stood silently by the sand tray, lowered her head, and began to eat the sand! I felt lost, thinking that I could do nothing to help this child in the few minutes that we had remaining. Partly out of desperation and partly out of wonderment, I placed my hand on her back, across from her heart chakra, and prayed. A most amazing thing happened. I found myself being drawn into a vortex of energy that took me up and away, into what felt like a far and distant realm that seemed to be some region in the astral plane. Once I arrived, I felt myself in contact with this child's soul. We began to converse in a telepathic manner:

"What are you doing out here when your body is walking around down on earth without anyone in it?"

She emphatically stated, "I'm not going into that body. Somebody made a mistake! I don't want to be down there!"

I quickly found myself saying, "There is a real disaster going on down there. You have to go into that body. Besides, it's not as bad as you think. (I was very optimistic in those years!) There are people who will help you to talk and learn things."

At this point in our conversation, I found myself grabbing her energetically and pulling her down into her body. We came in through the top of her head and, once in, her crown chakra closed, so she could not get out. I opened my eyes and found myself looking right at her, as she was now making clear and steady eye contact with me. Her eyes were no longer crossed. I asked her mother, Mary, if Jenny looked different. Mary thought she did. I asked Mary to come back in a week and report on any changes. In a week's time, Mary told me that her Jenny had begun to use words, was sleeping through the night, and was more relaxed and directed in her play. She also made eye contact. Mary left for another country after a few days, and I never found out what happened to little Jenny. However, it was my impression that she was now ready to learn.

Sometimes, more disturbed forms of psychopathology provide clearer examples. In the case of this little girl, the question remains, what was the source of her problem? Was it genetic, biological, social, psychodynamic, or spiritual? Stanislav Grof said that some believe autism to be a disease of the soul. If so, then perhaps that brief but profound experience I shared with Jenny was a healing directed at the soul. This idea gives rise to a logical wonderment as to how many mental and emotional problems also might be related to disorders of the soul.

The Power of Group Consciousness

Many years ago I conducted a weekend retreat with the focus on healing. I suggested that the group could try an experiment by focusing our attention on one individual and visualizing that person as being surrounded by golden light. One of the participants was a psychiatrist in residency at Napa State Hospital. The psychiatrist volunteered that she had a young boy patient who was about eight years old. We selected him as the recipient of our prayers and spent five minutes in this process. Two months later, I called this psychiatrist to find out what had happened. She had forgotten about the healing ritual and seemed surprised as she informed me that the boy had in fact changed since she returned. His behavior had improved, but most interesting of all, a foul odor that had been emanating from him prior to our group healing had vanished completely, and it was obviously easier for others to approach this child in the absence of the repulsive odor.

On an entirely separate occasion and with totally different people, I taught an extended class on healing. This group consisted of a variety of professional people, including two nurses and one pediatric cardiologist. One of the attendees, Sally, had a heart problem that had existed for several years, a heart murmur that could easily be detected by the trained medical ear. One evening we spent some time, under the direction of the cardiologist, listening to her heart with the aid of a stethoscope. The group spent one-half hour in focused energy healing on behalf of Sally. We simply placed her in the middle of a circle and placed our hands above her physical body. Each member allowed energy to flow through their hands and into her body. At the end of the time, there was no longer a detectable heart murmur.

Eminent Psychosis

Kathy called me because her *guru*, Swami Muktananda, had told her she needed to see a psychologist. She had obtained my name from a friend of hers. Coming into the session, she began to tell her story of marital disaster and personal pain. Her speech was very pressured, her thinking was paranoid and tangential, her hold on reality was tenuous, and her judgment was very poor. She was about to leave my office and initiate an affair with her next door neighbor. She had no insight into her problem and was unable to develop any observing ego (ψ) with which she might understand her situation. After twenty-five minutes I realized that my verbal attempts, listening, and interpretation were not useful, and that she would need medication and/or hospitalization if nothing were to change. I asked her if she was willing to do some energy work. Given her background in yoga, she was very comfortable with this idea. I spent fifteen minutes doing subtle energy work with her in total silence. At the end of the short time, she sat up and said, "I am not afraid!" Her fear and paranoid ideation had stopped. Her mood had shifted, and she was more relaxed; her thinking was intact, and her judgment was suddenly much better. She decided that it would be a bad idea to sleep with her neighbor and that she should go home and talk to her husband. Thereafter, she returned for a few visits in which she discussed her marital problems.

This intervention did not magically solve her problems, but it did keep her out of the hospital and restore some basic ego (ψ) functions, so she could continue the work in outpatient psychotherapy.

This type of intervention takes on even greater meaning in the light of current managed-care pressures to keep people out of the hospital. This fifteen-minute procedure was extremely cost effective!

The Power of *Shakti*

Jacquelyn had been mildly depressed all her life. She was in her early thirties and had never been married. She had just ended a very painful and psychologically damaging relationship with an individual with a borderline personality disorder. She had a poor relationship with her father and low self-esteem. She liked her work and was very well-respected by her customers. Jacquelyn had been in treatment for nine months, her ability to set boundaries had improved significantly, and her self-esteem was rising. She decided she wanted to explore meditation, and I was offering a short-term class on meditation and healing. During the third session of a six-week class, I suggested we demonstrate the power of the energy that is accessed during meditation. Jacquelyn was lying face up on a table, and five individuals were standing around her. I instructed each individual to allow energy to flow through them while directing loving thoughts and intentions to Jacquelyn. We chanted *Om* as a way to intensify the energy. This procedure lasted for approximately ten minutes. At the end of the "treatment," Jacquelyn sat up and, to her surprise, did not feel depressed. She informed us that "something" had lifted during the energy work and that she had simply felt her depression go away. She reported feeling lighter and a sense of joy.

Thereafter, I continued to see Jacquelyn once a week in individual treatment for several more months. Her depression never returned. She is now married and reports that she is able to cope with her life, and that if she feels a little down, she can deal with it and work things out.

Kidney Failure

John had an extraordinary life story, in that he had received three organ transplants, two hearts and one kidney. His physician referred him to me because of "stress." After his first heart failure, he received a heart transplant, but his body had rejected that organ. He was on his second transplant when he came to me. His kidney came from the same donor as his current heart. He was seen every six months at Stanford University Hospital to guard against organ rejection. I saw John on a weekly basis, and we did normal psychotherapy regarding his feelings about relationships, work, his sense of failure because he was not more financially successful, and his feelings about having three organ transplants. Most of the therapy was directed at his becoming more authentic in life, but we did spend a few sessions on meditation, self-healing, and some subtle energy work.

John showed no signs of rejecting his heart, but at one point his kidney began to lose function. Kidney function is measured by the excretion of a nitrogen compound, creatinine, and a rising level indicates loss of kidney function. It is very unusual for the creatinine level to fall, once it has risen. At this point, John was showing physical signs of kidney rejection, and the lab reports from Stanford showed an increase in his creatinine levels. In one particular session, we spent approximately fifteen minutes or less doing some subtle energy work on his kidney. John was familiar with this type of work, as we had used this method for his general state of well-being many times before. He also practiced some self-healing techniques that he learned in treatment and which he reinforced at home by listening to an audio tape, *Healing in the Light.*[38] At the end of the session, he reported feeling better, and the next Stanford lab report showed that his kidney had begun functioning better and that the creatinine level had declined. I asked several physicians about this change, and they all confirmed that it is very unusual for the level to decline once it has been elevated. His kidney and heart continue to function. Cost effective treatment? Care to estimate the cost of a kidney transplant?

Regeneration

A good friend of mine, Mitchell May, has a well-documented story that in my experience is one of the most amazing experiences of healing that has ever been reported. Mitchell was injured in an auto accident in Tennessee. He was the passenger in a VW bus and the accident impelled a shard of sheet metal through the tibia of his right leg. The lower portion of his leg was totally destroyed, and his foot and ankle had to be kept connected to his leg with the aid of a metal brace. Mitchell was in the local hospital, and they could not provide much treatment for him. He was in excruciating pain. His father was on the teaching staff at UCLA, so Mitchell was transported by air in a full body cast to UCLA Medical Center. The clinical staff at the hospital felt that they needed to amputate Mitchell's leg, because he was developing gangrene, he was losing kidney functions due to massive doses of antibiotics, and the morphine was not effectively controlling his pain. Furthermore, he was addicted to the morphine by this point.

Mitchell described pain so terrible at one point that it sent him out of his body. In this transcendent state, he saw the presence of two Beings, who spoke to him: "You have a choice to return to your physical body or leave. If you choose to return, the course of recovery will not be easy, but you will learn a great deal from it. The choice is yours." Mitchell shares that these Beings were very loving and totally without judgment. He did confide, however, that he could feel the preference that these Beings held. He obviously decided to return to his body.

Bernauer Newton, Ph.D., a noted psychologist associated with the California School of Professional Psychology in Los Angeles, was an expert in hypnosis. Mitchell's family heard about Dr. Newton and asked him if he could help Mitchell. He replied that Mitchell's problem was beyond his ability and suggested that they call Dr. Thelma Moss, a psychologist at UCLA who was studying parapsychology. (Please note the high level of ethical standards here, as Dr. Newton forthrightly made a referral when he recognized that he did not have the proper training in this matter.) As chance would have it, Dr. Moss was engaged in investigating the healing ability of Jack Gray. She asked Jack if he could help Mitchell, and he replied, "Of course I can, but I am tired of doing this type of thing and nobody believing me. I will help Mitchell if you document it."

Thus began a six-year healing process. The medical consensus was that his leg must be amputated in order to save his life. Mitchell would not sign the release for surgery, so the medical staff began the legal process to declare him legally insane so they could obtain a court order to amputate. With this drama in the background, Jack began his work with Mitchell.

Mitchell reported that Jack would spend all night with him, talking and sometimes yelling at him, in an attempt to break through his ways of thinking. Jack worked with Mitchell for six years. During the first year, he helped him regenerate bone, nerves, muscles, and skin. At the beginning of their work, he helped Mitchell control his pain and actually was able to end Mitchell's addiction to morphine within a few hours. Mitchell described the events of that evening. "Jack was creating some potion using water. He was chanting and passing his hands over this water. The energy became so thick in the room that a nurse could not push the door open to get inside. Jack gave me this stuff to drink, and the pain went away and so did my addiction to morphine. I had no withdrawal effects." Mitchell's story goes on and on, with incredible accounts of instantaneous changes in his physical condition. Early in the treatment, Jack did energy work over his leg, and the following day mushroom-like things began to appear as the skin began to form.

Today, Mitchell is walking around and helping others. Needless to say, he learned a great deal about healing through his own process of recovery. He has a gift in the subtle realms that is truly unique. He now is President of the Synergy Company, which markets a super-food, Pure Synergy, a nutritional supplement that he developed as part of his own healing process.[39] Mitchell's story is well-documented and has been on television. The physicians now admit that his case was a medical miracle, because they were unable to heal him. In fact, they were going to cut his leg off! It took many years before this story became available to the general public, but eventually Mitchell's story was highlighted in the December, 1996 issue of the *Yoga Journal*. Western medical thought has not provided a way to explain this kind of healing, nor has it investigated this type of phenomenon in order to include these cases in its healing traditions.

Post-Surgical Recovery

Subtle energy work has proven to be very effective for those who have just had surgery. A surgical operation is a traumatic experience to the physical body: it places a strain on the entire system, and the subtle fields of energy are also disturbed by this procedure. The trauma is most easily rebalanced immediately after surgery. A number of years ago a friend of mine was in the hospital because of a hysterectomy. When I went to visit her shortly after the surgery, I entered the room and found her to be very pale and in a great deal of pain. She was a *yogini* (yoga disciple) and very sensitive to subtle energy work. I began to open myself and allow the energy to flow through me as I prayed for her healing and well-being. She began to moan from the pain, as it seemed that something was being pulled out of her on a subtle level. In spite of her intense pain, she was adamant that I continue. After about five minutes, the energy completed itself and she look markedly different. The color had returned to her face, and she was smiling. The pain was gone, and she appeared more relaxed. At that point, her surgeon came into the room, took one look at her, and announced, "Well, you certainly appear to be getting better."

I have made a point of being in the hospital hours after surgery, helping friends and family members, and I had a similar experience with my father when he had open-heart surgery, receiving a five-artery bypass at the age of seventy-six. I spent a few hours over three days working with him. His physician then commented to him, "You know, you have made a very fast recovery for a man in your age group." He was discharged without any complications.

The Purification of Shame

Mary was severely abused both physically and emotionally as a child. She was a victim of incest, physically tortured, stabbed, starved, and constantly humiliated. As is often the case with children who have been so severely abused, she developed a multiple personality disorder as a way to protect and preserve her essential Self. Her core self became split off and had no contact with those "sick, disgusting people." In the course of treatment, her underlying sense of shame became the focus of attention. The split-off, "little girl" part of herself believed that she must be terrible, because she was always told that by her parents. She lived in terror and was fixated at that level.

With the use of hypnosis, the little girl aspect would emerge and actually believe that her parents were still alive and that she was a nine-year-old child. She could not comprehend being anything other than a soiled, castaway, worthless child. Her shame and sense of feeling dirty had permeated her cellular structure. I asked this little girl to close her eyes and imagine a great golden light above her. She did this with great ease. I suggested that this light had a wonderful healing power and that the light could and would come down through the top of her head and enter every aspect of her being. I further suggested that a great loving presence was in this light. At this point she began to feel a presence and visualized a female aspect of God that she called Divine Mother. She became very quiet and glowed with a radiance and beauty. She felt the love of the Divine Mother flow through her as she received solace and comfort. She informed me that she heard Divine Mother say that her parents were not her real parents, that She was her Real Mother, and that her earthly parents had only had her on loan and had done a very terrible job of raising her. She continued to explain how the Divine Mother expressed Her love for her. Prior to this session, this child had the physical hallucination that she was filthy and could not wash off the dirt. After the experience with the Divine Mother, she reported feeling clean and pure. This inner experience was far more powerful than any words or support that I could ever offer her, though my love and support did help her to go within and feel this presence. A good way to distinguish spiritual experiences from creations of the mind is by the result: transformation occurs from genuine spiritual experiences. If a person is changed, then something more than imagination has transpired.

An entire book could be written on the thousands of stories that exist concerning miraculous healing. I hope these few are sufficient to open your mind to greater possibilities.

Various schools of psychological theory address the individual only, as if it were a little drop of water, and fail to recognize that the relationship of that little drop to the ocean is also an important aspect of personal development and integration. Perhaps the limited nature of traditional approaches stems from the historically biological and pathological notions of disease. Psychotherapy, as a profession, has typically taken a medical perspective with the aim to cure disease. The possibility of addressing higher potentials and facilitating more creative aspects of the self has not been paramount. The limitation of Western rational empiricism has resulted in a total neglect and discounting of valuable data that address the hidden dimensions of consciousness that can facilitate the healing process.

Virtually no discussion exists concerning ways to access the spiritual properties of the Self which can help in the healing process; any discussion of these occurrences typically exists outside of the traditional healing professions. I believe that it is time to include these levels of reality into traditional health care. Good research needs to be done as a way to document and legitimize this healing potential. It works. We might as well make full use of spiritual methods, save the health care system a lot of money, and help to awaken civilization in the process.

The next chapter suggests some specific ways to integrate spirituality into clinical protocols.

Sacred Healing
in Psychotherapy

THIS CHAPTER CONTAINS some good, sound, practical suggestions regarding the integration of spiritual techniques and
concepts into the psychotherapy process. This information
can be useful for either professional therapists or non-professionals
interested in this topic. If you are in therapy, it might be helpful to
read the following material from the point of view of how your
therapist is working with you. If you are searching for a therapist, this
information will help you interview your potential therapist and find
the one who can offer you what you want.

First and most important, the therapist must regard spiritual
material—i.e., beliefs, ideas, experiences, visions, premonitions,
etc.—as real and legitimate areas for discussion. Once you embrace a
spiritual reality, an individual's subtle experience of God becomes as
important to discuss as his or her feelings about early childhood.

Initial Interview

During the first interview, as you are getting to know the individual, ask about his or her spiritual beliefs and experiences. It is

important to differentiate between spiritual and religious beliefs. Many individuals will quickly inform you they are not religious, frequently because of early negative experiences with their church. However, upon further inquiry, you will discover that they do have strong personal feelings about some force that guides and directs the universe. Attempt to discover how the individual conceives of this cosmic force. Is it loving or vengeful? Does it provide any order to life? Has this person ever felt any direct intervention or help from this cosmic force? When something strikes you as important, feel free to explore that area. It is also very useful to find out what actual, direct experience the individual has had with Spirit. As you probably know, having an internal relationship with God is very sustaining. An active and substantial spiritual inner life is the greatest source of strength in times of crisis.

It is also typical to find individuals who have very little direct experience of spiritual reality, but who are curious, interested, and open to new possibilities. Thus, the therapeutic relationship may provide a spiritual beginning for many individuals. The material presented in previous chapters regarding the therapist's level of personal spiritual experience becomes most relevant in this situation, as authentic spiritual help does not come from an intellectual discussion. If you have the ability to actually transmit subtle energy and embody spiritual consciousness, then you can help an individual have a direct experience of Spirit.

Once a person has been touched in this subtle way, he or she is never the same. You may be able to open a door and start someone on an inner quest that will lead to profound learning and help him or her to find a deeper source for both internal strength and coping resources. In fact, the greatest gift you can provide is to open, inspire, and empower an individual to follow the path that speaks to their heart. The true gift of healing is not simply to transmit something to another that relieves his or her suffering, although the person may be grateful when that occurs, but rather to help someone access the Spirit within themselves. Once they have touched that sacred place within, they are much more likely to do the necessary work that cultivates and deepens their connection with God. This lofty goal may take weeks, months, and sometimes years to reach. In the meantime, important clinical issues need to be addressed. The following discussion addresses a variety of possible situations from the perspective of Sacred Psychotherapy.

Overcoming Victim Consciousness

It is common for a new patient to complain about his or her life circumstances, especially if the person has been abused as a child. Let's be honest. Some individuals do have horrible life experiences where almost everything goes wrong. Unfortunately, the mental state of feeling like a victim generally does nothing to improve one's lot in life. If anything, it seems to draw additional negative experiences to the individual. An esoteric principle regarding magnetism suggests, "Like attracts Like." In essence, you draw to yourself similar circumstances, based upon your level of consciousness. However, this is not to say that one can be assured of a "wonderful" life by raising one's consciousness. We all get tested regarding our particular issues of development, and we all have different roles to play in life. Some of the highest spiritual Beings who have touched Earth, such as Jesus, did not have an easy life. The essential element here is to shift one's identification away from solely the physical/material reality, to include a spiritual perspective as well. The following dialogue suggests one way to help accomplish this shift:

Patient: I don't know why all these horrible things are happening to me! What did I ever do to deserve this? Am I cursed or what? This is not fair. I just don't know what to do. Sometimes I just want to give up!

Therapist: It sounds like you feel very helpless, very confused, and pretty lost. You also sound pretty hopeless about the future. Why do you think things happen in life? How do you explain all these difficult problems you are having?

Patient: I don't know; maybe I just have bad luck. Maybe I am a bad seed, some kind of rotten person; my dad always told me I was a loser and wouldn't amount to anything.

Therapist: You don't seem so rotten to me. Have you ever had any exposure to esoteric teachings, spiritual philosophy?

Patient: Not much, but I have heard of that stuff.

Therapist: Do you believe in any Greater Power or Intelligent Force that provides some order or structure to life?

Patient: Sure, there must be something. I don't know about a person running the universe, but something must be going on.

Therapist: What do you think our purpose is, our reason for being alive?

Patient: Have kids, help others, I'm not sure.

Therapist: Most of the great spiritual teachings that have been handed down over the years suggest that we are here to learn about Love. We are here to learn to be more loving and caring human beings and to learn about God's Love.

Patient: Well, God sure has a weird way of teaching. How can I learn about love when all I get is hate and misery? It looks like God must hate me!

Therapist: You know that section of the Bible that says, "What ye sow, so shall ye reap?" What do you think that means?

Patient: What goes around comes around?

Therapist: That's right. That is karma. The ancient teachings and my personal experience of God is that he or she is a very loving God. God does not want to punish us. God gave us free choice, and it is our free choice that has gotten us into these terrible messes here on Earth. The blessings and the problems that we have now are the result of actions that have happened somewhere in the past, this life or even further back in previous lives.

God wants to help us resolve our suffering and will help if we ask. God's Grace is very real, but we need to ask for the help. While you may feel really helpless because you cannot stop what is happening to you, you can begin to change and transmute the energy that has caused these terrible circumstances. Spiritual practice actually offers a way to deal with your past karma and free yourself from its effect.

This type of discussion can shift an individual's sense of despair and helplessness when hope and a light at the end of the tunnel are offered. Once a patient has opened their mind to some alternative possibilities, you can begin to teach them the spiritual technology of neutralizing negative karma and drawing upon God's Grace. This type of discussion also helps to bring up the issue of personal responsibility for one's actions, which can lead to an exploration of what the person is doing now that will result in positive or negative consequences in the future.

Abandonment Issues

Many people have deep-seated issues around abandonment due to early childhood trauma. Since no human relationship is perfect, you can expect that someone will ultimately disappoint you, betray you, be insensitive at the wrong time, unavailable when you really need them, or just not fully present when you feel the need to be connected. Those individuals with stronger ego structures tend to cope or deal with these situations, talk about their feelings, and tolerate the good with the bad. However, all of these typically human events tend to activate early childhood abandonment wounds in those who have poor coping skills. Along with good basic psychotherapy to help understand and heal inner child issues, spiritual interventions can be extremely helpful in providing another means of coping with these painful moments.

The reality is that God is omnipresent and can be continually felt as a real internal force of Love, Joy, and Peace. The resulting sense of wholeness that accompanies this Divine presence surpasses any human experience. The value of a rich, spiritual, inner life is that it depends only upon the effort of the individual. God is omnipresent and always waiting for us to open and receive that Divine Love. Once again, the pain of despair, helplessness, and hopelessness can be lifted when an individual realizes that there is a way to end suffering that is not based upon external forces.

This inner strength obviously is available only to those who have accessed the spiritual realms. This truth does not necessarily immediately solve someone's problems of loneliness, isolation, and feelings of separateness. The fact of the matter is that inherent in the spiritual experience is a deep sense of interconnectedness with all of humanity. Thus, even though an individual may not have a current primary relationship, he or she can still feel a tangible, bonded connection with the Universal at a spiritual level.

The therapeutic intervention is rather simple. Simply suggest that the individual begin to shift his or her focus away from outside expectations when they are feeling disappointed and hurt. Help the person learn to turn inward, in order to activate and deepen their relationship with Spirit. Various methods have been proven useful in this regard:

Practicing the presence of God is one technique that has been suggested by Brother Lawrence,[40] a Carmelite friar in the 1600s. It simply consists of constantly remembering God, by talking to that Divine Presence. For instance, one can simply say, "I love you, God," or "Let me feel your love." Any simple phrase will do. It simply needs to be repeated over and over again. The goal is to make the relationship with God very personal, very real, and constant. Imagine constantly being with God, in everything you do, making the Divine relationship a living reality in every aspect of your life. That is the goal. It is important to have a devotional attitude with this practice.

Several years ago I was on retreat in Maui, Hawaii, and watching the sunset at the Lahaina harbor. The sky was filled with brilliant colors, and several couples were caressing in this most romantic setting. As I began to feel sad about being alone, I turned inward. I spoke to Divine Mother from a place in my heart. "Dearest Mother, I don't have to feel so alone. Free me from this delusion of separation from Thee. You are my greatest love! Be here with me now." In that instant, my heart and entire consciousness filled with tremendous Love. I was in a state of reverie and ecstasy.

Another practical technique that is very useful when missing a loved one is to turn one's attention to the Heart chakra. This technique requires more advanced sensitivity to subtle energy. Since everything is energy and vibration, and since, in essence, there is no time and space, then it is possible to activate the soul consciousness of a loved one within our own consciousness. Every soul emanates a vibration that is unique, just as each snowflake is unique. We can become very attuned to the vibrational quality of our loved ones and learn to awaken that experience within our field of awareness. Our thought, our intention, can actually create this inner connection. It is very reassuring to know that time and space cannot keep us apart from our loved ones.

Intuition

Perhaps your greatest clinical tool is your intuition. It is an amazing resource that can help you perceive important aspects about your patient. Your intuition can be developed by learning to listen to your inner experience. Intuition typically works along three sense modalities: vision, feeling, and/or hearing, as well as through pure thought. You might see images, symbols, and/or words that explain, either directly or indirectly, the exact nature of an individual's difficulties. It is very common to feel impressions in your body that are related to your patient. For example, you might feel their emotional pain or physical pain in your own body.

Some therapists are afraid of this loss of boundary, because they are worried that they will not be able to release the energy that they have touched. However, there are techniques to release others' vibrations that can make the process relatively safe. At the end of the day, visualize a shower of white or golden light coming down through the top of your head and filling your entire body. Draw your attention into the center of your spine and ask that any energy you have picked up that is not your own, be released. Imagine that all the stress, density, and/or emotionality is being transmuted into light and flowing out of your body. Focus upon your breath, breathing deeply and slowly, letting each breath recharge your body with cosmic energy.

The reality of this work is, however, that it does take a toll on us. I believe that we must be inspired to help others due to the physical and emotional price we pay. I personally have found the rewards for helping others to far outweigh the energetic burden that it might temporarily place upon me.

Finally, you might actually hear an inner voice that provides you with important clinical information. Your intuition might also express itself to you just as a clear thought. Since thought is energy, intuition can often come in the form of direct knowing. This is perhaps the clearest and quickest way of intuitively knowing.

Projective Identification

The process of projective identification is probably one of the most interesting and clinically useful concepts in theoretical personality functioning.[41]

In the early years after my initial spiritual awakenings, as I began to explore integrating spiritual awareness into the psychotherapeutic process, I seemed to become estranged more and more from my traditional colleagues. It seemed that we had very little in common and certainly little to share in the way that our work was unfolding. On several occasions, I even tried to share things that I was discovering but with little success.

One afternoon in the park in Beverly Hills, I was enjoying a sack lunch when one of the most esteemed Kleinian analysts sat down to visit. I was delighted with this opportunity to share a new discovery that I had had, about the nature of projective identification. The theories about this particular defense system always interested me, because they were so clinically useful. Projective identification, as the theory suggests, is an unconscious attempt by the ego (ψ) to disown unwanted, infantile aspects of the self. For instance, if an individual has great difficulty accepting and experiencing helplessness, he or she would create a situation in which the therapist would feel helpless and the patient would be in control, thereby allowing the patient to feel more powerful.

There seemed to be a great mystery about how projective identification worked. Theories abounded regarding subtle nuances, facial gestures, and the unconscious perceiving of other people's unconscious. Bion himself suggested that it might be a *beta* element, beta standing for some unknown process.[42] Nobody really knew how it occurred. I tried to share my recent discoveries regarding the transference of subtle energy. The psychological theory and energetic theory appeared to be quite compatible in this situation.

Within the psychological realm, it is commonly understood that individuals can have emotional experiences that are beyond their capacity to integrate. As previously noted, helplessness is a good example. If a child, through severe abuse or neglect, is made to feel helpless to a degree that is beyond their ego's (ψ) capacity to function, then that state becomes intolerable. The ego (ψ) will find whatever means necessary for survival. In the process, the difficult and overwhelming feelings (such as, of helplessness) become split off from the self and projected onto others. The individual can then identify with a "stronger" position, since the unwanted state is now experienced as "out there." Hence the term, "projective identification," because the individual *projects* the unwanted aspects of the self and *identifies* with the typically opposite and stronger functions that result in the fantasy of mastery. The result is truly fantasy, because this primitive defense mechanism does not allow for the resolution of a problem, nor does it lead to a higher level of functioning. It is, in fact, a rather poor mechanism for effective adaptation to life. It does, however, provide some degree of protection for an overwhelmed ego (ψ).

Once again, there are no clear psychological theories regarding how the feelings actually become activated in the other person who becomes the focus of the projection. Certainly, behavioral and emotional manipulations can account for some of the phenomenon; however, it is common for this experience to develop within minutes at a non-verbal level, with hardly any interaction. It is here that I suggest that the subtle energy theories are useful.

The subtle energy theory suggests that a vibration can be transmitted through consciousness and received unconsciously or consciously by the recipient. I believe that psychologists and mystics alike would agree that the unconscious has mental aspects. Since thought is a form of energy, the term "thought form" takes on a clearer meaning in this context. The thoughts of the individual, in the form of unwanted thoughts and feelings, take on a subtle energetic form and are projected via energy onto an external recipient. The unaware receiver now feels and thinks something, but may have little awareness as to the source of the new feeling state. When one is privileged to access the clairvoyant state, this matter becomes greatly demystified, for one can actually see the transfer of energy as it leaves one person and travels into the energetic field of another. Upon observing this phenomenon, I found it easy to understand why I might feel like behaving in a certain way when in the company of a certain individual, when such actions are not characteristic of my style. For example, an individual who actually carries severe rejection complex, due to early childhood emotional abuse, often finds other people acting very rejecting towards them. This aspect of rejection is projected onto the other and activated. The therapeutic value of consciously perceiving this process is that it allows the therapist to perceive what is happening, contain the feelings, avoid acting out against the patient, and explore the split-off element within the patient.

Of course, it is possible to deal with projective identification without being conscious of subtle energy. One merely has to be very aware of his or her thoughts, emotions, and actions. The awareness of subtle energy merely becomes another intuitive skill for a psychotherapist. However, it was fascinating for me to watch these energies float through space and then to observe my emotions and thoughts change. I perceived myself acting or feeling in a way that was inside my patient and not of my experience, and I began to see that projective identification was the result of this energetic transmission.

Incidentally, my esteemed colleague seemed to have little interest in such esoteric theories. Sadly, I was not surprised. It only confirmed what I had been discovering—that most of my colleagues were trapped in the limited phenomena of the mind. They had no capacity to see the subtle and deep reaches of their experiences.

Years later, I feel that this statement and observation is still all too true. One year ago I returned to therapy because of the pain and confusion I felt when plans to be married fell apart. I had been engaged for two-and-a-half years and felt a tremendous loss and in need of some help and direction. The therapist I chose was a very kind and understanding psychologist, very helpful around specific problems, and quite active within a cognitive approach. After a few months I felt much better and did not have any outer problems to work on, so I thought it might be a great opportunity to creatively explore some inner realms. Ultimately, I had to quit therapy with this well-trained, highly competent psychologist, because every time I would become silent, close my eyes, withdraw my attention, and concentrate with my intuitive awareness, he would start talking. We discussed this matter for three weeks, and he could not drop into a deeper level. He was so identified with his mind that he was compelled to talk, even when I asked him just to be present. He could not.

With projective identification, the ego (ψ) of the patient may be protected, but the consciousness of the therapist can become contaminated with very difficult psychic energy. The following discussion will focus upon the emotional and mental states that become activated in the therapist during projective identification and various therapeutic approaches that include both energetic and interpretive responses.

Sleepiness

One of the situations that I find most difficult is when I become very sleepy in a session. This feeling can come upon me even early in the morning when I am well rested. It has taken me years to clarify the source of this reaction. I eventually found that this occurs as the result of a subtle energetic force that actually numbs my perception. This force has a downward-pulling effect that dulls my ability to think or even remain present with the patient. I have found that this is a result of a projection wherein I become the container for an unexpressed, split-off part of the patient. Specifically, it occurs when the patient has certain aspects within that are being avoided and suppressed. The patient appears bright and alert, while I am fighting with all my will to keep my eyes open and stay awake. As a defense, I have attempted to use my will to push this energy away from me, but that has never really solved the problem for more than a brief second, because the patient has not made any conscious connection of this energy to their own inner life. I have found it is more clinically useful to flow with the experience and forthrightly bring it into discussion:

Therapist: (It might be necessary to interrupt some superficial talk in order to begin.) Sorry to interrupt, but something is happening here that I wonder about. I am sensing this on an energetic, intuitive level and maybe you can help here. I notice that I am finding it hard to attend to what you are saying, and I wonder if there is something else that you are trying not to tell me? Do you feel like you are trying to block something out of our conversation?

Patient: I don't know. What do you mean?

Therapist: Is there something that you do not feel safe or comfortable to talk about?

Patient: Well, actually, there is something that I feel I cannot talk about.

At this point, the patient typically goes on to tell me why he or she cannot discuss some particular issue, and once the resistance is overcome, all the content comes flowing to the surface. Also, typically, as soon as the individual begins to acknowledge my observation, the force that is pressing upon me discontinues. The energy is now flowing, and a new life and vitality enters the room. The value of being a little more conscious about the energy is that you can see (and *feel*) how strongly the individual is attempting to avoid certain subjects.

Thus, a gentle pressure on your feeling state can serve to lead to a much quicker opening to the underlying issue. It is important to remember that you are not attempting to break through the patient's defenses. Rather, you are exploring, touching on the defense system that will naturally allow for the deeper material to emerge. This process allows for a nice integration of your subtle intuitive perception with your traditional psychotherapy skills. The essential point to remember is that your emotional and mental state may be what your patient is actually feeling but not expressing. Open yourself to a greater place within, and using your subtle perception, intuitively feel into yourself and your patient and compare the difference. Remember, the goal here is to feel subtle energy and vibration. If you have done your homework, you know what your own essential energy feels like, so anything different would be your patient. Remember the story about the Master who could hear his student thinking? Learn to discern emotion and thought on the subtle plane, using your intuition.

This phenomenon does not only occur in the face of suppression or avoidance, but also and equally for feelings of confusion, helplessness, and anger. It is striking how quickly you can begin to feel these things without much verbal interaction. As you begin to notice a shift in your state, when in the presence of a client, allow yourself to become more quiet and centered. Intuitively, compare your state with the state your patient seems to exude, moving back and forth between your experience and your patient's until you begin to sense what might be going on with them, by carefully identifying your feelings when in their presence. Then, attempt to calmly and sensitively bring this information into discussion. For example, if the experience is anger, you might say:

Therapist: As I am here with you today, I am noticing that I feel anger and resentment. I actually was feeling pretty good before our session so I wonder if I might be feeling something that you are feeling, but not talking about? Is there anything that you might be upset about right now?

Patient: There sure is. . . .

Vibrational Attunement

Intuition and healing can be facilitated through attunement with subtle energy. For the purpose of this discussion, let us refer to this process as vibrational attunement. The following simple exercise can help you develop finer perception for vibrational attunement.

First, begin by imagining that you are a musical instrument. Allow yourself to feel and perhaps even hear the note or chord that is being played by your consciousness. As you become more sensitive, you will perceive everything in creation as a vibrational quality. Your consciousness has a unique vibration, and everything else has a vibrational pattern as well. Each cell of the body, organs, plants, emotions— everything can be identified by this energetic signature. You can sensitize yourself to perceive these patterns.

Second, set the intention to open to a place in your consciousness that is totally neutral. This neutral state is timeless, open, and eternal. Practice being present in this state. Remember that energy follows thought, and your intention is what creates this inner experience or shift in your consciousness. Learn to be comfortable in this state, without the need or pressure to do anything. Just allow yourself to stay present and aware of all sensations in your body, feelings, thoughts, and visual images.

Third, learn to reach out with your will and match the vibration of someone else. You can do this by imagining a frequency scale, then moving up and down on that scale until you find the right harmonic and you actually feel a sense of resonance with the other person. Perhaps imagine that you are moving up and down on the rungs of a ladder until you find the right spot. It is possible to adjust your vibration to match an external vibration. Once you have come into synchrony with the other, just remain open and present and perceive what shows up on your consciousness. If you are really neutral, you will receive impressions from the other person. When you are ready to complete this exercise, simply release the connection, release the vibrations you might have absorbed, and return to neutrality. Then take some time to talk with the individual and explain what you experienced and see how that information matches the person's experience. Reality testing plays a valid part in developing a greater trust in your ability to discern.

This process of vibrational attunement will allow you eventually to discern very subtle qualities and changing states all around you, and you will learn to attend to the energy of a situation as well as the behavior, words, and emotions. Remember that the key to developing this heightened state of awareness is to become very present, stay in the moment, and be centered in consciousness, as opposed to your mind or emotions. The greater your inner peace, the easier it is to "hear" what is going on all around you. Your inner receptivity will be clouded by an overstimulated nervous system; therefore, reduce external sensory stimuli and allow silence to reign—silence also strengthens the nervous system. In addition, it helps to avoid drugs and chemicals like caffeine, which stimulate the nervous system, as well as mental agitation, which creates waves of distraction. Develop an inner life that is peaceful, a healthy body, and a calm emotional life to enhance your ability for this finer perception.

Often we hold past memories in our body, which also reduces the flow of energy and impairs our subtle perceptions. Various forms of deep tissue bodywork, which are designed to release blocked energy, open the structure, and align the skeletal system, can be very helpful. The vibrational realm becomes more available as we become balanced and open at all levels—mind, body, emotions, and soul.

The clinical usefulness of heightened intuitive ability is tremendous. Most important, with this advantage it is possible not to waste a lot of time trying to find out what is most important and to help the patient attend immediately to the most essential issues. The therapist can act as a guide to focus the session on the most relevant topics. In most cases, it is what the patient does *not* know that creates the problem, so the therapist can be of great service by guiding the patient into an area that will bring growth and development.

Since intention actually creates a mental magnet to create an experience, setting an internal intention with each patient to perceive the most important issues for that session will facilitate greater progress. Allow yourself to let go of any need to help, and trust that all the information you need will become available to you. Allow yourself to be comfortable with the silence and expand into the moment as you connect with your patient. It is very helpful to explain to your patient what you are doing, so that they do not think that you are bored or going to sleep.

Therapist: I want to let you know that I try to use my intuition in order to know more clearly what you are trying to tell me and what are the deeper sources for your problems. I do visually see images and pictures, which give me this information, so when I close my eyes, I am not going to sleep. Actually, I am listening more attentively.

Visualization

Considerable research has demonstrated the relationship between the mind and body. Some cancer patients have overcome their illness by visualizing the cancer cells being removed from their bodies. Great athletes have enhanced their performance by visualizing perfect results prior to and during their competition. The body responds to thoughts, and mental images hold powerful links to the body and emotions. In fact, there is no separation between the mind and the body, since the body can speak through these symbolic images. Hence, the great power of interactive, guided imagery, in which mental images can be used to effect changes in physical, mental, emotional, and spiritual states. Likewise, the body and soul can also communicate reciprocally through mental and kinesthetic images. We are a unified system of mind, body, and soul.

Guided imagery can be taken to another level when consciousness is brought into the relationship, because the therapist can do

much more than merely guide an individual along an internal dialogue, by being energetically present with a patient as well. This
facilitates the healing process because the joining of consciousness
enhances the energetic shifts that occur. For example:

Therapist: You were just telling me about feeling upset about
something. Can you feel that upset now?

Patient: Yes, I do.

Therapist: Where do you feel it? Where in your body?

Patient: I feel it in my chest and mostly in my gut.

Therapist: OK, I want you to close your eyes, relax, take a deep
breath, and relax. Now just breathe into that sensation. Allow yourself just to be with that sensation and describe its qualities. What is
the texture, the color, the size of the sensation. Just allow yourself to
describe it. Don't try to do anything with it. *(This is a good process
because it begins to teach an individual the ability to be an observer to an
experience. This process also teaches one how to be a neutral container
and simply allow an experience to exist, without having to act on it,
which can be a very valuable exercise for building patience and forbear-
ance in impulsive individuals.)*

Patient: (Patient provides some detailed description.)

Therapist: Good, now I want you to imagine that this sensation
can actually speak with you. Imagine that it has a voice; then, in your
mind, hear what it has to say. Ask it, what is it feeling, why is it there,
and if it has anything to tell you.

After some discussion and exploration, the patient will typically
discover more information concerning the deeper source for the
distress, such as feelings of hurt and grief. As these emotions are
discovered and explored, the pain in the gut might move to a feeling
of loss and grief in the heart. At this point it would be possible to
provide some direct healing on the remaining pain and trauma that is
lodged in the heart center.

Therapist: Would you like some help in healing the pain you feel
in your heart?

Patient: I don't know what you mean.

Therapist: Perhaps we can help you release the pain you still feel. You feel it as emotion, but it is essentially energy, too. We can work with that energy to help heal the pain.

Patient: All right. What am I supposed to do?

Therapist: Just relax and close your eyes. Keep breathing into the pain that you feel. Remember that *you* are not that pain. Now, let yourself imagine that there is a wonderful light above you. Perhaps it is like the sun, with rays coming down through the top of your head. Let those rays of light come right down into your chest. That light carries with it a wonderful, nurturing, healing, Divine presence. There is such an immense sense of love and peace in that light, and it dissolves all that pain in your chest. *(It is important to realize here that you can help only to the degree that you actually can experience and manifest this energetic experience. If you have done your spiritual homework, you are actually channeling this healing force into the room and into the patient. This is not an intellectual fairy tale; you are allowing yourself to be an instrument to help the healing process. As a result, you can help to ignite the same possibility in your patient.)* Just let that Love go into every place that you feel any hurt, and let it dissolve the pain. Let that love fill your entire being; every aspect of you is filled with this light and this love.

At this point the individual usually feels quite a bit of love and can remain silent for a few minutes as the energy continues to flow. It is essential to stay present with the patient and hold the energy. If you allow yourself to be distracted, i.e., read your mail, think about your next patient, etc., you will have withdrawn your conscious energy and support from the process, and your patient will feel this and be distracted as well. Continue to help the patient with your energetic support on the subtle plane as they deepen into the experience; you are "holding open the space" for a healing shift to occur. When the session needs to come to a close, allow a few minutes to talk about whatever happened.

Therapeutic Touch

Therapeutic Touch is a particular healing form that can be easily integrated into psychotherapy. I find it especially applicable, because it does not need to involve any physical touching. Given the intense transference reactions that are elicited in patients, physical contact can stir up either intense longings for physical intimacy or deeply repressed anxiety or terror. Either way, the positive therapeutic relationship becomes more complicated, and sometimes severely impaired, when physical contact is introduced into psychotherapy. In fact, many malpractice insurance companies specifically inquire whether the professional touches the patient in any manner. Therapeutic Touch, or subtle energy work, requires no physical contact but allows for a powerful way to facilitate changes at the level of mind, emotions, and body.

The process of Therapeutic Touch involves the subtle energy fields that surround the individual. In Chapter Five, the various layers of manifestation that encase the soul were discussed: physical, emotional, mental. Each of these aspects of manifestation exists as a subtle energy. Therapeutic touch is one way to engage these energy fields directly and to facilitate profound changes in a relatively short period of time. One of the great benefits of this practice is that it allows for the use of intuition, and the therapist often receives quite clear insights regarding the patient's core problems. This information can be used to help guide a patient to explore certain areas and issues. Once again, this direct knowing regarding essential concerns speeds up the therapy process. Less time is wasted in irrelevant, superficial chatter that holds no possibility of transformation.

The process for employing Therapeutic Touch is actually quite simple. Begin by becoming very centered and invoking the presence of Spirit. Whatever prayer works for you is perfect. I like the following prayer, which comes from the teachings of Paramahansa Yogananda: "Divine Mother, thou art omnipresent; thou art in all thy children. Manifest your healing energy in his/her mind, body, and soul." I also silently pray that my patient will receive whatever he or she needs in this moment. In essence, I try to get myself out of the way and to let God do the work. This is a wonderful state, because the energy begins to flow strongly, with waves of healing vibrations passing through the therapist's body. Now, place your hands about six inches above the patient's body. Then, allow your hands to move as the energy guides them. You will find that you are prompted to hold them over particular parts of the body. You can also scan all areas by passing your hands over a spot and noticing the quality of energy and any impressions you receive. You may explore each chakra and notice the quality of energy there.

Next, allow your intention to shift to the different layers of the individual, i.e., mind, body, and emotions. You may intuitively feel particular areas of conflict. Then, attempt to perceive the essential soul energy present, and sense how closely the patient is connected to that quality. Finally, let go and open fully to the flow of energy moving through you. At this point, you will probably feel very connected with the patient on an energetic level. You may notice sensations of warmth, cold, tingling, or pulsation. These all are related to states in the patient. I have observed over the years a sensation that feels like two similar poles of a magnet gently pushing against each other. This seems to signal some force being activated that seems to result in real shifts in the patient. On occasion, you might feel as though you have absorbed a specific feeling or physical pain from the patient. I encourage you to relax at this point, to continue to breathe evenly, and not to identify with the sensation, but merely to observe what is happening.

If you follow this practice, the energy will pass through you and release from your consciousness. This type of experience occurs when you are actually helping to pull something out of the patient's energetic field, and it is this process of energetic release that accounts for sudden changes in moods, emotions, and perceptions. The changes and insights that occur in this process can be discussed after the treatment. The entire session takes only between ten and twenty minutes to provide. Because of the short time involved, it is quite easy to integrate therapeutic touch in a typical, fifty-minute psychotherapy session. While is it possible to begin exploring this type of energy work on your own, great value can be received through training with someone who has been doing this work, because an accomplished practitioner can open healing channels within you through the direct transmission of energy. Thus, the healing you receive will deepen your ability to heal others.

Prayer

Prayer is a very powerful force that will help your patients. No one needs to know what you are doing within the privacy of your inner life. I have had many, many people thank me over the years for my prayers. They report significant changes following their requests for prayer. I am always interested to hear these reports, because I do not have any conscious knowledge of how they are being helped, but I continue to pray for people anyway.

Prayer is simply you talking to God from a sincere place within your heart. Devotion, according to the yogic teachings, is the important element in attracting God's response, and devotion is simply sustaining a sincere, loving, and loyal relationship with God. To pray, simply talk to God and ask God to help the individual in any way he or she might need. I find it very helpful, during a difficult session, to turn inward and ask God for help to understand what is going on. I find that my faith and trust in God gets rewarded time and time again as I turn inward during the most difficult moments in treatment, to ask for help. The following illustrates my inner dialogue:

> *Dear God, you created this universe, not me. You know, it is a real mess down here. We are so lost. This person needs your help. I can't do anything to fix this problem, but you can. I really want to help this person, who really needs the help. We are both trying so hard. We need your help. You can do it. Give this person some sign, some experience, to help them find the strength, the hope to resolve this crisis. You are so great; you created this universe. One little thought from you can change this person's life. I am counting on you to help!*

I do believe that it is acceptable to get tough with God. We are lost without Divine help, and I expect to receive it!

Spiritual Reality versus Psychosis

When integrating spiritual methods and awareness into psychotherapy, it becomes important to be able to discern authentic spiritual experience from primary process material. It is very common to be asked, "How do I know if my vision is real or if I just made it up?" You, the professional, must be able to advise the client as to whether to follow an inner vision or warn them against impulsive and potentially destructive actions.

First of all, spiritual experiences change our lives, and their "realness" gets revealed in our day-to-day life. We feel different after a superconscious experience also, and something tangible happens thereafter. It is very typical for a sense of Peace, Joy, and/or Bliss to accompany a spiritual experience, as God's presence is very healing. This Bliss is much different than the temporary high that one can feel with a drug, in which he or she gets elevated into an altered state for a brief time, only to return to familiar consciousness once the drug has run its course, without any permanent change in consciousness.

Spiritual contact can occur in a meditative state, dream state, or waking state. These naturally occurring spiritual experiences are the result of some previous effort, whether in this lifetime or another. It is common to feel uplifted and possible to visually perceive some angelic or saintly presence. Typically, we perceive Spirit in the form that we worship. A devotee may see his or her *guru*, a Christian will perceive Christ, and so on. Waking, dreaming, sleeping—all is the same to Spirit. We can be touched in any state, and it will have a profound impact on our lives.

During a therapy session in which guided imagery is being used to help facilitate a deeper connection to Spirit, individuals often ask if it is real. I suggest to them that it may not matter, although a real spiritual experience will definitely transform their life. I explain that the mind is going to great trouble to create the images and information that he or she is perceiving in this trance state. Even if it is only "psychological material," such as images that relate to sub-personalities or unconscious conflicts, it can be very useful as a way to further explore important themes in psychotherapy. This brief discussion usually serves to satisfy the patient's need for meaning and allows him or her to suspend the critical, judging aspect of the mind, so as to open the door for new experiences to emerge.

The energy of psychotic material, which originates from primitive aspects of the psyche, can easily be distinguished from the subtle energy of the superconscious. The superconscious flows from the higher centers of the brain and from the astral body. This state is often accompanied by the quiet cessation of breath and a flood of internal light. While a great surge of energy from the superconscious takes place, it is not physical in nature and does not agitate the nervous system. In fact, the energy may charge the nervous system with vitality, but it does not agitate the emotional body or mental body. The mind becomes calm within the superconscious experience.

In contrast, psychoses and mania have exceedingly agitating qualities. Sensations of anger, anxiety, and pressure are not typical of the sublime spiritual realms and are indications of the pathological aspects of a client's psyche. Also and to a lesser degree, the impression that one has a mission to save others, which is a very common feeling among spiritual people, may be more an expression of a psychological nature than of a spiritual one. The indicative factor in this case is the emotional fervor attached to the impression. Spiritual reality, ultimately, has a calming and uplifting effect.

Of course, the transformational process necessarily includes the fire of purification. This fire is not totally symbolic, since intense energies can be experienced that serve to purify the consciousness and eliminate the dross. This illustrates why a strong and well-integrated ego (ψ) is needed for serious spiritual work. Primitive shadow material, or aspects of the psyche that have been disowned, become heightened under the effect of these intense, purifying energies. The transformative value of these experiences lies in the fact that through them, an individual can be impelled into intense self-reflection and sincere soul-searching and eventually can learn to consciously recognize his or her own material and transform the negative qualities of hate, greed, lust, jealousy, and selfishness into the higher manifestations of forgiveness, contentment, non-attachment to the senses, and love. An observing ego (ψ) is required for this process.

On the other hand, a psychotic individual does not have the internal strength to maintain this observing ego (ψ) and therefore becomes lost and controlled by strong, inner forces. An individual's capacity to observe his or her experiences without the need for action is a good criteria to determine his or her ability to withstand the demands of spiritual unfoldment.

For example, an individual in a pathological state will justify destructive and impulsive actions on the basis of spiritual guidance. In 1989 one schizophrenic individual contributed to the destruction of thirty-five thousand acres in Nevada City, California, when he burned sheets of toilet paper and threw them in the air on a hot and windy day. He explained later that demons had appeared to him in a vision and directed him to do so. It is always important to maintain good common sense when dealing with internal visionary material. Dark forces can attempt to influence us and encourage us to perform actions that can harm ourselves or others.

Truth tends to repeat itself. I encourage individuals to be patient and also to listen to the consistency of an inner message over time. In this process, it is important to listen more from the heart than from the mind. The delusive aspects of creation, sometimes referred to as Satan, can be very tricky. I do believe that dark forces exist that attempt to keep us from the light. Since creation consists of the play of duality between the light and the dark, knowledge of this fact should only serve to push us deeper into our spiritual practice, so that we can strengthen our clarity and presence, and develop our ability to discern Truth from delusion. We can learn to look more deeply into the heart for answers, to listen for a response, and to develop an inner knowing regarding the messages we receive from our intuition. Since each of us may have a different way of perceiving, only through practice can we develop greater discernment regarding our own style of intuition.

Meditation

Most of the suggestions regarding spiritual intervention can be employed only with a receptive individual. In this regard, meditation is one of the best methods to help an individual open a direct relationship with Spirit. It is important to explain to patients that meditation is not a process in which you "make your mind blank." First of all, one cannot "make" the mind blank. The mind gradually becomes quiet, allowing consciousness to transcend the mind, when the proper techniques are used. Proper meditation practice encourages an individual to focus upon something, some aspect of the Divine, and merge with that object of attention. It is in the process of merging into the Divine experience that we transcend the mind and discover inner states of peace, love, joy, and bliss. These qualities are aspects of the soul and not products of the mind. In these transcendent states, inner clarity is increased and clearer intuition can be developed.

In any discussion about meditation, it is important to mention that many people, especially those in the fundamental Christian community, worry about being overcome by demons if their mind were to become blank. The fear is that dark forces will enter and take over the mind. The greater misconception is that meditation actually attempts to make the mind blank. This is a total misunderstanding of meditation since the concentration techniques always have the awareness focused upon the breath and a *mantra*. Without objects of concentration, the mind would just wander and consciousness would never transcend the contents of the mind. Meditation proper occurs when conscious awareness is merging with the Divine in the form of light, sound, energy, feeling (i.e., peace, love, joy, or bliss) and/or a sacred figure such as Jesus, a saint, or the *guru*.

It is common for patients to complain about being confused and not knowing what to do in life. In such cases, meditation can be a constructive technology for personal empowerment. The following dialogue might be helpful in presenting this idea:

Therapist: I know you feel very lost and do not know what to do. While you may not realize it, a part of you has all the answers for you. You seem so emotionally distraught and mentally upset that it is very difficult for you to actually hear what is best for you. However, when you are quiet, it becomes easier to listen and hear what your intuitive Self knows.

Patient: What are you talking about?

Therapist: I am talking about your soul and the wisdom that your soul has. Your soul knows everything you need and can help you solve your problems and make decisions. You just need to develop a better connection with your soul.

Patient: Well, how do I do that?

Therapist: Meditation is one good way.

Patient: What do you do to meditate?

At this point you can provide some basic instruction for meditation and actually spend a few minutes meditating with your patient. Of course, this implies that you must consistently meditate as part of your own spiritual practice, so that you can help calm your patient by your energy as well. I typically give my patients meditation audio tapes if they are interested in learning meditation. The tapes provide them with support to continue their practice at home.

Past-Life Regression

An interesting phenomenon that occurs in transpersonal work is past-life information. Western perspectives generally do not give much credence to the notion of reincarnation, so past-life information gets discounted if it arises in this context. However, ancient yogic teachings and mystical traditions recognize reincarnation as a real factor in the cosmic play. It is well beyond the scope of this discussion to provide a comprehensive review of the literature on reincarnation. My own experiences, both personally and professionally, have led me to believe in reincarnation as a very real factor to consider. Assuming some validity of this theory, the clinical application and usefulness of past-life regression will be considered here.

The great teachings of yoga and the mystery schools explain that our consciousness continues from one incarnation to another. The soul's awareness is eternal and simply adopts one form, then another, as it passes through various levels of existence. Death is just like a hand slipping out of a glove, as the consciousness departs the physical body. With birth, the soul consciousness reenters a new physical body, and the individual typically forgets all the past memories of life on the astral plane and the various previous incarnations. However, since consciousness continues and grows, each individual does not start anew and fresh each lifetime. As a soul, each one of us continues on the road of spiritual development. Each lifetime continues with fresh chances to conquer unresolved themes and issues. Every lifetime is an opportunity to fulfill old desires and complete whatever lessons the soul needs to learn for final emancipation.

When life is viewed from this perspective, the therapist, then, can hold a much broader and deeper understanding of the human condition. First of all, rather than merely thinking that each person is solely a product of genetics and social conditioning, the life patterns that may be involved from previous incarnations can also be considered, for it is highly possible that beliefs, feelings, and personality patterns are the result of past ingrained habits and tendencies that come with us into this lifetime! The Eastern teachings, in both the Buddhist and yogic tradition, suggest that this is so.

Furthermore, clinical evidence suggests that significant problems in this lifetime may be the direct result of previous past-life situations. Specifically, at the moment of death, our last dying thought is said to become the thread upon which an individual reenters life. This is why spiritual practice is often referred to as preparation for death. Our last thoughts become the template for our continued existence, because consciousness never stops, though it is somewhat misleading to call anything our "last thought." Since the consciousness never stops for an instant, the thoughts, desires, and tendencies we have developed and accumulated in a particular lifetime simply continue on with us, no matter what the form may be.

Our past actions, the seeds of our karma, may not ripen until a later incarnation; thus, an individual may have a situation occur in life that is totally the result of actions in a previous life. This larger perspective regarding the nature of reality and the continuity of life can provide for a more logical explanation of life's difficult circumstances as well as an individual's current tendencies.

Once again, as previously discussed, this frame of reference sheds a much different light on the notion of victimization. For example, I have a patient who suffered tremendous abuse from both her parents. One can only wonder what one might have done to deserve such terrible treatment. A past-life regression revealed an incarnation in which this person actually took great pleasure in hurting others. This information allowed her to come to terms with the abuse suffered in this lifetime and to feel that she had repaid her karmic debt. Past-life information can therefore be clinically helpful in the following ways:

1. *A patient can discover the unresolved issues that have been carried over into this lifetime and gain a clearer perspective on how to resolve them.* These issues can impact greatly both one's psychological and spiritual levels of functioning. The circumstances of a past life can create certain protective, reactive patterns in the current life, which become easier to shift once an individual recognizes the original source for the behavior style. Defensive personality styles are not always solely the result of experiences from this lifetime. For example, my previous life experience as a child in Nazi Germany left severe scars on my consciousness for this lifetime. I noticed that in this lifetime I would be reluctant to express the love I felt for

someone and could not understand why I would not want to verbalize it. Then, through past-life regressions, I remembered the reality in the concentration camps, in which loved ones were taken away to die. In fact, I remembered how the Nazi soldiers would select someone to kill and enjoy the pain it caused for those who loved that person. Their sadistic need was actually given greater opportunity when an individual would express affection for another, because the Nazi soldiers would then know who to kill. Thus, it became an act of protection not to openly express loving affection. Upon realizing this situation, it allowed me to be more appropriate in this life context and to overcome the tendency to withhold my expression of love.

2. *A patient can gain greater self-acceptance as he or she perceives the thread for personal tendencies.* For example, those individuals who have typically felt different and apart from others, often discover that they have had many past lives in monastic settings. This life, then, becomes an opportunity to find a balance between spiritual desires and human capacities for personal love and service. This information helps to dissolve self-blame and to shift one's perception away from the notion of a deficit to a more benign notion of personal growth and development.

3. *A patient can use guided imagery and the power of imagination to change the mental constructs of a past-life experience and find a resulting shift in his or her present feeling and mental state.* Though at first this notion may seem amazing, there appears to be some evidence that the quality of the present moment can affect both the future and the past. One theory is that time is an illusion, and modern physics has been suggesting something quite similar as well. If this is true, then our consciousness may be able to effect changes across time. Guided imagery that combines the power of imagination may be able to change the related memory-feeling state and result in a shift in one's current state of awareness. Perhaps, as some suggest, there are multiple simultaneous realities, and so, in effect, past lives are actually happening right now in a different dimension. Thus when we

make inner changes, we concurrently change what is/was/will be occurring in a different time-space continuum simultaneously. It is an interesting theory. Years ago I had a friend who developed claustrophobia. She had no history of any anxiety attacks or any previous discomfort within small places. Upon going into trance and exploring her inner realms, she began perceiving a scene in which a young woman was being buried alive, and she felt a great affinity for this woman. She used her imagination to recreate the scene so that the woman dug herself out and escaped unharmed. At the completion of this inner meditative experience, her claustrophobia vanished. Sounds like a story out of the X-files, but this is what she reported. She was also a healthy, functioning woman, with no psychiatric history, who was, in fact, a successful artist. This type of data certainly appears worthy of further clinical investigation.

Past Life Induction

The actual technique to facilitate a past-life regression is quite simple. Begin with a hypnotic trance induction, and then use any specific image that allows one to enter another time zone. For example, I typically use an elevator in a ten-story building that will automatically stop at a specific floor. I suggest that the elevator will go up, and the patient is to report which floor it stops on. I further suggest that as the door opens, a scene will unfold that has relevant information to help the patient in this life, and that the scene is about a past-life experience.

Another good technique is to have the patient imagine walking down a ten-step staircase, into a hallway with five doors—with two doors on each side and one at the very end. The patient will be drawn to a door, and behind that door, the past-life memory and experience will be revealed. The patient opens the door, and the past-life regression begins. In practice, whatever material comes up, whether related to a past life or not, always tends to be very useful. In closing, it is always good to bring the person back the same way they came, with verbal cues to return them back into this reality, in their current body, and in the current time and place. This closing helps to avoid any continuing sense of disorientation.

This chapter provides a glimpse at the many possibilities for therapeutic intervention allowing the integration of the sacred into psychotherapy. A sense of joy and wonder unfolds, since the work is inspired from the soul. This deeper expression of Self or soul on behalf of the therapist and patient results in a very dynamic and creative relationship. Once again, the required therapeutic skill is in trusting the inner wisdom of the soul and being able to allow its expression.

Given the intensity of consciousness, special consideration needs to be made regarding boundary issues in the therapeutic relationship. Transference issues and boundary concerns are constant factors to consider during depth psychotherapy. The added dimension of spiritual energy heightens the need to clearly establish manageable boundaries between therapist and patients. The next chapter addresses these issues.

14

Boundary Problems

Therapist-Patient Relationship

BOUNDARY PROBLEMS are the biggest ethical concern for the practicing psychotherapist, and most patient-therapist lawsuits are the result of these boundary violations. Sexual contact with a patient is the most obvious type of problem, and dual relationships pose another. A dual relationship results whenever any additional contact with a patient occurs that creates another type of relationship outside the therapeutic relationship. Psychotherapists are currently cognizant of these potential problems and are justifiably concerned regarding any potential for misunderstanding between therapist and patient.

Furthermore, even when no dual relationship exists, boundary issues exist in the therapeutic context. The nature of transference *guarantees* that a patient will distort his or her perception of an event, based upon the patient's prior experiences and current level of psychological development. Many therapists are extremely cautious with regard to any physical contact with a patient, because of the potential for misinterpretation of even a simple, comforting hug. Some patients arrive wearing "red flags" indicating severe personality disorders that leave them unable to accurately perceive reality, a tendency to project and blame others, and an uncontrollable, vindictive rage over any sense of narcissistic injury. Thus, if these boundaries issues are a given when engaging in the more-or-less concrete means of relating, such as spoken words, expressed emotions, and physical behavior, imagine the potential for confusion and turmoil when the therapist attempts to engage the patient in work in the realm of subtle energy!

The greatest potential for misunderstanding in this subtle work exists because healing is based upon the loving energy of the heart chakra. All healing comes from love. This type of love is unconditional and impersonal. Most patients have early wounds in which basic needs for love, nurturance, and understanding were not successfully met. These wounded individuals mistake an impersonal, universal love for the personal. They misinterpret the love and care of the therapist as the sign that their deepest longing can find fulfillment.

Most people in our culture know only personal, limited love. Love becomes the spark for relationship and marriage. We typically take home the one who shares this wonderful presence with us. The patient in this setting often does not know how to interpret being touched so deeply. Powerful early desires are activated and deep longings emerge. Some people run away from this experience, being too uncomfortable to acknowledge their feelings, and therefore they miss the opportunity to learn and progress. Others become deeply attached, and difficult transference reactions develop that can take months or years to fully resolve. In the latter circumstance, patients can become convinced that they are meant to be with the therapist and even vow to wait until he or she might become available at some future time. Some healing traditions such as bodywork evoke even more emotional responses, because of the added confusion and intimacy of the physical contact. Some professionals (and their lawyers) would argue that the best way to deal with these potential problems is to avoid activating them in the first place.

Hence the practice of keeping emotional and physical distance: with those patients who are unable to develop a strong and consistent working alliance with the therapist,[43] then it is advisable to maintain very strict physical boundaries and never breach them. However, this does not solve the problem of energetic transmission. It is possible to modulate the flow of energy, and the conscious therapist must take care never to fuel the fires of sexual passion by engaging the heat of *shakti* with those who do not have the psychological integration and emotional maturity to receive it.

On the other hand, many individuals can be educated to understand the powerful energies that are awakened when the heart center is activated. Consciousness is very intimate and allows for a profound interpersonal connection. A therapist must be very thoughtful in preparing an individual to receive this force and also be very active in educating and supporting the patient in understanding its dynamics and effects. One means is to actively discuss the effects, purpose, and value of this subtle energy. Here are some helpful suggestions regarding this discussion:

1. A powerful effect of the connection is that consciousness is being magnified because two individuals are consciously present in this field.
2. The strength and power of the connection is not a sign to fall in love or have an intimate sexual relationship. Rather, it is an opportunity to move to deeper aspects of the Self and allow the Divine hand to help in the process.
3. The purpose of this energy is for awakening and healing. Consciousness is energy, and if the patient can develop a receptivity to it and learn to attune his or her consciousness to a higher vibratory rate, then the process of change and growth will be quickened.
4. This energy is dedicated entirely to healing and spiritual awakening. It is not intended for a personal relationship. The patient needs to learn to regard the energy as an omnipresent force that is available to anyone who learns to become aware of it. The therapist is not the origin, owner, or director of this force. The therapist becomes a *mirror* to reflect this energy and

an *amplifier* to help create a healing environment in which the patient can immerse his or her consciousness to absorb the vibration.

5. The value of this energy is that it provides a living experience quite beyond the power of words and also beyond the limits of the mind, physical body, and emotions. For some individuals, it becomes the first doorway to exploring spiritual realities. The inherent value in this type of work is that the direct transmission of energy can shift consciousness in a second, for time dissolves in the energetic realms. If an individual can be open and receptive to subtle energy forces, then great work can be accomplished very quickly at deep levels of being.

I would encourage professionals to seek out spiritual training and to become comfortable with the intensity of the energetic realities so that they do not shy away from using this powerful healing force.

Furthermore, it is critical that the therapist be very clear about his or her own level of neediness or sense of deprivation, for one cannot go further than one's own uncleared issues in the therapeutic relationship. One's sense of emotional deprivation, loneliness, and/or sense of emptiness can lead to acting out with a patient, because the patients are so vulnerable. It is so easy. There is no need for either party to go out and take the risks of finding and developing a new relationship.

The intimacy is touching and the love is profound at the subtle energy level. Unfortunately, the basic foundation of the therapeutic relationship is unequal, and hence the inherent prescription for difficulty. One of the most difficult challenges facing the conscious therapist is that one must attain the ability to be nonattached to the love and intimacy that is generated when working on this level—first, in order to open to such a deep level, and then, to be able to completely let it go. A patient will feel the desire and need of the therapist in this state, and the therapist must be prepared and capable of maintaining a correct therapeutic relationship in the face of the deeply intimate love that constitutes the work in the subtle energy realms.

Equally, I have come to realize that patients will intuitively know a great deal about the therapist in the course of this type of treatment, because they naturally tune in to the shared energy in this open field. Again, there are no secrets in consciousness. I remember a time many years ago when I was in the midst of an extremely difficult personal relationship. I had never spoken about this matter to any one of my patients. At the end of one session, as the patient was walking out the door, he stopped, turned around, and said, "Whoever she is, don't marry her!" He then walked out and closed the door. He was right, too!

There is another type of boundary problem that deserves discussion, which is the difficulties that can arise between a spiritual teacher and the student. This particular relationship warrants consideration because any psychotherapist who practices Sacred Psychotherapy will probably have patients who are involved with spiritual teachers, and problems can arise. An enlightened psychotherapist can help his or her patients deal with these difficult relationships. The next section sheds light on this subject.

Spiritual Advancement and Pathological Narcissism

During the last decade, many prominent spiritual teachers in the U.S. have become sexually involved with their community members. Some teachers have fraudulently used the finances of the community, and many have used their position of power for their own personal gain at the expense of the followers. Many followers have been bewildered over the discrepancy between the heights of spiritual development reached by the teachers and the depths of psychological pathology that have been subsequently revealed. It is important to understand this apparent paradox in development, not only because it has been so rampant in the United States, but also because of its implications in the realm of Sacred Psychotherapy.

This problem can best be approached through a blending of Western personality theory with yogic knowledge of the soul. First, the soul and the personality evolve in different ways. While they do influence each other, they still have some degree of autonomy. This distinction might be more easily understood if we first consider the relationship between the soul and the physical body. First of all, the body is the house or temple of the soul. Certain yogic practices such as physical postures, fasting, and cleansing techniques can be employed to assist with the process of transcending body consciousness. In the case of a spiritual Master, once having reached a high level of spiritual advancement and having become totally detached from the pains and suffering of the physical body, he or she may elect to take on the illnesses of others, using the body as a sacrificial object for the well-being of others, without accruing additional karma on his or her own behalf. For example, the physical form of a spiritual Master may appear to be in poor health, whereas his spirit glows with the ever-brilliant light of the soul, powerfully untouched. It is common for a Self-realized master to continue healing others, even though his or her own physical body may be very sick from cancer or some other disease. Paramahansa Yogananda could scarcely walk during the latter part of his life, as he took on the karma of many devotees. Similarly, Ramana Maharshi had advanced cancer yet still continued healing others.

The personality holds a similar relationship to the soul, in that the personality, like the physical body, is subject to change, growth, and disorder, while the soul is eternal and belongs to the realm of the changeless, omnipresent Truth.

Intensive spiritual practice awakens the *kundalini* energy, a subtle dormant force in the base of the spine, which, upon activation, sends a current of energy up the astral spine and thereby activates the various spiritual centers in the spine *(chakras)*. Great spiritual power typically results. Through dedicated practice, individuals can touch profound states of bliss and develop powers *(siddhis)* for healing, intuition, and manifestation. The presence of these spiritually advanced souls is quite tangible, as one can feel the intensity of their higher vibratory states. Also, profound states of love and peace are common around such individuals. Such highly spiritually advanced individuals have learned to focus upon their soul consciousness and express the rewards that come from intensive and prolonged spiritual practice.

However, attaining realization of higher spiritual awareness does not negate one's personality any more than it negates a physical body. In fact, a real danger appears when the *yogi* ignores the perfection and refinement of the personality as an aspect of his overall spiritual progress. Psychotherapy, as a Western method, has not been recognized as a part of the larger yoga system, and many *yogis* believe that it is not necessary to attend to personality issues while developing spiritual power. They mistakenly believe that yogic practice will solve all problems and purify all aspects of the personality.

However, it is my experience and observation that this is simply not true. A complicated and socially dangerous situation can and does result when an individual with an underlying personality disorder continues to achieve spiritual power, with the nature of their self-delusion continuing unchecked, and individuals under these people's influence get hurt in the process.

It is important at this point to understand the distinction between a personality disorder and a neurotic disorder. An individual who suffers from a neurotic state feels anxiety and conflict. Various aspects of the self oppose each other, and the mind is filled with the turmoil of the cognitive struggle. Forces in the psyche are juxtaposed and inner peace is lost. Guilt, shame, and resentment are common results of such inner conflicts. When this psychic energy cannot be resolved, psychosomatic concerns become generated as the unresolved energy lodges in the physical body. Also, as emotional energy becomes blocked, the body may symbolically express what the conscious mind cannot.

In neurotic processes, repression is the most common defense mechanism. Repression results when personal thoughts and feelings are regarded as "ego-dystonic," or not in harmony with the conscious mind, as when the mind rejects feeling angry at someone, believes the self to be at fault, and therefore attempts to repress the angry feeling.[44]

A personality disorder, on the other hand, results when the thoughts, feelings, and behaviors of the individual are "ego-syntonic" (ψ) and are regarded by the person as perfectly fine. An individual with a personality disorder does not feel anxiety or internal conflict. Rather, it is more likely that people who have close personal contact with such an individual will feel conflict and upset. The defenses employed in a personality disorder are primitive, such as denial, projection, and splitting. These defenses are considered "primitive" because they do not solve problems and do not lead to higher levels of functioning, serving only to protect the ego (ψ). The individual with a personality disorder does not possess the internal resources and strength to recognize their own personal problems and responsibly solve them.

Pathological narcissism is a personality disorder that has received much attention and consideration in Western psychological circles over the last ten years.[45] In the case of the narcissistic individual, the wound to the psychological self is so great that overwhelming shame and despair are avoided by rage, denial, and projection. Since internal psychological forces cannot be consciously acknowledged and contained, great "acting-out" occurs, in which impulsive behaviors emerge as internal pressures become too strong to manage. The narcissistic individual feels a heightened sense of importance and entitlement. The self is over-inflated, which is actually a cover-up and reversal of a deeper sense of failure and worthlessness. The narcissistic individual looks to the world to provide a mirror for his or her heightened self-image. Criticism to the narcissist is perceived as an attack, not as an opportunity to learn and mature psychologically from valued information. Furthermore, the narcissist may feel that their life has a special purpose or a sense of mission and any individual who obstructs their plans and programs will be perceived as disloyal and undermining of their work.

The importance of individual development at the level of the personality becomes quite obvious when we consider the result when someone dedicates his/her life to spiritual development, yet ignores deep-seated narcissistic aspects in their personality. As we have discussed, a highly evolved spiritual Being has great power and typically attracts a following of devotees who wish to learn and evolve spiritually. These followers will go to great measures to spend time with their *guru* or spiritual teacher. Spiritual communities become a natural outgrowth of this tendency as a way of providing support for aspiring devotees as well as helping to organize and promote the work.

Another common effect among those on the spiritual path is that once they have achieved some degree of spiritual awakening, they tend to want to become teachers. This motivation to teach may come from a genuine desire to help others evolve and transcend the delusion of physical/material reality that brings so much misery and pain to the world, but it can also result from a sense of personal inflation—and both factors can exist at the same time.

The great problem results when an individual rightfully achieves a degree of spiritual development with all the resulting powers or *siddhis* but has done little work on his or her own personality. That person's siddhic magnetism quickly draws a following of devotees who want to learn but who can then become caught in the disordered personality's web of control, confusion, and acting-out. The world does need spiritual teachers, and many such individuals do have valuable contributions to make to individuals and society. Their work is important and they may have a true mission in life to help the evolution of this planet. Unfortunately, once an individual has moved into the role of a spiritual teacher, he or she may be "alone at the top," since these individuals may have lost the mirror of their own teachers to help them perceive their shadow material.

Once they have progressed to the point where they feel "so great," an over-inflation of the ego (ι) results, wherein they will predictably give little or no credence to any constructive criticism that may be offered. Quite typically, their "greatness" is mirrored back by a group of loyal devotees in an inner circle who want to stay in good stead and avoid receiving the wrath of the teacher that might result from some personal disagreement or confrontation. The delusion becomes greater and greater, with no one to hold the teacher accountable.

It must be borne in mind that personal development appears to flourish best within the context of relationship. A *relationship* serves to provide an individual with a mirror and clarity to perceive the Self. Once the student has lost the teacher, then life must be the mirror, and the dilemma occurs at this point, because the narcissist has great defenses against life's reflection of personal shadow material. Sometimes it takes a great or highly public personal drama to break through the highly developed defenses that serve to protect the underlying vulnerability in the self.

The difficult combination of spiritual advancement and pathological narcissism results in a preoccupation with one's own position and a serious loss of empathy for others. For example, even though the leader of a community may eventually be confronted by community members with his behavior and accused of acting in inappropriate and irresponsible ways, it is rare that he will openly admit that he did something wrong and apologize to those individuals to whom he caused harm. In this type of case, it is more typical for the resident "guru" or teacher to write a series of letters and hold community meetings in which his feelings and needs are discussed. His personal problems may be cast in the light of a noble battle to overcome temptation, while he works to reframe the perspective so that he, the resident "guru," appears to be the victim of undeserved, unmerciful attacks. The pain, confusion, and betrayal of trust of the injured, devoted members are never discussed, because the narcissistic "guru" has such limited ability to empathize with the traumatized devotee.

In addition, such a "guru" has very limited understanding of the powerful transference relationships that develop between his followers and himself and takes little responsibility to manage those situations once they occur. Community members are typically viewed as instruments of God to help the work and are not related to as people, but rather as things that can be used to accomplish a goal and satisfy a spiritual need. Given the nature of spiritual communities and the vulnerability of individuals who leave their homes and families to join them, it is to be expected that individuals will tend to idealize the "guru" as they project their early family patterns onto the leader and hope to receive gratification for early, unfulfilled needs of love and acceptance. These types of individuals, who are very commonly found in spiritual communities, are quite vulnerable and susceptible to manipulation and abuse. They may tend to give away their material things and their sense of self in an attempt to gain love, spiritual blessings, and acceptance, and they often have deep unresolved issues around individuation. The narcissistic leader will eat them up and spit them out, after having digested what they can offer to support the goals of the community and to fulfill the leader's own personal needs. It is important to note, however, that in healthy spiritual communities, the process of surrendering and relinquishing material possessions can be a profound aspect of spiritual practice that leads to tremendous growth and awakening of soul consciousness.

It is rare that such a leader can be held accountable by his community. If it is attempted, the over-inflated "guru" will distort the facts, deny the truth, and change the rules of the community in order to justify his position and actions and maintain his standing. It is important to note that these teachers feel they are behaving correctly and actually feel justified in their actions, because of the existing over-inflation of self. Such defensive actions often are accepted by the community members, because they must maintain a level of denial in order to maintain their relationship with the teacher. The members' lack of individuation makes it impossible for them to think clearly and discern finely the full facts of a situation. The members often are unable to maintain "whole object relationships," in which the "good" and "bad" aspects of the teacher can be openly discussed and integrated. In the end, the integrity of the community becomes sacrificed through this process of splitting and denial.

In conclusion, the spiritual realities of expanded states of awareness, increased magnetism, profound states of love, and increased power all serve to create very sophisticated and complicated transference issues and boundary problems, both within the professional office and in spiritual communities. The challenge for the enlightened psychotherapist and the spiritual teacher is to become more conscious and more responsible in helping patients and students deal with these powerful forces. These potentially difficult circumstances also hold the potential for great learning and transformation when addressed with honestly, integrity, and skill.

The practice of Sacred Psychotherapy places the professional in the role of healer and spiritual guide. To this end, it is helpful to know some guided meditative techniques that can be integrated into psychotherapy. The next chapter provides some examples for meditation instruction.

Guided Meditations for Healing and Spiritual Development

THIS CHAPTER PROVIDES SOME SUGGESTIONS and direction for healing, both psychologically and spiritually. The reader is cautioned, however, not to become fixated on these various processes, as they are offered simply as examples, or as a place to begin. In practice, the best strategies or interventions for each situation come from intuition that arises in the moment. Experience will teach that your consciousness will tell you exactly what is needed in that moment, and that you must trust this subtle form of communication. When you use your intuition in interactive guided imagery, you will be led to or presented with the right symbols and images, exactly appropriate for the situation. I have used the following guided meditations with my patients and on my audio tapes. They were conceived and produced in a meditative state, and their impact results from the power of the soul that is communicated through the voice vibration. The reader could either purchase the meditation tape or record the dialogue in your own voice and use it as a guide to deepen your inner experience.

Preparation

The first suggestion is for the psychotherapist and consists of a process that will help the therapist deepen his or her connection to the patient and enhance the therapist's intuitive ability to "know" what the patient needs. If you are in therapy, you might want to consider how consciously your therapist attempts to quiet down and tune in to you. There are several ways to come into this state, but here is one approach:

> *Allow yourself to quiet down at the beginning of the session. Do not be concerned about making polite talk and social contact. You have only fifty minutes in which to help transform this person's life, and every precious minute holds the possibility for a life-changing experience. Hold this possibility firmly and brightly in your consciousness. Each moment is sacred. Open to the eternity that exists in the present. Breathe and relax and let go of time and space. All possibilities exist right now. Let go of any compulsion to "do" anything. Remember that God is working through you. Let God tell you what to do. Listen with your heart. Look with your inner vision. Feel with your kinesthetic body and absorb the energy that is in the room, the energy of your patient. Set the intention that you will receive information regarding the most essential issue concerning your patient. Listen past anything he or she might be saying. Trust your intuitive knowing. Feel the sensations of texture and density in your subtle energy body. Center yourself and let go of any identification with your body, mind, feelings. Be still, let go, open to the moment, and listen to your inner experience—then consider the possibility that what you sense is your patient. Allow your consciousness to be a screen, onto which your patient projects his or her issues for you to perceive.*

Inspiration for Meditation: Good Basic Instruction for Meditation

This next suggestion consists of good, basic instruction for entering a meditative state. The text is taken from the audio tape *Inspiration for Meditation*.

Close your eyes, take a deep breath, exhale, and relax. Open your heart to receive Divine blessings of Love, Peace, and Joy. Remember to keep your spine relaxed and straight. Whether sitting on a chair or on the floor, keep your shoulders back, and as your eyes close, let your gaze go up to the point between your eyebrows. Continue this gaze without straining your eyes, easily looking upward to the spiritual center between your eyebrows. Now begin breathing evenly to the count of ten. Draw in your breath, hold it for the count of ten and then exhale. Continue breathing evenly to the count of ten. Allow yourself to become even more quiet. Focus on your breath, breathing through your nostrils, always breathing through your nostrils, and as your breath just naturally begins to come in, simply watch your breath . . . just as though you are watching somebody else breathe, allowing your body to breathe, however it wants to. As you watch your breath, you might add a mantra *to your breathing, mentally saying on the in-breath, "I am" and on the out-breath, "Peace" or "Love." So, as your breath comes in, mentally say, "I am," and as the breath goes out, "Peace" or "Love."*

However your breath wants to go, just allow it to go. Remember that there is no time, there is no space. You are pure consciousness, pure light. Perhaps, just mentally affirm, "I am Love," "I am Light," "I am Joy."

As you continue to follow your breath, you may find there is a space between your in-breath and your out-breath. In this space, you may find that you do not need to inhale immediately. If so, simply allow yourself to melt and relax into this breathless state, enjoying the peace and the calm that comes when your body and mind becomes so quiet. Remember, you are not this body; you are not your thoughts; you are pure consciousness.

Now, as your breath comes in, place your awareness right at the base of your spine, and focus your awareness in your first chakra or center of energy, breathing in and out through that center. This is the center for survival. It is our grounding to the earth. As you breathe into the first chakra, feel it open. All your awareness is focused right at the base of your spine.

Now, as your breath comes in, imagine a current of energy coming up your spine to a point just below your navel. This is your second chakra, the center for life force energy, sexuality, and creativity. So, just keep your awareness focused at this point, breathing in and out. . . . As you breathe, feel that center open.

And now, as your breath comes in, follow that current of energy up your spine, right into your solar plexus, your third chakra, the center of personal power. Focus your awareness right in your solar plexus, breathing in and out, opening that center, feeling the energy, drawing it up your spine.

Now, as your breath comes in, draw that current of energy up into your heart, into the very center of your chest, into your heart chakra, the center for unconditional love . . . and continue breathing in and out, through that center, as your heart opens to Love for all humanity.

And now, as your breath comes in again, draw the current of energy upward through the very center of your spine, into your throat, the center for expression and expansion. Breathe in and out through your throat.

Now, as your breath comes in, draw the energy up to the point between your eyebrows, to your spiritual eye . . . simply breathing in and out, with all your awareness focused right at that center, perhaps seeing light and reaffirming "I am Love," "I am Light," "I am Peace," "I am Joy." Always draw your awareness back to your breath, staying focused on your spiritual eye. If your mind should wander off, just come back to your breath, staying focused at that point between your eyebrows.

And now, when your breath comes in, imagine that there is a current of energy that comes from the very base of your spine, all the way up into your spiritual eye, and then, as your breath goes out, the current of energy descends right down the very center of your spine, which allows you to be drawn deeper and deeper within your spine.

As you go deeper and deeper into meditation, you will see an inner light, perhaps it will be white, maybe gold. When this light comes, just melt into this light, and allow this light to penetrate every aspect of your being, every cell, every place in your awareness. Just let yourself melt into this light. As this light continues to flow within you, feel yourself expand. As your heart opens, feel a deep sense of Love and Joy, deeper than you have ever felt before, and let this love fill every aspect of your being. Allow this Love to flow to all those you know, surrounding them all with this Light, feeling this Love flow to everyone you know— friends, loved ones, even those with whom you may have difficulties. See them all surrounded in this healing Light, this Divine Love.

And now, just feel yourself melt into this Light, into this presence. If you have any concern, just place it in this Light. Allow its presence to come to you, to heal your concerns, to quiet your mind, and to touch

your soul, comforting you, feeling a deep sense of Peace and Love. Let
yourself be transformed by this Light. You are filled with Wisdom, you
are filled with Love, you are filled with Peace and Light. As you focus on
this presence, attune your will into the Divine Will, asking for that
sacred presence to guide and direct your life, with every aspect of your
life being guided by this Divine Will. May you always be blessed and
guided on your way. May you always find ever greater Peace, ever
greater Love, and ever greater Joy.

Guided Meditation for Physical and Emotional Healing

This next meditation is taken from the audio tape, *Healing in the*
Light. The focus here is upon the healing power of inner Light and the
ability of consciousness to transmute unbalanced physical and emotional energy. The goal in this experience is to learn to perceive all
inner states as vibration and energy, and to then re-create a sense of
harmony and well-being in all aspects of the mind, body, and soul.
The result is a powerful skill in preventive healing as one develops the
ability to draw upon the subtle healing forces that are encoded in our
Divine nature.

As a way to begin, help your client become relaxed, using either
hypnosis or simple muscle relaxation techniques. Once the client is
relaxed, you might want to explain what you are going to do. The
following may give you some idea of what to say.

Now I am going to show you how you can use your consciousness to
effect changes in your physical body and how you can use imagery and
imagination to discover the link between your emotions and your
physical health. A relationship exists between mind, body, and spirit.
You can learn techniques to help you maintain your health and your
sense of well-being. There is so much light and so much energy available
to you on the subtle planes, and you can learn to draw that light and
energy into your physical body and into your emotions.

It is often said that disease is a state of imbalance. When you are in
perfect harmony, you can be very healthy. Your subtle energy body
actually contains a blueprint for your health and perfection. You can

learn to draw on that blueprint, to bring that vibration of health into your body, by entering a deep state of meditation. It will bring you a light and an energy, as it comes into your body, that sustains life itself. It feeds your cells and keeps you healthy.

Everything you are learning about meditation and the true essence of your consciousness can be used in a very practical way to keep you strong and healthy. When you are feeling well, this is a perfect time to meditate and draw life force energy into your cellular structure, to recharge your immune system, feed your cells, and keep strong and healthy.

Now continue with some concentration-deepening techniques:

Focus on your breath and place your awareness at the point between your eyebrows. Just watch your breath as it comes in and out, staying concentrated on your breath. As your breath comes in, and as the breath goes out, remember that you are not your body, you are not your mind, you are not your emotions. You are pure consciousness, consciousness that is floating on your breath. You are pure awareness. The breath comes in, and the breath goes out. Pure consciousness, pure awareness. Whatever may be happening in your physical body, or your emotions, is not who you really are.

Remember, you are pure consciousness; you are Light. Be aware of what is happening in your body and perhaps your emotions. Don't get lost into identifying with those experiences. Breathe into those aspects of your body, and let yourself imagine that there is a golden light above you, perhaps like the sun. Imagine that there are rays of light that come down from the sun. Slowly they come down, entering through the crown of your head, filtering down into your entire body. It may be golden light; it may be white light. Whatever it is, it's fine. Allow that Light to come down. Feel it go into every cell of your body, recharging every cell with health and vitality. This Light has a perfect sense of balance that heals every aspect of your Being. As you merge and melt into this Light, you are one with this Light, everything is at ease, there is nothing to do—only to open and receive this Light. It sustains your body, touches your heart and your soul. There is perfection in this Light, and every cell of your body is drawn into that perfection. Your cells begin to vibrate in harmony with this Peace and this Light. All tension melts and leaves your body as you continue to breathe into this Light, into this Peace, and your body opens and releases all tension as you flow into this Light, this healing Light.

There is such a sense of being at ease. It is like having a long, long rest, where you just let go. Don't hold on. Just breathe into the Light and into the Peace, and let it flow through your body, through every cell. The greatest gift you can give to your own health is to reduce your level of stress. Whatever stress you pick up in your life may be held in your body, and it creates the potential for disharmony. So just melt and let it all go. Every breath releases more and more tension, as you are drawn into a deeper state of Peace. Feel the perfection in every cell of your body.

And now, notice if there is any particular place, a particular organ or certain parts of your body, that you need to speak with. You may be having some kind of difficulty, somewhere in your body. Allow yourself to put your attention on any particular place that you want to heal, again being the observer. Pay attention to the sensation, and allow yourself to have an internal dialogue with your body. Let it speak to you through your imagination. Let it have a voice, whether it is an organ, a cell, whatever it may be. Find out about it. Perhaps there are memories stored in your body. Perhaps a part of your body has a particular emotion, a particular need, or something that it is trying to communicate to you symbolically. Just open to receive that information. Just allow yourself to observe. Allow the wisdom of your body to speak to you. Pay attention to what your body wants to tell you. Perhaps there is a message of how you need to change your life, or something is unfinished and must be attended to. Or perhaps there are emotions that have not been processed. Whatever it may be, just make note of it.

If there is some situation you want to improve in your body, I would like you to imagine some kind of image, some symbolic image to represent that situation in your body. It doesn't matter what it is. And now imagine whatever needs to happen to bring your body back to its perfect state of health. Allow your body to return to your state of perfection, and as you breathe, see that perfection coming back into your body. It is all Energy. It is all Light. Remember you are Energy, you are Light, you are Pure Consciousness. As you continue to breathe, just imagine any physical problem dissolving out of your body as you return *to a perfect state of health. You keep coming back to a perfect state of health. See and feel yourself in that perfect state of health. Visualize yourself as being vibrant, alive, healthy, and strong. Imagine yourself going through the course of your day with ever greater vitality, with an ever-deeper sense of Peace.*

An ancient memory of perfection is encoded within you. Let your body remember and allow that sense of perfection to emerge, expanding your awareness, filling you with Love.

At this point you can help your patient gently and gradually return to his or her normal state of waking consciousness.

Guided Meditation for Exploring One's Life Purpose

This meditation is designed to use the imagination and intuition to access the soul's knowledge about its unique purpose in life. The script is taken from the audio tape *Soul Journey*. Every life has purpose, and every soul has its own unique direction and meaning for each lifetime. When an individual is able to discover this purpose, he or she will find greater meaning and direction in life. Knowing this purpose helps an individual keep on track and often provides a deep sense of fulfillment.

Once again, help your patient relax through any method with which you feel comfortable. Once the patient has closed his or her eyes and appears comfortable, initiate the following suggestions:

Now, as a way to help you become even more relaxed, just take a deep breath, hold it for a moment, and then let it go. As you breathe out, just breathe away any tension that you might feel in your body, just allowing yourself to relax and go as deep as you want to go . . . feeling peaceful, calm, and safe. If for any reason during this guided experience there is some external emergency where you would have to come out to attend to, you will do so automatically. You will be perfectly safe, and you will return to your normal waking state. So, just continue to breathe and let every breath take you into deeper and deeper relaxation, focusing on the muscles in your face, relaxing your eyes, your mouth, the throat—

and feeling that sense of relaxation flow all the way down your shoulders, down your arms, your hands, and your fingers. Every breath, every beat of your heart helps you go deeper and deeper as you relax. Just let go. More and more relaxed . . . going deeper and deeper within, to a place that feels safe and secure, peaceful and calm . . . letting that sensation flow all down your back, with all the muscles letting go, just melting . . . feeling more peaceful than you have ever felt before, more and more relaxed. Now let that relaxing sensation go all the way down into your abdomen, into your pelvis, through your buttocks, down your legs, all the way down into your feet into your toes . . . ever more deeply and deeply relaxed, as deep as you want to go . . . and deeper still, feeling so wonderful, so safe, more and more relaxed with every breath.

Now imagine that you are standing at the top of a staircase that has ten steps. It is fully carpeted. It has a nice railing on either side, and there is a hallway at the bottom. Now gently step from the tenth to the ninth step, allowing yourself to go deeper still . . . deeper within . . . to a place that feels like the core of your very being. Here it is safe and secure . . . peaceful and calm . . . and now step down to the eighth step, just slowly, step-by-step, going down to the seventh . . . and, counting down the steps . . . six . . . five . . . four . . . deeper and deeper, more and more relaxed, just being drawn within. . . . And now, as your inner world opens to greater clarity, all impressions become clearer and clearer . . . all sensations, sounds, and colors—all the way down to the fifth step, step-by-step . . . the fourth step . . . deeper and deeper still . . . to the third . . . and to the second . . . and finally all the way down to the bottom.

Now let yourself step into the hallway, and as you walk down that hallway, you notice that at the end there is a spiral staircase that goes up, up, and up into the Heavens . . . and you find yourself being drawn to that staircase, and the closer you get to it, the greater the sense of Peace that descends throughout your entire Being.

Now let yourself step onto the staircase and begin to ascend. Each step takes you higher and higher, up and up . . . into another realm, a realm of Spirit, a realm of Light, a realm of intuitive Knowing. It is a realm of Love, Serenity, Compassion, and Understanding. It is a realm of great Wisdom, where all things are known—past, present, and future. . . . There are Beings who live in this realm whose sole purpose is to help you understand yourself and your life. . . .

Continue to go up and up, step-by-step being drawn higher and higher. Each step you take, the vibration becomes lighter and lighter. It becomes effortless, as you are drawn up the spiral staircase... just gently going around and up... being drawn up and up... into this wonderful, celestial realm... of Peace and Love. The Bliss that is here is so gentle that it touches your very soul... and you finally make it to the top... and as you pass through white, wonderful, billowing clouds, you come out, stepping onto the clouds, which provide a foundation upon which you may walk.

And now, as you walk, you will see a golden palace with large doors. Allow yourself to walk right to that palace. Inside this palace you will find an ancient and wise Being, who is there only to help you, to guide you, to answer your questions, and to share ancient Wisdom and Divine Knowledge. You can ask anything you want, and you will receive answers to all your questions. Perhaps your soul's purpose will be revealed. If it does not happen this time, do not worry, for you can return over and over again... and either through this experience or through a dream. As you continue to ask, someday the answer will come!

So now, let go of all expectations and open to the possibilities that await you here and now. The doors begin to open, opening inward and allowing you to enter. As you walk inside, you are greeted by a wise and ancient Being. You will have all the time you need to ask any question you want. This ancient Being is filled with unconditional Love. There is total Love and Compassion in this sacred place. There is more Love here than you have ever known before. So now, allow yourself to be guided by this teacher and spend some time in sacred communion. You will have all the time you need. I will return in a little while. (Allow five to ten minutes of silence.)

And soon it will be time to return... so, allow yourself to finish your conversation... knowing that you can always come back to this sacred place. Once the inner doorways have been opened, you may return as often as you need. For now, let yourself say good-bye and give thanks for all the blessings you may have received.... So, gently, slowly, let yourself walk back out through those doors, back to the spiral staircase along the path, gliding along the clouds... and, when you return, you will remember whatever you want to remember, bringing with you the *sense of peace and love that you felt on this journey. As you finally come to the spiral staircase, allow yourself to descend, just gliding down, step-by-step, all the way to the bottom, such an easy, effortless journey.*

Now you find yourself back in the hallway, and now coming back to the ten stairs and stepping up, one at a time, all the way back to the top. Now come back to normal consensual reality, oriented in time and place. Move your body a little bit, let yourself reconnect with your body, moving your arms and your hands, legs and feet, feeling connected with yourself, and perhaps feeling deeper and expanded by this experience.

These meditative scripts are offered as suggestions. I hope they stimulate your imagination. I encourage you to be creative in developing your own meditative experiences. The thoughts and images that spontaneously flow from your consciousness are often the best for the moment.

The work we do in each moment, when we are conscious, holds unforeseen potential. We cannot separate the individual from the collective, nor the microcosm from the macrocosm. This work is sacred because it not only touches the soul of those individuals with whom we consult, but it also holds the potential to transform society as well. The final chapter speaks to this greater possibility.

16

Conclusion:
The Individual Therapist's
Contribution

THE AIM OF THIS BOOK has been to present sufficient information to open your mind and heart to the possibility that we have a much greater opportunity in this life than conventional Western psychological methods and thought may provide. We are more than our physical bodies, more than our personalities, more than the thoughts that pass through our consciousness. There is something enduring in our nature that transcends all time and space—our Soul. When we identify with our Divinity, we can open to the possibility for our consciousness to expand far beyond the limited conceptions of Western psychological thought. In truth, our human possibilities for love, healing, and creative manifestation are potentially unlimited.

Identifying with our Divinity does not mean the end of personal challenges and psychological struggles. It simply means the beginning of a realization that God directs all of creation and that we are able to access Divine Grace to help and guide us. We can realize our soul nature and consciously use life's difficulties to deepen our relationship with God as we turn to the Divine for help in every aspect of our life.

The delusion that we are limited to the physical/material plane is very strong and is embraced by many; however, a smaller but steadily growing number of individuals, both in the professional health care community and the lay public, embrace the perspective that our earthly life is embedded in a spiritual context. Because the collective delusion is so strong, the process of spiritual awakening requires a tremendous degree of presence in order to stay conscious of our true spiritual nature and not be drugged by the collective amnesia that discounts and denies Spirit. Nonetheless, each moment provides us with the opportunity to love, serve, and surrender, and to allow God's Grace to unfold and flow through us ever more deeply. Any miraculous ability to heal that we may seem to manifest comes only from this Divine source.

Despite living in difficult times, the opportunity for change is great, and individual transformation leads, one person at a time, to planetary transformation. In the 1980s, after three years of international meetings, events, and travel as director of Projects for Planetary Peace, I developed an ever-greater appreciation for the one-on-one process of personal transformation. I began to feel that bringing individuals together was useful but insufficient. After all, each of us brings to each interaction our strengths as well as our weaknesses. In fact, our difficulties and shadow material actually became more magnified with the intensity of the global work. Ultimately, each of us had to return to the deep, inner work of personal transformation to become more open, more centered, and less attached, in order to continue the collective international work.

Through this, I developed great appreciation for the individual psychological work that occurs in private offices all across the country. We all play an important part in the evolution of humankind. I believe that psychotherapists have an important contribution, because we are so intimately involved in shaping the lives of children, adolescents, adults, and families. As each one of us embraces the

Light and opens to the beauty and wonder of the Divine, we help to ignite this evolutionary process.

Much of our population lives in a sea of alienation and utter hopelessness about the future. The economics of our country continue to change as the middle-class becomes smaller, and the separation between the wealthy and poor becomes greater. The basic human values of honesty, integrity, respect, and consideration often have gone by the wayside in favor of material gain and violence.

Despite these significant problems in America and throughout the world, we continue to move in a positive direction. The consciousness of the planet is shifting. We can see the influence in health care, where people are seeking complementary approaches that honor the spirit along with the mind and body. As individuals begin to discover that no separation exists between their mind, body, and soul, then it is easier to realize that, in essence, there is no separation between people. The perception of the Truth of the soul unites us and creates a common bond that transcends cultures and national boundaries. I have been to many international gatherings that have been centered in Spirit, where people felt close, open, loving, accepting, and cooperative. There is a better way to live and resolve conflicts than through violence, but we must shift our perception of reality in order to find it.

This message is not new. The momentum for such a shift is increasing, and this book may be a part of that momentum. The theory about the hundredth monkey, who creates the impetus for a collective shift in consciousness, is described in *The Hundredth Monkey* by Ken Keyes:

> The Japanese monkey, *Macaca justcata*, has been observed in the wild for a period of over thirty years. In 1952, on the island of Koshima, scientists were providing monkeys with sweet potatoes dropped in the sand. The monkeys liked the taste of the raw sweet potatoes, but they found the dirt unpleasant.
>
> An 18-month-old female named Imo found she could solve the problem by washing the potatoes in a nearby stream. She taught this

trick to her mother. Her playmates also learned this new way, and they taught their mothers too.

This cultural innovation was gradually picked up by various monkeys before the eyes of the scientists. Between 1952 and 1958, all the young monkeys learned to wash sandy sweet potatoes to make them more palatable. Only the adults who imitated their children learned this social improvement. Other adults kept eating dirty sweet potatoes.

Then something startling took place. In the autumn of 1958, a certain number of Koshima monkeys were washing sweet potatoes—the exact number is not known. Let us suppose that when the sun rose one morning, there were 99 monkeys on Koshima Island who had learned to wash their sweet potatoes. Let's further suppose that later that morning, the hundredth monkey learned to wash potatoes.

THEN IT HAPPENED!

By that evening, almost everyone in the tribe was washing sweet potatoes before eating them. The added energy of the hundredth monkey somehow created an ideological breakthrough!

But notice. The most surprising thing observed by these scientists was that the habit of washing sweet potatoes then spontaneously jumped over the sea. Colonies of monkeys on other islands and the mainland troop of monkeys at Takasakiyama began washing their sweet potatoes![46]

Each one of us may be that hundredth monkey. Every thought we put into the ether, every loving action and deed, may create that critical mass to bring us all to the next level. Every action has in it the potential to transform the planet, when viewed from this collective reality. It is easy to feel helpless in a political reality where power seems to be held by only a few. When we shift our reality to the Truth of spirit and the oneness of our inner connections, all power is returned. There is nothing more powerful than the power of our Love. Gandhi brought a powerful nation to its knees through his simple actions and his love. The problems of violence, disease, and social alienation will dramatically shift in perspective, as each one of us becomes more spiritually conscious and heart-centered.

Our task, if we are to facilitate this planetary evolution, is to shift our own consciousness. We are God's instruments. Once we make the shift and realize that our true nature is lodged in our spirituality, we can no longer be trapped in the delusion of duality and the limitations of the physical/material plane. We can, as Christ said, "Be in the world, but not of the world."

In closing, I would like to end with a few simple reminders that are helpful in sustaining a spiritual life. These principles have been used to transform consciousness and obtain spiritual realization for centuries. You can change your life with these simple, yet powerful techniques, and your ability to help others will exponentially expand to the degree of your spiritual awareness.

1. **Listen from the depth of your soul.** Your heart is a valuable instrument for gaining wisdom. There is a quiet but powerful voice within you that resides in your heart. Learn to access this intuitive intelligence that originates from the subtle, discriminative capacity of your soul.

2. **Trust your intuition.** Your deeper Self has a tremendous sensitivity to perceive the world around you.

3. **Let the Divine help you.** Do not feel that you have to solve all your problems by yourself. Develop a collaborative relationship with God.

4. **Live in the moment.** Bring your full attention into the present. Your consciousness will be magnified when attuned with your soul. Hold the intention that your presence, in each moment, creates an energetic environment in which miracles can happen.

5. **Invoke the power of prayer.** Invoke the presence of unity and perfection in your consciousness. You are interconnected with the universe; there is no separation. Your thoughts and prayers have unseen power. Pray for others and pray for the world.

6. **Always look for the unseen spiritual opportunity for awakening.** Even the most difficult circumstances can provide an opportunity for profound deepening and spiritual development.

7. **Attune your will with the Divine.** You will be amazed by the results.

Samadhi

T HIS POEM WAS WRITTEN BY PARAMAHANSA YOGANANDA. In it, he attempts to give the reader a glimpse of the state known as *samadhi*. Far beyond the body and mind, consciousness flows to Light itself. Bliss and Wonder, Joy and Love—all components melt into one.

Vanished the veils of light and shade,
Lifted every vapor of sorrow,
Sailed away all dawns of fleeting joy,
Gone the dim sensory mirage.
Love, hate, health, disease, life, death:
Perished these false shadows on the screen of duality.
The storm of *maya* stilled
By magic wand of intuition deep.
Present, past, future, no more for me,
But ever-present, all-flowing I, I, everywhere.
Planets, stars, stardust, earth.
Volcanic bursts of doomsday cataclysms,
Creation's molding furnace,
Glaciers of silent X-rays, burning electron floods,
Thoughts of all men, past, present, to come,
Every blade of grass, myself, mankind,

Each particle of universal dust,
Anger, greed, good, bad, salvation, lust,
I swallowed, transmuted all
Into a vast ocean of blood of my own one Being.
Smoldering joy, oft-puffed by meditation
Blinding my tearful eyes,
Burst into immortal flames of bliss,
Consumed my tears, my frame, my all.
Thou art I, I am Thou,
Knowing, Knower, Known, as One!
Tranquilled, unbroken thrill, eternally living, ever-new peace.
Enjoyable beyond imagination of expectancy, *samadhi* bliss!
Not an unconscious state
Or mental chloroform without willful return,
Samadhi but extends my conscious realm
Beyond limits of the mortal frame
To farthest boundary of eternity
Where I, the Cosmic Sea,
Watch the little ego floating in Me.
Mobile murmurs of atoms are heard,
The dark earth, mountains, vales, lo! molten liquid!
Flowing seas change into vapors of nebulae!
Aum blows upon vapors, opening wondrously their veils,
Oceans stand revealed, shining electrons,
Till, at the last sound of the cosmic drum,
Vanish the grosser lights into eternal rays
Of all-pervading bliss.
From joy I came, for joy I live, in sacred joy I melt.
Ocean of mind, I drink all creation's waves.
Four veils of solid, liquid, vapor, light,
Lift aright.
I, in everything, enter the Great Myself.
Gone forever: fitful, flickering shadows of mortal memory;
Spotless is my mental sky—below, ahead, and high above;
Eternity and I, one united ray.
A tiny bubble of laughter, I
Have become the Sea of Mirth Itself.[47]

Glossary

ahamkara. Ego, the aspect of self that experiences a separation from God.

Akashic records. The vibratory realm in the subtle ethers in which all of God's thoughts, past, present, and future are written.

asana. A physical posture in the system of Hatha yoga.

ashram. A spiritual, monastic center.

astral body. The subtle energy body composed of light or *lifetrons.* It is one of three bodies that encase the soul: physical, astral, causal.

astral plane. The subtle plane of existence just beyound the physical realms. This plane consists of light and energy and holds the blueprint for the physical/material world.

Aum. The sound of God that permeates creation. In deep meditation one can be baptized as one becomes immersed in the cosmic sound; also considered the sound emanating from the Holy Ghost.

bhajans. Devotional songs to God.

buddhi. The discriminative aspect of the intellect that is able to perceive Truth.

causal body. The subtle energy body that is composed of pure thought and encases the soul.

causal plane. The subtle plane of existence that is beyond the astral. Existence on this realm is composed of pure thought.

chakra. The *chakras* are spinning vortices of conscious or subtle energy. Each *chakra* corresponds to various physical glands or organs and is imbued with different states of awareness.

chitta. The spiritualized aspect that has condensed from God's consciousness and is centered in the Heart. *Chitta* contains the power of feeling and the ability of the soul to experience its existence. The ego evolves out of *chitta* when the consciousness is distorted by delusion.

darshan. Literally means receiving the blessing of having the vision of or seeing the Divine, but is also often used to refer to being in the presence of the Divine.

dharma. Duty or spiritual obligation.

gunas. Three qualities inherent in Cosmic Nature: *sattva*, the spiritual, uplifting, positive attribute; *tamas*, the negative attribute towards evil and darkness; and *rajas*, the neutral, activating attribute.

guru. Dispeller of darkness. The *guru* brings light and is sent by God to help the disciple obtain Divine realization.

hatha yoga. One aspect of Patanjali's system of Asthanga Yoga, the eightfold path. *Hatha yoga* addresses the body with a system of physical postures, *asanas,* which prepare the student for meditation without distraction from the physical body.

ida. One of the subtle currents along the astral spine. It is one of two astral *nadis*, both auxiliary to the *sushumna*, which constitute the primary channels of the astral sympathetic nervous system. The *ida* corresponds with the in-breath and the current runs up the left side of the spine.

jnanendriyas. The five organs of sense: smell, taste, sight, touch, and hearing.

karma. The cosmic law of cause and effect. Past actions in previous lifetimes as well as this life create consequences that are experienced in our present situations. Karma continues from lifetime to lifetime until one completes the cycle or spiritually neutralizes the energy.

karmendriyas. The five organs of action: excretion, generation, feet, hands, and speech.

kriya yoga. An ancient, advanced *pranayama* technique handed down from Krishna to Mahavatar Babiji of the Self-Realization Fellowship. The devoted practice of this technique leads to God-realization.

kundalini. The *kundalini*, according to yogic philosophy, is a dormant energy located at the base of the spine. When this force is activated, either as the result of yogic practice or as a spontaneous movement, a current of energy proceeds up the astral spine and opens the corresponding *chakras* along its path. The higher centers of the spine and brain are typically activated when this energy is drawn up from the base of the spine, often resulting in the experience of unconditional Love, deeper intuitive perceptions, and superconscious transcendental Bliss.

mahabhutas. Five subtle elements that appear as gross matter in solid, liquid, fiery, gaseous, and etheric form.

Mahavatar Babaji. Known as the "deathless Master" because he always keeps the form of a twenty-five-year-old young man, Babaji is one of the fully enlightened Masters of the Self-Realization Fellowship. He made the previously lost technique of *kriya yoga* once again accessible to humankind.

manas. The aspect of Divine consciousness condensed from *chitta* that becomes the mind and is identified with the senses.

mantra. Repetition of sacred sounds or the name of God.

maya. The repulsive force of God that results in the delusion that physical/material reality is the only true existence. Also known as Satan.

muni. A yogi who is able to withdraw his consciousness from external sense objects and from the mental and emotional attractions towards them.

nadis. The astral sympathetic nervous system that controls the physical sympathetic nervous system.

Om. See AUM.

panchatattvas. These five electricities produced from *chitta* are the cause of all other creations.

pingala. One of the subtle currents along the astral spine. It is one of two astral *nadis,* which are auxiliary to the *sushumna* and constitute the primary channels of the astral sympathetic nervous system. The *pingala* corresponds with the out-breath and the current runs down the right side of the spine.

prakriti. That aspect of God as Cosmic Nature that creates the cosmic dream-universe.

prana. Yogic philosophy describes the subtle life force energy that sustains living organisms as *prana.* The universal *prana* is the pure Nature (*prakiti*) that permeates and sustains the universe.

pranayama. Prana is "life force energy," *yama* is "control." *Pranayama* is the control of the life force energy through specific yogic breathing techniques.

purusha. Conscious Being, conscious Soul, essential Self.

raja yoga. The "royal" or highest path to God-realization. It includes all as aspects of yoga practice with an emphasis on meditation.

sadhu. A seeker of God who has renounced wordly life.

samadhi. The last step in Patanjali's system of yoga. *Samadhi* is obtained when the life force energy has been withdrawn from the outer senses, and the meditator then becomes one with the object of meditation, God.

samskaras: Past tendencies of thought and action that have been ingrained in our consciousness. These tendencies become habit patterns that carry over from one lifetime to another.

satsanga. Fellowship with Truth.

shakti. Powerful energy force that emanates from the soul and is directed by the will.

siddhis. Yogic powers obtained along the course of spiritual development.

sushumna. The main astral spine of subtle energy that controls the gross function of the astral life force energy, which creates and sustains the physical body. The two other astral currents related to the *sushumna* are the *ida* and *pingala.*

vrittis: The waves of thought and emotion that constantly arise in one's consciousness. Literal translation is "whirlpool."

yogini: A female student of yoga.

Bibliography

Bion, W., *Introduction to the Work of Bion*. New York: Jason Aronson, Inc., 1977.

Castaneda, C., *Teachings of Don Juan: A Yaqui Way of Knowledge*. New York: Simon and Schuster, 1968.

Fairbairn, W.R.D., *Psychoanalytic Studies of the Personality*. London: Routledge & Kegan Paul, Ltd., 1972.

Frawley, D., *Ayurvedic Healing: A Comprehensive Guide*. Salt Lake City: Passage Press, 1989.

Greenson, R., *The Technique and Practice of Psychoanalysis*. New York: International Universities Press, Inc., 1967.

Guntrip, H. *Schizoid Phenomena, Object Relations and the Self.* New York: International Universities Press, Inc., 1969.

Iyengar, B.K.S., *Light on Yoga*. New York: Schocken Books, 1966.

Kernberg, O., *Borderline Conditions and Pathological Narcissism*. New York: Jason Aronson, Inc., 1975.

Keyes, K. Jr., *The Hundredth Monkey*. Coos Bay, OR: Vision Books, 1982.

Lawrence, Brother, *The Practice of the Presence of God*. J.J. Delaney (transl.). New York: Doubleday, 1977.

Masterson, J., *The Narcissistic and Borderline Disorders: An Integrated Developmental Approach*. New York: Brunner/Mazel, 1981.

Masterson, J. *The Search for the Real Self: Unmasking the Personality Disorders of Our Age*. New York: The Free Press, 1988.

Sandweiss, S.H., *Sai Baba, the Holy Man . . . and the Psychiatrist*. San Diego, CA: Birth Day Pub., 1975.

Satchidananda, Yogiraj Sri Swami. *Integral Yoga Hatha*. San Francisco: Holt, Rinehart and Winston, 1970.

Segal, H., *Introduction to the Work of Melanie Klein.* London: The Hogarth Press, 1973.

Shapiro, D., *Neurotic Styles.* New York: Basic Books, Inc., 1965.

Tompkins, P., *Secret Life of Plants.* New York: Harper & Row, 1973.

Walsh, R. & Vaughan, F. (Eds.), *Paths Beyond Ego.* New York: G.P. Putman's Sons, 1993.

Watson, L., *Lifetide.* New York: Bantam Books, 1980.

Winnicott, D.W., *Playing & Reality.* New York: Basic Books, Inc., 1971.

Wolf, F. A., *Taking the Quantum Leap: The New Physics for Nonscientists.* San Francisco: Harper & Row, 1981.

Wolf, F.A., *The Body Quantum: The New Physics of Body, Mind, and Health.* New York: Macmillan, 1986.

Yogananda, Paramahansa, *The Autobiography of a Yogi.* Los Angeles: Self-Realization Fellowship, 1971.

Yogananda, Paramahansa, *God Talks with Arjuna: The Bhagavad Gita, Royal Science of God-Realization.* Los Angeles: Self-Realization Fellowship, 1995.

Yogananda, Paramahansa, *Whispers from Eternity.* Los Angeles: Self-Realization Fellowship, 1975.

Yukteswar, Sri, *The Holy Science.* Los Angeles: Self-Realization Fellowship, 1977.

Suggested Reading

THE BIBLIOGRAPHY LISTED REFERENCES that were directly quoted or mentioned in the text of this book. The list is relatively small compared to the vast volumes that have been written on this and related topics. I believe that it is important to clarify that, for several years following my initial spiritual awakening in Hawaii, I spent hours each day in meditation receiving information regarding the nature of consciousness and the deeper spiritual teachings. I found that I learned more from direct inner experience than by reading about others' thoughts, theories, or personal experiences. I recommend to the reader that he or she try to find a balance between reading and meditation and learn to achieve the direct inner knowing for that which you wish to learn. In spite of my own particular inclination for direct inner knowing, many find it extremely useful to explore the available literature. The following books are recommended for further study.

Chopra, D., *Quantum Healing: Exploring the Frontiers of Mind/Body Medicine.* New York: Bantam Books, 1989.

Chopra, D., *Perfect Health: The Complete Mind/Body Guide.* New York: Harmony Books, 1991.

Chopra, D., *Unconditional Life: Mastering the Forces That Shape Personal Reality.* New York : Bantam Books, 1991.

Chopra, D., *Return of the Rishi: A Doctor's Story of Spiritual Transformation and Ayurvedic Healing.* Boston: Houghton Mifflin, 1991.

Chopra, D., *Creating Health: How to Wake Up the Body's Intelligence.* Boston: Houghton Mifflin, 1991.

Chopra, D., *Ageless Body, Timeless Mind: The Quantum Alternative to Growing Old.* New York: Harmony Books, 1993.

Chopra, D., *Creating Affluence: Wealth Consciousness in the Field of All Possibilities.* San Rafael, CA: New World Library, 1993.

Chopra, D., *Perfect Weight: The Complete Mind-Body Program for Achieving and Maintaining Your Ideal Weight.* New York: Harmony Books, 1994.

Chopra, D., *Restful Sleep: The Complete Mind-Body Program for Overcoming Insomnia.* New York: Harmony Books, 1994.

Chopra, D., *Journey into Healing: Awakening the Wisdom Within You.* New York: Harmony Books, 1994.

Chopra, D., *The Seven Spiritual Laws of Success: A Practical Guide to the Fulfillment of Your Dreams.* San Rafael, CA: Amber-Allen Publishing, 1994.

Chopra, D., *The A-to-Z Steps to a Richer Life.* New York: Barnes & Noble, 1994.

Chopra, D., *The Return of Merlin: A Novel.* New York: Harmony Books, 1995.

Chopra, D., *Boundless Energy: The Complete Mind/Body Program for Overcoming Chronic Fatigue.* New York : Harmony Books, 1995.

Chopra, D., *Perfect Digestion: The Key to Balanced Living.* New York: Harmony Books, 1995.

Chopra, D., *Deepak Chopra's Infinite Possibilities for Body, Mind & Soul.* New York: Crown Publishers, 1995.

Chopra, D., *The Way of the Wizard: Twenty Spiritual Lessons in Creating the Life You Want.* New York: Harmony Books, 1995.

Chopra, D., *The Path to Love: Renewing the Power of Spirit in Your Life.* New York: Harmony Books, 1997.

Chopra, D., *The Seven Spiritual Laws of Success for Parents: Daily Lessons for Children to Live By.* New York: Harmony Books, 1997.

Chopra, D., *Overcoming Addictions: The Spiritual Solution.* New York: Harmony Books, 1997.

Cornell, J., *Mandala: Luminous Symbols for Healing.* Wheaton: Quest Books, 1994.

Gyanamata, Sri, *God Alone: The Life and Letters of a Saint.* Los Angeles: Self-Realization Fellowship, 1984.

Haich, E., *Initiation.* Palo Alto: Seed Center, 1974.

Joy, W.B., *Joy's Way: A Map for the Transformational Journey: An Introduction to the Potentials for Healing with Body Energies.* Los Angeles: J. P. Tarcher, 1978.

Joy, W.B., *Avalanche: Heretical Reflections on the Dark and the Light.* New York: Ballantine Books, 1990.

Kübler-Ross, E., *On Death and Dying.* New York: Macmillan, 1969.

Kübler-Ross, E., *Questions and Answers on Death and Dying.* New York, Macmillan, 1974.

Kübler-Ross, E., *To Live Until We Say Good-bye.* Englewood Cliffs, NJ: Prentice-Hall, 1978.

Kübler-Ross, E., *Living with Death and Dying.* New York: Macmillan, 1981.

Kübler-Ross, E., *Remember the Secret.* Millbrae, CA: Celestial Arts, 1982.

Kübler-Ross, E., *Working It Through.* New York: Macmillan, 1982.

Kübler-Ross, ., *On Children and Death.* New York: Macmillan, 1983.

Kübler-Ross, E., *AIDS: The Ultimate Challenge.* New York: Macmillan, 1987.

Kübler-Ross, E., *On Life After Death.* Berkeley, CA: Celestial Arts, 1991.

Kübler-Ross, E., *Death Is of Vital Importance: On Life, Death and Life After Death.* Barrytown, NY: Station Hill Press, 1995.

Kübler-Ross, E., *The Cocoon & the Butterfly.* Barrytown, NY: Barrytown, Ltd., 1997.

Kübler-Ross, E., *Say Yes to It.* Barrytown, NY: Barrytown, 1997.

Kübler-Ross, E., *Healing in Our Time.* Barrytown, NY: Barrytown, 1997.

Kübler-Ross, E., *The Meaning of Suffering.* Barrytown, NY: Barrytown, 1997.

Kübler-Ross, E., *The Wheel of Life: A Memoir of Living and Dying.* New York: Scribner, 1997.

Levine, S., *A Gradual Awakening.* Garden City, NY: Anchor Press, 1979.

Levine, S., *Who Dies?: An Investigation of Conscious Living and Conscious Dying.* Garden City, NY: Anchor Press/Doubleday, 1982.

Levine, S., *Meetings at the Edge: Dialogues with the Grieving and the Dying, the Healing and the Healed.* Garden City, NY: Anchor Press, 1984.

Levine, S., *Healing into Life and Death.* Garden City, NY: Anchor Press/Doubleday, 1987.

Levine, S., *Guided Meditations, Explorations, and Healings.* New York: Anchor Books, 1991.

Levine, S., *Embracing the Beloved: Relationship as a Path of Awakening.* New York: Doubleday, 1995.

Levine, S., *A Year to Live: How to Live This Year As If It Were Your Last.* New York: Bell Tower, 1997.

Moore, T., *The Planets Within: Marsilio Ficino's Astrological Psychology.* Lewisburg: Bucknell University Press, 1982.

Moore, T., *Dark Eros: The Imagination of Sadism.* Dallas, TX: Spring Publications, 1990.

Moore, T., *Care of the Soul: A Guide for Cultivating Depth and Sacredness in Everyday Life.* New York: HarperCollins, 1992.

Moore, T., *Soul Mates: Honoring the Mysteries of Love and Relationship.* New York: HarperCollins, 1994.

Moore, T., *Meditations: On the Monk Who Dwells in Daily Life.* New York: HarperCollins, 1994.

Moore, T., *The Re-enchantment of Everyday Life.* Thorndike, ME: G. K. Hall, 1996.

Moss, R.M., *The I that Is We.* Millbrae, CA: Celestial Arts, 1981.

Moss, R.M., *How Shall I Live: Transforming Surgery or Any Health Crisis into Greater Aliveness.* Berkeley, CA: Celestial Arts, 1985.

Moss, R.M., *The Black Butterfly: An Invitation to Radical Aliveness.* Berkeley, CA: Celestial Arts, 1986.

Moss, R.M., *The Second Miracle: Itimacy, Spirituality, and Conscious Relationships.* Berkeley, CA: Celestial Arts, 1995.

Myss, C., *Anatomy of the Spirit.* New York: Harmony Books, 1996.

Shah, I., *Wisdom of the Idiots.* London: Octagon Press, 1969.

Sri Daya Mata, *Only Love.* Los Angeles: Self-Realization Fellowship, 1976.

Sri Daya Mata, *Finding the Joy within You: Personal Counsel for God-centered Living.* Los Angeles: Self-Realization Fellowship, 1990.

Tsu, L., *Tao Te Ching* (G. Feng & J. English, Transl.). New York: Vintage Books, 1972.

Vaughan, F.E., *Awakening Intuition.* Garden City, NY: Anchor Press, 1979.

Vaughan, F.E., *The Inward Arc: Healing in Psychotherapy and Spirituality.* Nevada City, CA: Blue Dolphin, 1995.

Vaughan, F.E., *Shadows of the Sacred: Seeing Through Spiritual Illusions.* Wheaton, IL: Quest Books, 1995.

Walsh, R.N., *Towards an Ecology of Brain.* Jamaica, NY: Spectrum Publications, 1981.

Walsh, R.N., *Staying Alive: The Psychology of Human Survival.* Boulder: New Science Library, 1984.

Walsh, R.N., *The Spirit of Shamanism.* Los Angeles: J.P. Tarcher, 1990.

Wilber, K., *The Spectrum of Consciousness.* Wheaton, IL: Theosophical Pub. House, 1977.

Wilber, K., *No Boundary, Eastern and Western Approaches to Personal Growth.* Los Angeles: Center Publications, 1979.

Wilber, K., *The Atman Project: A Transpersonal View of Human Development.* Wheaton, IL: Theosophical Pub. House, 1980.

Wilber, K., *Up from Eden: A Transpersonal View of Human Evolution.* Garden City, NY: Anchor Press/Doubleday, 1981.

Wilber, K., *A Sociable God: A Brief Introduction to a Transcendental Sociology.* New York: New Press, 1983.

Wilber, K., *Eye to Eye: The Quest for the New Paradigm.* Garden City, NY: Anchor Books, 1983.

Wilber, K., *Transformations of Consciousness: Conventional and Contemplative Perspectives on Development.* Boston: New Science Library, 1986.

Wilber, K., *Grace and Grit: Spirituality and Healing in the Life and Death of Treya Killam Wilber.* Boston: Shambhala, 1991.

Wilber, K., *The Spectrum of Consciousness.* Wheaton, IL: Theosophical Pub. House, 1993.

Wilber, K., *Sex, Ecology, Spirituality: The Spirit of Evolution.* Boston: Shambhala, 1995.

Wilber, K., *A Brief History of Everything.* Boston: Shambhala, 1996.

Wilber, K., *The Eye of Spirit: An Integral Vision for a World Gone Slightly Mad.* Boston: Shambhala, 1997.

Wilber, K., *The Marriage of Sense and Soul: Integrating Science and Religion.* New York: Random House, 1998.

Williamson, M., *A Return to Love: Reflections on the Principles of* A Course in Miracles. New York: HarperCollins, 1992.

Williamson, M., *A Woman's Worth.* New York: Random House, 1993.

Williamson, M., *Illuminata: Thoughts, Prayers, Rites of Passage.* New York: Random House, 1994.

Williamson, M., *Emma and Mommy Talk to God.* New York: HarperCollins, 1996.

Williamson, M., *The Healing of America.* New York: Simon & Schuster, 1997.

Williamson, M., *Illuminated Prayers.* New York: Simon & Schuster, 1997.

Yogananda, Paramahansa, *Man's Eternal Quest.* Los Angeles: Self-Realization Fellowship, 1975.

Yogananda, Paramahansa, *Sayings of Paramhansa Yogananda.* Los Angeles: Self-Realization Fellowship, 1980.

Yogananda, Paramahansa, *The Science of Religion.* Los Angeles: Self-Realization Fellowship, 1982.

Yogananda, Paramahansa, *Songs of the Soul.* Los Angeles: Self-Realization Fellowship, 1983.

Yogananda, Paramhansa, *Whispers from Eternity.* Los Angeles: Self-Realization Fellowship, 1986.

Yogananda, Paramahansa, *The Divine Romance.* Los Angeles: Self-Realization Fellowship, 1986.

Yogananda, Paramahansa, *Where There Is Light: Insight and Inspiration for Meeting Life's Challenges.* Los Angeles: Self-Realization Fellowship, 1988.

Yogananda, Paramahansa, *Wine of the Mystic: The Rubaiyat of Omar Khayyam: A Spiritual Interpretation.* Los Angeles: Self-Realization Fellowship, 1994.

Yogananda, Paramahansa, *Journey to Self-Realization: Discovering the Gifts of the Soul.* Los Angeles: Self-Realization Fellowship, 1997.

Yukteswar, Swami, *The Holy Science.* Los Angeles: Self-Realization Fellowship, 1972 [c1949].

Additional Resources

The following is a list of nutritional products and Website locations that may prove helpful to you and your patients.

I have found food supplements to be very helpful for balancing the physical body, enhancing the immune system, and stabilizing minor mood shifts that may be the result of poor nutrition. Because our soil has been so depleted, we do not receive sufficient nutrients from the foods we eat. The abundance of "green" food supplements helps to recharge our pranic life force. In the Ayurvedic School of Medicine, green foods are highly recommended in this regard.[48]

Food Supplements

Pure Synergy: An excellent product that contains over fifty ingredients. The main elements include various forms of algae, juices, Chinese herbs, American herbs, enzymes, Asian mushrooms, royal jelly, and anti-oxidants. This product was developed and is marketed by Mitchell May, whose story is related in this book.

Klamath Lake Algae: An excellent source for Klamath Lake algae. This particular algae grows naturally in the pristine waters of Washington. The lake is fed by runoff from the surrounding volcanic mountains and contains numerous nutrients from the volcanic ash. The algae provides an excellent source of essential amino acids, anti-oxidants, protein, and chlorophyll. While individual reports vary, many people find increased energy, greater mental clarity, and an enhanced sense of well-being. Both products are also available directly through the Synergy Company. To order, or for a complete brochure, contact:

The Synergy Company
CVSR Box 2901
Moab, Utah 84532
1-800-723-0277
http://www.synergy-co.com

Spirulina: A beta carotene-rich food with essential vitamins and minerals. This product can be found in your local health food store.

Melatonin: An excellent supplement with anti-cancer and anti-aging properties. Can be found at your local health food store.

Ginkgo: A supplement to help blood flow to the brain for increased mental alertness. Can be found at your local health food store.

Related Websites:

http://www.ronmann.com: Ronald L. Mann, Ph.D. Home Page. It contains a variety of information and audio tapes designed for the healing of mind, body, and soul.

http://www.newmed.com/complete.htm: New Medicine Home page. This site has an extensive list of audio and video tapes to purchase. Listed by audio/video tapes, subjects, speakers, and writers. Tapes include Jon Kabat-Zinn, Ph.D.; Bernie Siegel, M.D.; Ram Dass; Kenneth Pelletier, M.D.; Larry Dossey, M.D.; Robert Johnson; Rollo May, Ph.D.; Carl Rogers; H.H. Dalai Lama; and many more. They deal with psychology-spirituality, death and conscious dying, spiritual emergence, wellness work, shamanism, men and women, identity and relationship, and much more.

http://www.yogananda-srf.org: Self-Realization Fellowship Home page and information about the Self-Realization Fellowship and Paramahansa Yogananda. It includes a variety of information about the Self-Realization Fellowship, has excerpts from Yogananda's writings (these change, so check here often), and much more. Discusses Christianity, yoga, meditation, more. Very informative, helpful site.

http://www.samata.com: User Friendly Yoga was created in response to the needs of Westerners, both men and women, in the 35–65 age range. The focus is on safe postures for backs and necks, stress reduction, proper breathing, and balancing the strength and flexibility of the spine. User Friendly Yoga is taught for groups and in private lessons. Private lessons are taught as part of the Healthy Back Healthy Mind Program. 1-310-306-8845.

http://www.abwam.com/nalybi/email.html: New Beginnings Store. Many tapes and CDs are available here for vocal/chant music; several by Paramahansa Yogananda as well as his disciples, Gregorian chants, Enya,

Benedictine Monks, Ronald Mann, Ph.D., many original songs, and much more.

http://www.skdesigns.com/internet/spirit/index.htm: Website of Shirley Kaiser. A great resource for Spirituality and Alternative Healing.

http://www.HealthAtoZ.com: A search engine with many, many links to health sites in the realm of complementary medicine and the healing arts.

http://www.healthy.com: HealthWorld Online is the most comprehensive natural health and wellness site on the Internet, integrating both natural and conventional health information into a synergistic whole. HealthWorld Online provides the resources needed by individuals to make health choices and opens the door to Self-Managed Care™.

Audio Tapes by Ronald L. Mann, Ph.D.

The author has produced a series of audio tapes for self-healing and spiritual development that are available at selected bookstores. All tapes are professionally produced in digital stereo with original synthesized music. The current tapes are as follows:

Inspiration for Meditation: This tape was originally produced in Kauai, Hawaii. The guided meditation focuses upon the *chakra* system and the life force energy in the spine. The breath and *mantra* are used to develop concentration and redirect the life force energy away from the outer senses into the deeper centers of the brain. The intent is upon the direct experience of the self as love, joy, and light, not merely the physical, emotional, or mental. Original music composed and performed by Aryeh David. (60 minutes. Music continues for extended meditation on side B.)

Zen Meditation: This meditation tape arises out of the Zen tradition. Simple bamboo flute music becomes the backdrop for mindful awareness. The focus is upon becoming aware of the contents of the mind and emotions without being identified with them. The feeling is simple and elegant. Original music composed and performed by Aryeh David. (60 minutes. Music continues for extended meditation on side B.)

Om Mani Padme Hum: This ancient and sacred Tibetan chant is combined with the Classical Indian Tambura. Chanting is a profound way to shift the consciousness because the vibration in sound directly affects the nervous system. A profound sense of peace and a deepening of the meditation state is obtained when one merges the mind with the sound. The words *Om* (Cosmic sound of creation) *Mani* (Lotus) *Padme* (Jewel) strongly impact your consciousness. (60 minutes: 21 minutes of chanting and 19 minutes of Tambura music for meditation. Same on both sides.)

Jai Ram Sri Ram: This sacred Indian chant comes from the tradition of Yoga. Chanting the name of God is an ancient practice that draws the Divine presence to us. This melody is slow and devotional. It helps to open the heart and prepare you for meditation. (60 minutes: 20 minutes of chanting and 10 minutes of music for meditation.)

Coming Home: This guided meditation helps one to transcend the identification with the physical body and gently let go into the Light. The focus is upon feeling the love and bliss of one's true nature and melting into the Divine. The music takes the listener into a very deep, meditative state. (25 minutes on Side 1. Music continues on Side 2 for extended meditation.)

Healing in the Light: This guided meditation begins with the induction of a gentle trance state and then calls upon visual imagery to activate the presence of inner light. This subtle force is used to direct healing energy into the cellular structure and the immune system. Directions are also given for a direct, intuitive, internal communication to discover the underlying cause for any disease process. Original music composed and performed by Aryeh David. (60 minutes. Music continues for extended meditation on side B.)

Soul Journey: This guided experience begins with a comprehensive trance induction and then takes the listener on a journey into a heavenly realm to meet an inner teacher in a golden palace. Time is given for inner communion to explore one's soul purpose and other questions of personal importance. Original music composed and performed by Aryeh David. (60 minutes. Music continues for extended meditation on side B.)

Sleep: This tape provides a hypnotic induction to fall asleep. Suggestions are given for a wonderful, restful, healing sleep in which the unconscious will work to solve any problems the listener might have. Children love this tape. Original music composed and performed by Aryeh David. (60 minutes. Music continues for extended sleep on side B.)

Self-Hypnosis for Stress Release: An intensive hypnotic induction that helps you to totally relax and release all stress. The process focuses upon entire body relaxation and visual imagery for a safe haven in nature. (60 minutes. Music continues for extended relaxation on side B.) Original music composed and performed by Aryeh David.

Business Break: Stress Reduction for Corporate America: Side one provides a quick way to relax when the pressure builds up at work. This gentle music and soothing, guided relaxation will quickly release tensions from both mind and body. Side two provides a guided experience to enhance creative, intuitive problem solving. Original music composed and performed by Aryeh David. (Five minutes on each side.)

For further information, Dr. Mann may be contacted at 1-800-405-7332.

Training Programs in Sacred Psychotherapy

Dr. Mann offers intensive training programs in the integration of spirituality into psychotherapy. These programs are organized by the Institute of Alternative Healing, a nonprofit organization dedicated to the scientific investigation and dissemination of information regarding ancient healing methods. For more information regarding this professional training program, which leads to certification by the Institute, please call (800) 405-7332.

Chapter Notes

[1] *Guru* means dispeller of darkness. The *guru* brings light and functions as a spiritual teacher.

[2] George Bernard Shaw. Letter, 19 Aug. 1909 to dramatist and patron Lady Gregory (published in *Collected Letters*, vol. 2, 1972).

[3] The patterns of life's circumstances that are the result of causes from past actions.

[4] J. Kornfield, Even the Best Meditators Have Old Wounds to Heal: Combining Meditation and Psychotherapy. *Paths Beyond Ego*. R. Walsh & F. Vaughan (Eds.) (New York: G.P. Putnam's Sons, 1993).

[5] The last step in Patanjali's system of yoga. *Samadhi* is obtained when the life force energy has been withdrawn from the outer senses, and the meditator then becomes one with the object of meditation, God.

[6] Yogic philosophy describes the subtle life force energy that sustains living organisms as *prana*.

[7] The *kundalini*, according to yogic philosophy, is a dormant energy located at the base of the spine. When this force is activated, either as the result of yogic practice or as a spontaneous movement, a current of energy proceeds up the astral spine and opens the corresponding *chakras* along its path. The higher centers of the spine and brain are typically activated when this energy is drawn up from the base of the spine, often resulting in the experience of unconditional love, deep intuitive perceptions, and transcendental bliss associated with the angelic realms.

[8] *Sankhya* philosophy is an Indian philosophy that details creation from Spirit to matter. See also the diagram on page 125.

[9] Pantanjali was a wise sage who created the *Yoga Sutras*, which outlined the eight steps of the yogic path.

[10] See, for example, Yogiraj Sri Swami Satchidananda, *Integral Yoga Hatha* (San Francisco: Holt, Rinehart and Winston, 1970); B.K.S. Iyengar, *Light on Yoga* (New York: Schocken Books, 1966); and Paramahansa Yogananda, *Autobiography of a Yogi* (Los Angeles: Self-Realization Fellowship, 1971).

[11] This quote is attributed to Sri Gyanamata, a direct disciple of Paramahansa Yogananda and a renunciate of the Self-Realization Fellowship.

[12] Phoenix Rising Yoga Therapy can be contacted at 1-800-288-9642.

[13] Paramahansa Yogananda, *God Talks with Arjuna: The Bhagavad Gita* (Los Angeles: Self-Realization Fellowship, 1995), p. 559. All quotations are used with the permission of the publisher.

[14] Yogic cosmology is very elaborate and discusses many elements that compose the universe. An excellent discussion of these forces and their interrelationship can be found in *The Holy Science* by Swami Sri Yukteswar (Los Angeles: Self-Realization Fellowship, 1977).

[15] Martin Seligman, Ph.D. *Consumer Reports* Study Provides Good News for Psychotherapy. *California Psychologist,* January, 1996.

[16] Sri Yukteswar, *The Holy Science*, p. xiii.

[17] Yogananda, *God Talks with Arjuna: The Bhagavad Gita.*

[18] Yogananda, *The Autobiography of a Yogi.*

[19] Yogananda, *God Talks with Arjuna: The Bhagavad Gita,* p. 204.

[20] *Ibid.,* p. 204.

[21] *Ibid.,* p. 212.

[22] W. Ronald D. Fairbairn, *Psychoanalytic Studies of the Personality* (London: Routledge & Kegan Paul Ltd., 1972).

[23] D. W. Winnicott, *Playing & Reality* (New York: Basic Books, Inc., 1971).

[24] H. Guntrip, *Schizoid Phenomena, Object Relations and the Self* (New York: International Universities Press, Inc., 1969).

[25] J. Masterson, *The Search for the Real Self* (New York: The Free Press, 1988).

[26] Yogananda, *God Talks with Arjuna: The Bhagavad Gita,* p. 211-212.

[27] *Ibid.,* p. 264-265.

[28] *Ibid.,* p. 268.

[29] *Ibid.,* p. 268-269.

[30] *Ibid.,* p. 269.

[31] *Ibid.,* p. 270.

[32] The DSM-IV is a collection of descriptions and codes used to classify various mental and emotional disorders. It is the handbook for insurance billing.

[33] Fred A. Wolf, *Taking the Quantum Leap: The New Physics for Nonscientists* (San Francisco: Harper & Row, 1981) and *The Body Quantum: The New Physics of Body, Mind, and Health* (New York: Macmillan, 1986).

[34] e.g., Peter Tompkins, *The Secret Life of Plants*. (New York: Harper & Row, 1973).

[35] See pages 87-90, Chapter 6, for a detailed description of the *chakra* system.

[36] Fred A. Wolf, *Taking the Quantum Leap: The New Physics for Nonscientists* and *The Body Quantum: The New Physics of Body, Mind, and Health*.

[37] Please refer to the diagram on page 86 for the explanation of the astral body.

[38] R. Mann, *Healing in the Light* (audio tape). Copyright 1995.

[39] Please refer to Additional Resources for information regarding Pure Synergy.

[40] The reader is referred to the following book for a more complete discussion on this approach: Brother Lawrence, *The Practice of the Presence of God*, John J. Delaney (Transl.) (New York: Doubleday, 1977).

[41] Projective identification is a specific defense mechanism discussed by Melanie Klein. Hannah Segal, *Introduction to the Work of Melanie Klein* (London: The Hogarth Press, 1973).

[42] W. Bion, *Introduction to the Work of Bion* (New York: Jason Aronson, Inc., 1977).

[43] Ralph Greenson, M.D., has an excellent discussion regarding developing and maintaining the good working therapeutic relationship in his book, *The Technique and Practice of Psychoanalysis* (New York: International Universities Press, Inc., 1967).

[44] An excellent resource on this subject would be D. Shapiro, *Neurotic Styles* (New York: Basic Books, Inc., 1965).

[45] The reader is referred to Otto Kernberg, *Borderline Conditions and Pathological Narcissism* (New York: Jason Aronson, Inc., 1975) and James Masterson, *The Narissistic and Borderline Disorders* (New York: The Free Press, 1988).

[46] This story was cited from *Lifetide* by Lyall Watson (New York: Bantam Books, 1980), pp. 147-148.

[47] Paramahansa Yogananda, *Whispers from Eternity* (Los Angeles: Self Realization Fellowship, 1975).

[48] D. Frawley, O.M.D., *Ayurvedic Healing: A Comprehensive Guide* (Salt Lake City: Passage Press, 1989).

Index

Note: Page numbers in italics indicate diagrams

About
the Author

R ONALD L. MANN, PH.D., offers a unique integration of traditional psychological expertise with the profound wisdom of spiritual and mystical traditions. His work with Elisabeth Kübler-Ross, M.D., prompted a spontaneous spiritual awakening in 1977. One result of this experience is the gift for subtle energy transmission for healing the mind, body, and soul. Dr. Mann continues to deepen his spiritual life through *Kriya Yoga*, the meditation techniques and yoga philosophy taught by Paramahansa Yogananda, founder of the Self-Realization Fellowship. He has conducted intensive workshops on healing and spiritual development in the United States and abroad.

Dr. Mann shares his wisdom and healing presence through a collection of ten audio tapes. Selections from these tapes have been heard on the audio program, *Serenity*, which aired on both the domestic and international flights of American Airlines.

He was the Executive Director of Projects for Planetary Peace, a non-profit organization involved in Citizen Diplomacy specializing in the difficulties between the United States and the Soviet Union. His international conflict resolution work resulted in appearances on television and radio. He is currently the Director of the Institute of Alternative Healing, a non-profit organization dedicated to the scientific exploration and dissemination of ancient healing methods.

Dr. Mann is currently in private practice and provides spiritual guidance, healing, and transformational work for individuals, couples, and families. He offers a vast collection of healing resources on his website at http://www.ronmann.com.